AMERICAN CHRISTIANITY'S
ADULTERY WITH SECULAR CULTURE

Register This New Book

Benefits of Registering*

- ✓ FREE **replacements** of lost or damaged books

- ✓ FREE **audiobook** – *Pilgrim's Progress*, audiobook edition

- ✓ FREE information about new titles and other **freebies**

www.anekopress.com/new-book-registration

*See our website for requirements and limitations.

AMERICAN CHRISTIANITY'S ADULTERY WITH SECULAR CULTURE

THE TRUTH ABOUT OUR DANGEROUS COMPROMISE WITH THE WORLD

You adulterous people! Do you not know that friendship with the world is enmity with God? Therefore whoever wishes to be a friend of the world makes himself an enemy of God.

– James 4:4

MICHAEL D. LEMAY

ANEKO
PRESS

We love hearing from our readers. Please contact us at www.anekopress.com/questions-comments with any questions, comments, or suggestions.

Visit Michael's website: www.michaeldlemay.com

American Christianity's Adultery with Secular Culture – Michael D. LeMay

Updated Edition Copyright © 2018

First edition published 2012

Cover Design: J. Martin

Cover Image: Olga Terestsenko /Shutterstock

eBook Icon: Icons Vector/Shutterstock

Printed in the United States of America

Aneko Press

www.anekopress.com

Aneko Press, Life Sentence Publishing, and our logos are trademarks of

Life Sentence Publishing, Inc.
203 E. Birch Street
P.O. Box 652
Abbotsford, WI 54405

RELIGION / Blasphemy, Heresy & Apostasy

Paperback ISBN: 978-1-62245-104-3

eBook ISBN: 978-1-62245-105-0

10 9 8 7 6 5 4 3 2 1

Available where books are sold

Contents

Dedication

I dedicate this book to my Lord and Savior, Jesus Christ, upon whom I depend for every breath I take. He called me home when I had strayed so far. He taught me how to be a true disciple, father, and husband, and loved me when I was unlovable. While I see my human depravity as filthy and disgusting, He sees me as beautiful and wonderful. How does one react to such love without gratitude and joy?

I want to thank my wife, Nancy. Her love and courage led me back to God and His truth. She is what Eve was created to be for Adam.

I thank the board, staff, and supporters of the *Stand Up For the Truth* radio program for their dedication to and passion for God. All of you have blessed me in many ways.

I thank the Watchmen on the Wall ministry people who have been sounding the alarm over the past forty years as the American church has started to slowly die. I apologize to each of you for arriving so late to the battle. I hope what I have lacked in timeliness will be made up for with passion and courage.

Foreword

Mike LeMay is a true watchman on the wall. This book addresses many issues that currently plague our nation and American Christianity. As a Christian coming from a Muslim background, and a fellow watchman, I see how the culture is infecting American Christianity when just the opposite should be happening. Mike points this out accurately and clearly, challenging the church to once again be a beacon of light.

This book accurately addresses the taboo subject of Islam that most will not talk about. Islam is a cancer and a vicious virus that America and many of its churches seem to be having a love affair with, unaware of the destruction they are courting.

Mike reveals how our education system is indoctrinating our children into secular humanism, and how some Christian colleges and seminaries seem to be embracing a similar agenda.

This book not only takes a hard look at these and other dangerous movements, but it also asks some serious questions about why many Christian leaders are silent about, or even embracing, these movements. Mike questions if many of our churches are beginning to look more like IBM or Starbucks rather than houses of worship.

A growing number of people see an emerging pattern of "nice theology" being promoted by Christian leaders, but it comes with a very heavy price: the truth about God's perfect nature, the pure gospel, the absolute truth of Scripture, and moral clarity. Mike points out the severe consequences this is having on American Christianity.

Mike also challenges every Christian to take a good hard look in the mirror, questioning our own motives and behaviors as Christians. He asks if we are attempting to redefine God into an image more acceptable to our human desires of the flesh rather than worshipping Him in His entirety.

This book will challenge you as Mike asks very difficult questions ignored for too long by many. Every Christian needs to read this book and ponder its warnings.

Elijah Abraham
Founder, Living Oasis Ministries

Introduction

You adulterous people! Do you not know that friendship with the world is enmity with God? Therefore whoever wishes to be a friend of the world makes himself an enemy of God. Or do you suppose it is to no purpose that the Scripture says, "He yearns jealously over the spirit that he has made to dwell in us"? – James 4:4-5 (ESV)

"For whoever is ashamed of me and of my words in this adulterous and sinful generation, of him will the Son of Man also be ashamed when he comes in the glory of his Father with the holy angels." – Mark 8:38 (ESV)

American Christianity is in the midst of a torrid, adulterous affair with secular culture. Instead of preparing herself to become a spotless bride of Jesus Christ, she is cheating on Him and setting herself up for eternal disaster, leading others astray, and themselves being just like those Jesus warned in Matthew 7:22-23.

American Christianity as we know it is gasping for its last breath of biblical relevancy. It is slowly deteriorating, and at our current rate of degeneration it may only be a few years before it will be unrecognizable when held up against the Word of God. This should come as little surprise to anyone who truly understands the teachings of Christianity and who has been watching the American church wither away over the past fifty years.

The church is under attack externally from a powerful Enemy, Satan. He has assembled a strong, passionate army to neutralize and even destroy American Christianity. This army includes some very powerful institutions that together form a very formidable foe for Christianity in this nation.

The most obvious pawn of the Enemy is a rapidly degenerating secular culture. It is being augmented by a growing progressive government, a strongly biased media, a public education system bent on indoctrinating our children into secular humanism, and a radical religion bent on destroying Christianity at every turn – Islam.

Fifty years ago a child in the womb was considered a life with a right to be born. Now the child in the womb is disposable property. Up until the day of delivery its life hangs on a thread as the mother contemplates whether she wants to be a mother or dispose of the "inconvenience" within her.

Fifty years ago, homosexuality was considered sinful. Now it is accepted as normal and is even celebrated. In 2015 the Supreme Court legalized homosexual marriage and since that time we have seen aggressive actions by the LGBTQ lobby to enforce acceptance within churches. Today, public schools encourage young children to explore their sexuality and consider the possibility that they might actually *be* homosexuals.

Pornography used to be shunned as unacceptable behavior, but now it produces more revenue than all major sports in this nation combined. Adults and children access it from their smartphones and download it at will.

Islam, clearly a religion of antichrist as defined in 1 John, has become the darling religion of American culture. Islam, a religion that teaches that homosexuals, adulterers, and abortionists should be put to death, is somehow embraced as a "religion of tolerance" in America. Islam, a religion that commands every Muslim to kill Christians, Jews, and every infidel who will not convert to it, is somehow seen as a "religion of peace" in American culture.

American secular culture is disintegrating by the day, becoming increasingly hostile to biblical Christianity. It is bolstered by a radically progressive court system that supports evil and shuns Christian values at every turn. Polls show that an increasing number of Americans find abortion and homosexuality perfectly acceptable, and a shrinking number of Americans consider themselves Christians.

In the midst of this deteriorating secular culture, we should be seeing Christianity standing firmly against it, pointing out its sinful ways, and calling Christians to live differently. But instead, we see American Christianity being seduced by this increasingly evil culture, even wedding itself to it in hopes of still being "relevant." In a twist of spiritual insanity, we somehow think we will affect secular culture by becoming more like it.

The book of Hosea is a fascinating account of God calling out His people for their adultery against Him. When you read Hosea with American Christianity in mind, it is easy to see the parallels. God calls on Israel to abandon their whoring ways and return to Him as His beloved. While we are not to be confused with Israel, I am sure God hopes America, formed upon His law and principles, will abandon our whoredom with secular culture and return to Him also. But that is our choice, and it is a choice that has eternal consequences.

In a nation where 86 percent of its citizens still claim to be Christians, read these verses from Romans 1 and see if they might apply today:

> *The wrath of God is being revealed from heaven against all the godlessness and wickedness of people, who suppress the truth by their wickedness, since what may be known about God is plain to them.*
>
> *For although they knew God, they neither glorified him as God nor gave thanks to him, but their thinking became futile and their foolish hearts were darkened. Although they claimed to be wise, they became fools and exchanged the glory of the immortal God for images made to look like a mortal human being and birds and animals and reptiles. Therefore God gave them over in the sinful desires of their hearts to sexual impurity for the degrading of their bodies with one another. They exchanged the truth about God for a lie, and worshiped and*

served created things rather than the Creator—who is forever praised. Amen. (Romans 1:18-19a, 21-25)

Sound like America to you?

Make no mistake, American Christianity is at war, whether we wish it or not. It is being marginalized to the point that it is no longer a worthy opponent for the onslaught of secular humanism taking over this nation. Our nation was founded on Judeo-Christian laws and principles, and the church was seen as a force to keep the culture and the government in check, making sure they did not stray from those laws and principles. For nearly two hundred years the church performed admirably. When the culture or government would begin to stray from Christian values, the church would rise in unison and shout, "Not on our watch!" But all that started to change in the 1960s. As the secular culture made inroads with our children, the church was suddenly not there to push back. This ushered in a gradual decay to where we are now: a secular humanist culture on the rise and a church that seems to be in rapid decline.

This external battle force put together by Satan is powerful and committed to destroying biblical Christianity in America. Yet with all its force, it should be no match for the church. The church has two powerful weapons that should render the Enemy obsolete: the truth of God's Word and the power of the Holy Spirit. But sometime in the past fifty years, we began to leave those weapons behind and tried to fight this battle with our own strength and tactics.

Many powerful human empires of the past all came to ultimate destruction, no matter how powerful they seemed to be. On the exterior they had superior military forces and were in a position to continue domination for many more centuries, and no enemy could stand against them on the battlefield. But the demise of great empires or civilizations usually starts from the inside. Rome's status as a world empire began to wane as internal strife and corruption consumed her from within. Nazi Germany started to show the first cracks in its armor when a powerful underground was formed in Germany by its own citizens who were enlightened about the evil they previously supported. This underground movement started to work secretly with Germany's enemies to coordinate internal attacks and weaken the Nazi terror machine.

But an example worth noting for the purpose of this book is the Aztec civilization of Central America. Once a powerful empire reaching its height in the early sixteenth century, the Aztec civilization was decimated quickly with the arrival of the Spanish explorer Cortés. He quickly found allies within the empire who wished to gain power on their own and worked with Cortés in waging war against the Aztec leaders. They did find some early success in weakening the Aztec Empire, but according to several historians, Cortés brought another weapon with him that finally destroyed the Aztec leadership and culture: smallpox. This deadly disease was injected into the Aztec culture and destroyed it from within by weakening the empire and allowing the Spaniards and their allies to destroy this once-powerful empire. The great Aztec Empire was destroyed by an external virus introduced to it by foreigners.

This is happening to American Christianity today. Satan, armed with powerful allies, is waging a vicious attack on the church, a church that is already weakened by a foreign virus it has willfully ingested over the past fifty years: tolerance. If American Christianity does not defeat this virus immediately, we will become so weakened internally that we will be easy pickings for the powerful army Satan has assembled.

This virus is being spread by two internal groups within the camp of American Christianity: weak, unprincipled leaders and those that follow them. Many of our leaders are tolerating and even embracing the poisonous virus of tolerance that is internally weakening the church. We see fewer Christian leaders calling homosexuality sin, fewer leaders standing up to the murderous scourge of abortion, and fewer leaders even talking about sin anymore. These leaders are less interested in a pure, holy church and more interested in popularity, fame, and "nickels and noses." They are leading American Christianity to the brink of spiritual confusion, but they are only leading us to where we as "consumers" want them to lead us.

Yes, Christian church members are equally to blame for secular culture creeping into American Christianity. We no longer want leaders who preach about sin and our human depravity; we prefer teachers who make us feel good about ourselves. We no longer want leaders who challenge us to pursue righteousness and holiness; we want leaders who tell us how to have our best life now. We no longer want leaders who tell us we should fear falling into the hands of an angry God; we want leaders who coddle us and assure us that God loves us just the way we are – rebellious sinners.

Weak, compromised Christian leaders and those who follow them are knowing or unknowing agents of the Enemy sowing dissent and the virus of tolerance within our own ranks. We are weakening the church to the point it may soon fall to the Enemy pounding at the door.

We can blame the secular culture for the demise of American Christianity, but they are only doing what is expected of people blind to God and His nature and character. Just what leads us to expect these people would behave in a different manner? Their very nature hates or denies God and deep down they wish to be their own gods.

We can blame our Christian leaders who compromise and support the secular culture with their cowardly leadership, but they are merely a reflection of what we truly desire in our leaders. American Christians these days are more interested in feeling good about ourselves than we are in being challenged to walk away from our sins and seek righteousness and holiness. We are more interested in being seen as open-minded and tolerant than we are in speaking the truth to the lost who desperately need that truth. So we appoint leaders who reflect our spiritual laziness and apathy.

The sad truth is that rank-and-file Christians are ultimately responsible for the demise of American Christianity. We cry out against the evils of our culture while secretly embracing its values, and we often behave no differently than the lost. We desire leaders who will help us feel good about ourselves instead of confronting our sinful depravity.

It is absolutely crucial that we view this battle in the proper context. The spiritual death of American Christianity will not be a murder, it will be a type of spiritual suicide. The secular humanists have the poison to kill us but it can only happen if we willingly ingest that poison. Too many leaders are promoting the very poison which will kill us, encouraging us to consume it. But we alone will choose whether to reject it or partake of it.

Witnessing Suicide

My mother committed suicide. The death certificate states the cause as liver failure, but that was simply the effects of thirty years of abuse from addictions to cigarettes and alcohol. A once strong, beautiful, and vibrant woman, my mother withered away as she turned to cigarettes and alcohol, willingly consuming the poison that would eventually kill her. American Christianity was also once a strong, beautiful, and vibrant woman, but she is now drinking the poison of secular humanists.

My mother was once a strong rock of virtue and conviction, just like American Christianity used to be. She was attacked externally by my father, just like American Christianity is being attacked by the culture. Under attack and abuse, she slowly began to think there was something wrong with *her*, that she was no longer beautiful and lovable. So she began to "medicate" herself, thinking it would ease the pain. She slowly believed the lies that she was unattractive and worthless, and she gave up, just like American Christianity is now doing.

American Christianity is following a similar path of self-destruction. Secular culture has convinced her that the Bible's truth is unattractive and undesirable. So American Christianity, believing the lies, is changing to look more "beautiful" to this evil secular culture. She has abandoned her first love for a new lover, committing spiritual adultery against God.

My mother ignored the advice of those who loved her enough to point out the truth and chose to remain on her self-destructive path. American Christianity is doing the same.

Christianity in America looks more like the culture these days than it does the church in the book of Acts. Compromising at every turn when Jesus warned us against compromise; seeking the love and admiration of the world when Jesus told us the world would hate us because it hated Him first; and a growing embrace of, and even a love for, American culture that is destroying the church itself.

In Isaiah 7:9 God warns us: *"If you do not stand firm in your faith, you will not stand at all."* Just what does Christianity in America stand for these days? Is it light and salt to the disintegrating culture? Or is it embracing the culture, allowing this all-consuming cancer to slowly kill us? There is time to rescue the church. But it will take courage, dedication, and repentance from our leaders and those they lead.

American Christianity is on spiritual life support, and we are preparing to pull our own plug. Will we sit by idly as she commits spiritual suicide? Or will we summon the courage to question the path many Christian leaders are taking us down? Will we discover the biblical meaning of true love or will we continue to treat love as never having to say "you're wrong"? God is giving American Christianity a choice: continue to remain silent and question nothing we are taught, or be a good Berean and take everything to the Word of God to see if what we are being taught is truth. The second choice will lead us back to where we belong. The first choice will lead to spiritual death.

We will look at the poison the culture is offering to us as Christians. But remember, we are not forced to consume that poison; it will be our choice if we choose to ingest it.

This book will be critical of some in Christian leadership who are embracing and offering us spiritual poison. But this book is also directed at you and me because we are just as much to blame for the adultery of American Christianity. Every time we sin or accept sin, every time we fail to hold others accountable or allow them to hold us accountable, and every time we turn an apathetic eye of acceptance to the virus infecting the church, we are every bit as responsible as anyone for the spiritual death of the church in America.

On November 18, 1978, in Jonestown, Guyana, 918 "Christians" committed suicide by drinking poison. They chose to follow a leader who was leading them away from the truth of God's Word and who convinced them to follow him instead of God. A man of great charisma and charm, Jim Jones convinced his followers to do the unthinkable: take their own lives. They, not the culture or their leader, were ultimately responsible for the choice they made. Our evil secular culture is the poison today, and some of our leaders are presenting it as an acceptable and even beneficial drink these days. Will we drink it?

I hope this book lights a fire in you to become a true biblical scholar.

If you are solely depending on your pastor or Christian media to teach you the Word of God, I hope this book wakes you out of your sleepy, apathetic state. Whether or not American Christianity can escape its own self-inflicted demise is debatable. What is not in question is your ultimate responsibility to hold onto biblical truth no matter the fate of American Christianity. Read God's Word as if your life depends on it, because, my friend, it does.

Chapter 1

Awakening Out of a Deep Spiritual Sleep

A Call to Battle

It was a pleasant, warm Friday in June 2010. The previous thirteen months were quite the journey. After locating our studio in the basement of a chiropractic office for fifteen years, we were ready to move into our own brand-new facility. As a listener-supported station, we are very judicious with the financial support our listeners provide. We had put a fleece out before the Lord: if He wanted us to build a new facility we could own, He would have to provide a way for us to do so without increasing our budget and needing to ask for additional support from our listeners. God provided in an amazing way.

Here I sat in our brand-new building with 70 percent more space, in a near-perfect location, and paying less monthly than we were while renting! God accomplished this through a group of individuals and businesses who donated a lot of time and flooring, cabinetry, windows, and the roof. A year of sixty-to-seventy-hour workweeks had finally come to an end, and at the age of fifty-six, I looked forward to a little less hectic pace.

I sat at my desk contemplating what Nancy and I should do for the weekend. She talked about taking a drive to Door County, walking through the beautiful parks, and catching lunch and coffee. Then I received a phone call that would rock my world.

A pastor from Appleton, twenty miles south of Green Bay, was on the phone. We had never met or spoken but I knew of him. He introduced himself and asked a question that would mark my future in a challenging, wonderful way. "Mike, is Q90 FM planning on supporting Lifest with Jim Wallis scheduled as the key speaker?"

My answer showed how I had been lulled to sleep spiritually. "Uh, who is Jim Wallis?"

The pastor sent me some website links to Wallis and his organization, Sojourners. Quite frankly, my initial thought was to dismiss this as a legalistic pastor who would figure out some way to protest an historically successful Christian rock-music event. The event drew tens of thousands of Christian youth and parents every year, and the organization that holds the event is an organization bringing the hope of Jesus Christ to youth around the country.

I investigated the links the pastor sent me and quickly realized it would take a lot more than a couple hours of research to determine what, if any, actions we should take. Q90 FM has been a title sponsor of this event every year, and we partner closely with Life Promotions, the organization putting it on, to reach hurting youth for Jesus. I was not about to make a snap decision on such an important issue.

I informed my bride that we would probably have to forego our trip to Door County because I would need her help researching sites. She responded in the way I had come to expect: God wanted some more of our time, so let's answer the bell. Lifest was rapidly approaching and this issue required our immediate attention. We spent much of the weekend going through research, double-checking information out there to verify or refute the opinions of many people who believed Wallis and his organization had no business speaking to Christian youth.

I informed my board of the potential situation and continued researching, cross-checking and assessing the situation. I also texted a message to my friend who heads up Life Promotions, informing him we were investigating opinions and information about Wallis and Sojourners. His response was kind and gracious.

By the following Tuesday, after sharing the information we found with our board, we decided the best thing to do was to talk with the organization and share our concerns. My research had led me to some very troubling information on Wallis and Sojourners.

Jim Wallis is, to say the least, a Marxist sympathizer. He was a student chapter leader in the sixties for the Students for a Democratic Society, an anarchist organization that protested pretty much everything American. Wallis led the cheers as the United States went down to defeat in Vietnam and publicly spoke glowingly of communist regimes around the world.

He was hired after the 2004 presidential election to help the Democratic party garner more evangelical Christian votes. To say the least, he has been too successful. Evangelical Christians, in my opinion, were largely responsible for the election of Barack Obama, the most pro-abortion, pro-gay marriage president in American history, and they continue to support candidates who directly oppose God's stances on life and marriage. At the time, Wallis was one of President Obama's chief spiritual advisors.

An important disclaimer here: I consider myself a conservative, politically and spiritually. Politically, I believe the federal government has grown into an almost uncontrollable monster, choking the freedom and liberties of American citizens. I believe through a well-intentioned "war on poverty" our government is systematically squelching our free-enterprise economy and making more and more Americans addicted to government support, creating a narcissistic, lazy electorate.

I see the federal government as an increasing enemy to religious freedom. Through an overload of extremely progressive judges, the government has brought us tragedies like abortion. What was incredibly ruled as a woman's right to privacy, abortion has killed more than fifty-five million children under the guise of "choice." Sadly, the American church has for the most part chosen to sit out this battle for life.

A careful, objective study of our founding documents shows that the majority of our founding fathers were Christians. While a few of them were deists, the number of deists was far less than progressive education and the media spin that number into these days. Our democratic republic is, I believe, the one form of human government that comes closest to getting it right with God. Our founding fathers recognized and eloquently stated that man's rights come from God alone, and the focus of the federal government should be to protect those individual rights. The laws of the United States were fashioned after the law of God – the Ten Commandments. Our founding fathers would spin in their graves if they saw how the government has grown into what many believe is a monster of oppression these days.

I make this disclosure because of this: Jim Wallis and his organization strongly support expanded "cradle-to-grave" government and extreme "social justice." Both of these rub against my beliefs as a conservative. But they are not the reason I was concerned about him speaking at Lifest.

As I carefully studied the Sojourners website, I saw some alarming spiritual content that I did not think was appropriate to present to young Christians. Sojourners, which claims to be a Christian organization, referred to several "sins" on their site including:

- immigration laws

- the Gulf oil spill

- global warming

- poverty and disparity between the rich and poor

What was sadly lacking on their website were two crucial Christian issues they did not refer to as sin: abortion and homosexual marriage.

If Jim Wallis wants to preach his Marxist propaganda and beliefs, I suppose that is his right as an American citizen. What concerned me most was that he would be a keynote speaker at an event where thousands of young Christians would hear his eloquent appeal for social justice and be attracted to an organization that claims to be Christian but is anything but, and that youth would connect to Sojourners and the other sham "Christian" organization Wallis founded with Tony Campolo called Red Letter Christians. This would lead youth down a destructive path that would undermine the Word of God as absolute truth.

I conferred with our board and they instructed me to meet with the organizers and see if we could reach an agreement. I cannot overstate the painful decision this was for our leadership. We were risking a public disagreement with a fellow Christian organization that we had partnered with for over a decade. But after much prayer and thought, we knew it was the right thing to do.

Our discussion with the organization led me to two direct conversations with Jim Wallis as we explored possible compromises. The first discussion was pretty cordial. We offered to fly Wallis up at our expense where we would introduce him to area pastors who could vet and discern his stances and teachings. I agreed that if the pastors gave him the green light, we would acquiesce. That was rejected out of hand by Wallis during our first conversation. We hung up from our first talk, agreeing to pray and think about the dilemma we faced.

Later that week, with a deadline less than eighteen hours away to bring this to resolution, I sat in my office on a Thursday afternoon, quite frankly getting cold feet. I started to justify that perhaps we were making too big a thing out of this, and I was worried about causing division by having to take a public stance against a brother in the Lord, a man who tirelessly flies around the country sharing a message of hope with teens. I knew we had to publicly announce our reason for not supporting the event this year, and we had decided to be as low-key yet honest as possible, by not mentioning anything on air and simply announcing it on our website. Nancy and I were preparing a statement to be posted the following day.

My cell phone rang – it was Jim Wallis. I answered the phone expecting a reasonable conversation like our previous one, but instead he began ripping into us, accusing us of being right-wing fanatics and trying to silence progressive Christian viewpoints. I assured him politics had nothing to do with our decision and it was made purely on the fact that Sojourners is very weak spiritually in their stance on sin and the absolute truth of God's Word. They are an interfaith organization, partnering with people of all religions to promote religious syncretism and a dangerous humanist agenda. We were concerned that young, impressionable Christians would be drawn to Sojourners by the social justice call and find spiritual affinity in an organization that called themselves Christian yet refused to make right calls on obvious sin, and was also yoked spiritually with pagan religions in their quest to achieve economic equality and justice.

I explained to Wallis that we were opposed to his call for wealth redistribution through higher taxes for two reasons: First, that charity should be voluntary with the donor choosing which organizations to support as Christians. Secondly, their call for more and more government involvement in wealth redistribution and picking what causes and charities to support would be dangerous to Christianity, because the federal government requires that money given to charitable organizations cannot be used to push a religious agenda. In essence, Christians would be forced, through higher taxes, to support organizations at best neutral, and at worst hostile, to sharing the gospel of Jesus Christ.

Now, I am a warrior. I don't ever mind a good fight or argument. But as Wallis tried to attack me as bigoted or uncaring, strangely I felt no rise in blood pressure or tension. I felt the peace of God guiding and calming me. It was Wallis, the "enlightened and reasonable" one, who was boiling mad. I felt the Holy Spirit lead me to ask Wallis a couple questions:

First, "Mr. Wallis, do you believe homosexuality is a sin?" Three times I calmly asked and three times he refused to answer.

Second, "Jim, do you believe abortion is a sin?"

He yelled, "I am the most pro-life person you will ever know!"

I said, "Good, then my question is an easy one – do you believe abortion is a sin?" Again, three times I asked and three times he refused to answer.

I told Wallis I was deeply concerned with his position as chief spiritual advisor to President Obama, but Wallis adamantly defended Barack Obama as a committed Christian. I pointed out that Obama was the most pro-abortion, pro-homosexual marriage president in our history. I irritated him when I suggested that he either agreed with that definition of Christianity or he was an ineffective advisor based on Obama's stances.

The Holy Spirit led me to offer one more piece of bait to expose his real agenda. "Jim," I said, "I suppose you buy into all this global warming propaganda too." His answer told me all I needed to know about Sojourners and the social justice movement.

An Unchristian Worldview

When I asked Wallis about his thoughts on the need to aggressively fight global warming, his answer betrayed his worldview. "Absolutely! We need to have a pristine planet before Jesus can return!" There is the bottom line: Wallis is a left-wing *dominionist*: someone who believes we can control the final saga of this world's story, and that the fate of this world rests upon man's ability to clean up his act and usher in economic equality, justice, and an end to poverty and pollution. Once we have purified the earth, Jesus can return to save all mankind and rule in peace. Dominionism is the height of human arrogance, thinking we can actually rewrite prophetic Scripture and control our own spiritual destiny. I pointed out to Wallis that we must be reading two completely different Bibles because mine says that when Jesus returns there will be wars, rumors of war, poverty, pestilence, and chaos. Wallis did not back down, reaffirming man's responsibility to clean up the earth of poverty and pollution before Jesus can return. Forget the prophetic Word of God because man can do this on his own!

Our conversation ended abruptly with him hanging up. I informed my friend, the leader of Life Promotions, that we would post the decision on our website to sit the event out because of Jim Wallis being the key speaker to Christian youth.

I met with the staff the next morning and informed them of the leadership's decision. I reiterated that while we had to take this difficult stance, our ministry partner affected was still our partner in spreading the gospel and that we hoped this was just a blip on the radar screen in our longtime relationship. We prayed as a staff that God would be glorified by whatever transpired at the event.

With that, we moved on, or so I thought. Life would soon return to normal and we could go back to simply being a radio ministry that played positive, uplifting music for youth. I viewed this as an end to a difficult chapter in my life as a Christian. Life would return to a more normal state. But God had other plans.

Fasten Your Seatbelts!

A few days later, I was enjoying my usual Wednesday morning breakfast with a board member and two other Christians when my cell phone rang. It was my lovely bride with a warning: "You'd better head into the station. Glenn Beck just read our statement about Jim Wallis on his national radio program."

I quickly returned to the office. I was receiving phone calls and emails from around the country. A few were critical of our stance, but most were thanking us for taking the stand we did. Locally, as word got out, I was receiving hundreds of emails and phone calls. Some were supportive and some were in opposition to our stance. Most wondered why we decided to take a stand on such a relatively "minor issue." How could we not be at Lifest when so many youth would be there for us to interact with and minister to? Others accused us of "dividing the local church" by making so much out of something like this. Some listeners were furious, telling me they would never again support Q90 FM because of our stance.

Pastors were calling and wanting more information on why we made the decision we did. Listeners wondered, considering our longstanding partnership with the event, what could we possibly have found out to lead us to take such a stance? What we came to understand after a lot of research and prayer is this: the social justice movement in this country is anti-Christian. Its destructive, forced-wealth redistribution policy aside, it is a movement that is dismissing the Word of God as absolute truth and promoting religious syncretism.

As I continued to research and monitor Sojourners, I found connections with many other "Christian" organizations that had been questioned by Watchmen on the Wall over the years. Organizations like Red Letter Christians, founded by Wallis with Tony Campolo. We will discuss their agenda later.

I saw that a member of the Sojourners board was one Brian McLaren. McLaren, quite frankly, is a dangerous heretic. He denies the substitutionary atonement of sins by Jesus on the cross, which is the central truth of Christianity.

In a lighter but serious moment, I read on their website that Sojourners was offering a special gift if people joined their organization: a poster of Mohandas Gandhi. So why would a Christian organization offer a poster of Gandhi free to new subscribers?

As I explored the social justice movement further, I saw a disturbing pattern. The movement, which claims Christian roots, is more accurately a political activist organization. Virtually every political candidate they support is pro-abortion and pro-homosexuality. Now, we are all sinners in need of God's grace, and all sin is an offense to God, but I believe abortion and homosexuality cut right to the heart of God. The murder of the most innocent of people and a sexual sin that seeks to destroy the biblical foundation of the family are very serious offenses. So why would a "Christian" organization promote political candidates who continually vote to support abortion and homosexual marriage?

I discovered an unofficial alliance between the social justice movement and the emergent church movement. Leaders of one were closely knit to leaders of the other. I started seeing the list of usual suspects tied together in these and other movements that seemed to have one thing in common: a discounting of anything as absolute truth, including the Word of God. Experience and emotion were beginning to replace biblical knowledge and wisdom on the throne of American Christian intellect. Gradually, what we feel is right is trumping what God says is right.

I Was Blind, but Now I See

A year and a half earlier I received a tremendous blessing from God that seemed anything but a blessing at the time. Little did I know what God was preparing me to do in His perfect timing.

I was recovering from reconstructive shoulder surgery. Shoulder rehabilitation is probably one of the closest things a man will ever experience to the pain of childbirth. There were times when the physical therapist would push and crank on my shoulder that I wanted to punch him. But, in November of 2008, my rehabilitation was complete. One day on my way back from a breakfast meeting, it began to "snow" while the skies were bright and sunny. My right eye was seeing what looked like steady snowflakes falling from the sky, making vision out of that eye close to impossible.

I had undergone cataract surgery in both of my eyes years earlier, and every couple years I would have to go in when I saw a few "floaters" in an eye. It was a pretty routine outpatient surgery where they use a laser to clean up the lens. I figured this new experience was just another routine visit to the eye doctor.

When I arrived, the physician sent me next door to a retinal specialist who confirmed I had a detached retina in my right eye. Surgery was scheduled for a few days later and the retina was successfully repaired. At the end of the surgery they place a gas bubble in the eye to prevent infection while the eye is healing. The bubble severely impairs your vision, but gradually lessens over a two-to-three-week recuperation period. So I was blind in my right eye, but hey, no problem, that's why God gave us two eyes.

I was scheduled for a checkup ten days after the surgery to make sure everything was healing properly. The night before the checkup, Nancy and I went out to dinner. Usually I pray before we eat, but for some reason this night I asked my bride to pray for us. This was early December and we had easily met our five-thousand-dollar annual deductible on our health insurance plan with the shoulder and eye surgery. Here is a summary of Nancy's prayer:

> "Father God, we thank you for the blessing of this food, our
> marriage, and most of all, the sacrifice of Jesus, by which
> we are your children. We thank you for all you have pro-
> vided for us. Father, if there are any further medical needs
> planned for us, please allow them before the end of the year
> since our deductible is met. We thank you in the name of
> Jesus. Amen."

The next day I found out that indeed the prayer of a righteous woman is heard. I sat in the doctor's office and he said that my right eye was healing very nicely, saying that in about four or five days I should have a complete recovery of sight in that eye. I reported that I was seeing a couple small floaters in my left eye. "Well, it looked fine two weeks ago when I checked it, but I'll take another look," the doctor said. Then I heard two words you never want your doctor to mutter: "Oh, crap!" He told me somehow I now had a central detachment of the retina in my left eye and that he needed to perform surgery immediately because a blow to the head might lead to permanent sight loss in my left eye. I had surgery that night and Nancy drove me home, same as ten days earlier. But things were much different this time. The new gas bubble in my left eye, combined with the one in the right eye, left me virtually blind for three days. I sat there unable to read the Word or a book or watch television. It was just God and me.

As I prayed, I was beginning to "hear" some very strange things. Messages like "I will bring this nation to its knees economically so it chooses if it will worship money or Me." That is certainly coming about. But the one message I kept hearing was a chilling one that I just could not understand at that time: "I have taken your sight; I will restore it so you can connect the dots."

My memory raced to try and remember anywhere in God's Word where "connecting the dots" was mentioned as a spiritual gift or even mentioned at all, and of course, I came up empty. I tried to dismiss the message but I could not over the following months. I had no idea what God meant by "connect the dots."

As usual, God prepares us in advance for the work He ordains within us. As I look back now, I see what He meant by "connect the dots." We tend to look at movements like social justice, the emergent church, universalism, or New Age Christianity as separate entities. They are not. They are all different but connected components of Satan's master plan to deceive many in these final days. In fairness, most of the leaders of these movements do not realize they are pawns in Satan's chess match with God, and in truth, every one of us at times is used by Satan. But leaders of these and other movements are unknowingly advancing Satan's agenda to deceive millions in America. They are people who do love Jesus but have been led astray from the absolute truth of God's Word and His true character and nature. They are people who often mean well, but lack or reject the knowledge of the Word or seek to repackage God to fit the times or their vision of who God should be.

Standing Up for the Truth

As I shared information we uncovered about Jim Wallis, Brian McLaren,

Tony Campolo, and others with our board, God began to speak to us as a team. He encouraged us to continue the battle and to get out of our mindset of being a radio station that just plays music. He was opening our eyes to be His vessel for opening the eyes of other Christians who had also been lulled to sleep. On December 6, 2010, after a lot of prayer and preparation, *Stand Up For the Truth* debuted on Q90 FM and I have hosted the show ever since. The show is loved by many and hated by some, but it is not dismissed or ignored. We are asking the tough questions too long ignored by Christians and our leaders. We share the news and encourage people to take everything they hear back to the Word of God to see if it is true. The only measure man has for real truth is the written Word of God. It must be the plumb line upon which every opinion and issue is measured.

There are no sacred cows on this show. No issue is ignored. From Islam to the emergent church, from New Age Christianity to biblical illiteracy, and from abortion to homosexuality, the issues are discussed and the Word of God is the sole star of the show.

I am often asked just what we are trying to accomplish with *Stand Up For the Truth*. We are accused of dividing the body of Christ at times and stirring up dissension within the ranks. Some pastors report that every week a listener is coming up to them and sharing something they heard on the show, wondering where their church stands on the issue. And quite frankly, some pastors do not like the added questions and scrutiny. They would prefer to remain "ostrich Christians," just sticking their heads in the sand, believing evil and deception will just pass them by if they can't see it.

So why do we air *Stand Up For the Truth*? Barna Group research reports that only one in three self-professed born-again believers actually believes that the Bible is absolute truth, with more and more Christians believing truth is relative and not absolute. We seem to have returned to the pre-Reformation days, where biblical illiteracy is the norm. Far too many Christians are going to church on Sunday to hear what the pastor or priest says is in the Bible (if he reads from it at all), rather than being like the Bereans in Acts 17:11 who searched the Scriptures daily to ascertain real truth. That is the reason we air *Stand Up For the*

Truth and why over the last eight years it has accumulated loyal listeners throughout the world. Dedicated Christians are hungry for truth in a world of lies. They have been lied to by the government, public schools, the media, and even by some of our church leaders. Spiritual death is creeping into American Christianity, and a growing number of discerning Christians refuse to be a part of it.

We *Are* in a War!

In 2009 I was as blind as anyone to the great deception infecting American Christianity. But God used what I first saw as suffering to reveal the truth to me: American Christianity is in the midst of an adulterous affair with secular culture, slowly committing spiritual suicide. My mother's suicide could have been prevented if she had listened to her doctors and to those of us who loved her, but she chose to remain on a slow suicidal path. Will the church listen to those who are warning her of the effects of her adultery with the world? Or will she continue a slow spiritual death by dismissing the Word and truth of God?

We are in a war. Make no mistake about that. We face a tough, experienced, powerful enemy in Satan. He has a strong, committed army at his disposal and they are pounding at the walls of American Christianity. But this army would have no power over us if we stood on the truth of God's Word by the power of the Holy Spirit. But unfortunately, the Enemy has sympathizers within our camp, and they are weakening us from within through Christian leaders and followers who are in love with the trappings and values of this sinful culture.

I hope what you read will challenge you and awaken you if you find you have been lulled to sleep. I would prefer to write a happy book about how we are defeating the Enemy at every turn, but that book would be a fiction novel. I am a watchman on the wall. I did not ask for this assignment, and at times I wish God would give it to someone else. But He is God and I am just Mike. Where He leads, I will follow. But whether you want to accept it or not, we are all called to be watchmen. We have been entrusted with the truth of God's Word and the indwelling of the Holy Spirit. So read the command the Lord your God gives you as a watchman – and read it carefully.

*"Son of man, I have made you a watchman for the people of Israel; so hear the word I speak and give them warning from me. When I say to the wicked, 'You wicked person, you will surely die,' and you do not speak out to dissuade them from their ways, that wicked person will die for their sin, and **I will hold you accountable for their blood**. But if you do warn the wicked person to turn from their ways and they do not do so, they will die for their sin, though you yourself will be saved."* (Ezekiel 33:7-9, emphasis added)

Chapter 2

The Duties of the Watchman

Life was a lot easier in 2009. I was leading a Christian radio station that played music twenty-four hours a day. No teaching programs and no controversy except the occasional caller who warned we were playing the devil's music and telling us every translation except the original King James Version was invalid and deceptive.

I had just turned fifty-five and life was settling down after a year of seventy-hour workweeks as we began moving into our brand-new ministry facility. Nancy and I were doing wonderfully as a couple, and the ministry was growing and doing very well as we embraced our core values and principles, challenging one another to draw closer to God individually and as a team. Life would start to slow down now and I welcomed normal workweeks once again.

I often hear that if you want to make God laugh, tell Him your plans for tomorrow or next year. If true, I must have provided Him with a real hearty laugh, because He indeed had other plans. He called us as a ministry – and me personally – to step up our commitment to Him and the truth of His Word. Well, so much for a return to normality.

While the workweeks remained long and at times disruptive, I wouldn't trade them for all the tea in China. God has lit a passion in me to know Him intimately and to challenge Christians to turn away from our biblical illiteracy that is causing confusion in the church and allowing dangerous teachings to lead many astray. I look at life now with a new sense of peace in my own mortality. Now at age sixty-four, I realize statistically I have about another twelve years to live, since men born in 1954 live to an average age of seventy-six. If God allows me more years in this life, I will praise and thank Him. If He calls me home earlier, I will still praise Him because as Paul said in Philippians 1:21, *To live is Christ and to die is gain.*

This sense of my own creeping mortality has renewed my passion for God and the calling He has given me. Like an astronaut on a one-way journey to a new world with no worries about saving fuel for the return trip, I am going full speed to wherever God is leading me. I used to look at growing old as a problem, but I now see it as a great blessing. Every day I am one day closer to being with my Lord and Savior. "Retirement" is no longer something I desire. I will continue in my role as a watchman until God calls me home.

Sound the Alarm – but Sound the Right One!

Our calling as watchmen carries serious responsibilities. A gift or calling from God that is misused can quickly turn into a burden and can be destructive to the wrong people if not wielded properly. No matter what our calling or gift, we must use it with biblical knowledge, discernment, and a desire to restore rather than destroy.

We must resist the temptation to go on "witch hunts," always remembering that every one of us falls short of the glory of God and that none of us will ever figure God out completely. We will all be in error on something when we stand before Him. We must always err on the side of caution before screaming "heretic" over a leader or teacher we disagree with.

However, we must also resist the temptation to sit back in silence as dangerous teachings and leaders seem to be straying from biblical truth. Picture a watchman on the top of a wall. Inside are God's people who still believe that His Word is absolute truth. Outside the wall are people who either hate God, are ambivalent to Him, or who desire to dismantle the truth of His written Word. This is the great battle for American Christianity these days.

But there is also another group of people outside the great city of truth. They may have been lured away by slick teaching that tickled their ears. They may have decided a long time ago to remain neutral in this great battle, wanting to just live and let live. One day they decide to enter the great city. As they approach from a distance, the watchman sees them approaching the wall, but he cannot determine if they are enemy combatants or innocent pilgrims. So he sounds the alarm, but what alarm does he sound? "The enemy approaches"? Or "Strangers approaching"? What he announces carries huge ramifications. If he announces them as enemy combatants, the soldiers inside the city open fire, but if they are not enemies but rather innocent pilgrims, we have innocent blood on our hands.

However, if that watchman just lets these strangers inside the wall without at least sounding the alarm, and they turn out to be enemy combatants, the result could be catastrophic for the citizens inside, as an enemy has been turned loose inside the wall. The blood of the innocent citizens would be on the hands of the watchman.

This is a burden watchmen must carry. We must be careful to not open fire on innocent people who are not a part of the Enemy's army, but we must also be vigilant so we do not let enemy forces inside the camp where innocent people will be destroyed.

What we must not do is automatically sound an alarm to open fire. We must first sound an alarm for the leaders of the great city to discern if the approaching people are enemies or innocent pilgrims. If it is clearly established that these people are enemy combatants, then we go to war. But we must always be cautious before we call to unleash an attack.

As I was writing "The Demise of Christian Leadership" chapter to this book, I suddenly felt anger toward those I was writing about. How could they call what they are doing biblical leadership when the gospel was being twisted or compromised, and leaders with worldly beliefs were being brought into church and exalted? The anger was welling up in me with each keystroke. On a Sunday afternoon as I was completing that chapter, the anger reached a fever pitch and I was starting to feel hatred seep up in me. I immediately stopped typing and asked God to forgive me. My attitude was clearly wrong.

Some of you reading this book may think it is hateful as we name names and ask questions that need to be asked about our leadership and ourselves. However, we must not fall into the trap of thinking it is wrong to question leadership and hold them accountable to the Bible. We must be faithful to the Word of God at all times, holding every teacher to the standard of the written Word. We must start asking questions that have been ignored by too many for too long. Our desire should never be to tear down, but to restore. Also, I do not think the leaders I mention in this book are necessarily evil, nor do I question their salvation in Jesus Christ; only God is qualified to make that decision. And like every Christian leader, they are targeted by a ruthless Enemy every day. Their positions as leaders make them very vulnerable to the subtle attacks of the Enemy, and we must pray for them and give them the benefit of the doubt if we see something questionable in what they say or do. However, we must never allow them to be above reproach. When we start to see a pattern of words or actions that are not lining up with the Scriptures, we must have the wisdom and courage to confront them.

We mention names because we need these men of influence to become strong leaders for such a time as this, when the church needs them desperately. We must pray that God opens their eyes to their dangerous compromise with a sinful culture. However, we must never fall for the lie that leaders should not be questioned or challenged. Leadership must always be held accountable for their words and actions. Jesus did it and so did Paul. We must also.

Taking a Stand

It is painful to have to question Christian brothers and sisters. Like anyone, I would rather just believe the best in people and trust that God will shake things out. In fact, that is a common argument and critique we hear all the time regarding *Stand Up For the Truth*: "Just let God sort this out." There is only one problem with that argument: It flies in the face of Scripture.

Jesus called out the Pharisees who were abusing the law and acting like hypocrites. He called them *whitewashed tombs*. The Pharisees were the leaders and teachers of their times. Paul publicly called out

Peter in Galatians for being two-faced and trying to appease both Jews and Gentiles.

Second Corinthians 11 is a chilling chapter in the New Testament, where Paul begins a message of confronting false teachers who preach a false gospel and preach a different Jesus or present false spirits as truth:

> *But I am afraid that just as Eve was deceived by the serpent's cunning, your minds may somehow be led astray from your sincere and pure devotion to Christ. For if someone comes to you and preaches a Jesus other than the Jesus we preached, or if you receive a different spirit from the Spirit you received, or a different gospel from the one you accepted, you put up with it easily enough.* (2 Corinthians 11:3-4)

Talk about hitting the three major illnesses infecting American Christianity these days:

- a different Jesus

- a different gospel

- a different spirit

Jesus is being "refashioned" into a loving Jesus who accepts sin and would never judge anyone. He has now become our buddy instead of our Lord and King. And the gospel of salvation is being minimized into a simple "Ask Jesus into your heart" prayer, rather than a sincere confession of sin, repentance, and a commitment to turn away from the sinful nature by the power of the Holy Spirit.

There are false spirits being introduced into the church through Buddhism, Hinduism, mysticism, and New Age Christianity everywhere we look. If we do not stand against these false teachings and movements, we are just as guilty as those who teach them.

Naming Names

A common argument we hear is, "Talk about the issues, but you don't have to point fingers at specific people." If you were a Mormon or a Jehovah's Witness member, wouldn't you want someone pointing out the error in your leadership? Wouldn't you take what Joseph Smith taught and hold it against Scripture, pointing out the error? Funny, we have no problem naming names of cult leaders but we cringe at the sound of a Christian leader being called out for questionable teaching. If you were a new Christian who had fallen under the influence of a leader who told you that there were ways to eternal life other than through Jesus, wouldn't you want a friend to sit you down and point out the error?

It's as if we believe Christian leaders should get a pass from account-ability and scrutiny when in fact, leaders should have *greater* accountability and receive *greater* scrutiny because of their influence over thousands and even millions of Christians. Should we not discuss Barack Obama's hypocrisy in claiming to be a born-again believer while supporting the murder of innocent children through abortion and fighting for homo-sexual marriage? What about Mitt Romney claiming Mormonism is Christianity? What about Nancy Pelosi, who says she is a Catholic, yet pushes for greater and greater access to abortion, including sponsoring legislation that would allow physicians to kill a child who survived an abortion attempt and was born?

Should we not question George W. Bush's beliefs as a Christian when he states that Muslims and Christians worship the same God, and when he calls for the division of Jerusalem in an attempt to bring peace to the Middle East? If Brian McLaren or Jim Wallis calls out a conservative Christian politician over his views, the left applauds them. If conservative Christians call out progressive Christian leaders, we are called mean-spirited and divisive.

See folks, the beauty or disgust in "naming names" is in the eye of the beholder. When the opponent is called out, we cheer; when our guy is called out, we call it mean-spirited.

Word of Faith preachers like Joel Osteen, Kenneth Copeland, and Benny Hinn, along with influential pastors like Rick Warren and Bill Hybels, are powerful public figures with great influence. They are open about their beliefs and programs and they are leaders. We must not cower from challenging them when we feel they have strayed from the truth of God's Word, whether they do it intentionally or unintentionally.

Another argument we hear is the "Matthew 18" argument. First of all, Matthew 18 talks about going to a brother who sins personally against you, not a public figure or teacher who shares questionable beliefs or teaching. And Matthew 18 is a message of the importance of church discipline against a professing believer in unrepentant sin.

When we have attempted to contact people like Rick Warren, Bill Hybels, and Rob Bell before we shared our concerns on air, our numerous calls or emails have gone unanswered. So should we not discuss serious issues and the people who teach them until we sit down face to face and get to "know their hearts" as we have been encouraged to do? Well, if we follow that logic, these teachers can hide behind their entourage and voice mails perpetually and avoid any public scrutiny. Besides, as Solomon prayed at the dedication of the temple, only God truly knows the human heart. *For you alone know the human heart* (2 Chronicles 6:30).

Naming names is important when the person discussed wields tremendous influence. No one had a problem mentioning Harold Camping when he wrongfully predicted the date of Jesus' return. He was publicly rebuked as he should have been. So who determines whose name is mentioned and who is exempt? Usually it depends on our personal view of the person and the subject discussed.

A local pastor who is a wonderful brother in the Lord and has been a friend for years is a Pentecostal pastor. He even classifies himself as a Word of Faith pastor, but his views are soundly biblical on what the role of faith is in answered prayer. He realizes God alone decides who will be healed, but he believes our level of faith in God plays an important role when we approach His throne. I agree completely.

When I paid him a visit to tell him we were preparing shows about some of the outrageous claims of some Word of Faith pastors and leaders like Kenneth Copeland (there I go naming names again), and I was seeking his counsel and thoughts, he paused for a moment. He looked up smiling and said something like "Keep on exposing the false teachers of the social justice and emergent church movements but leave the Word of Faith Movement alone." He knew, of course, I could not do that and he was not serious in his request.

We are all often selective in whom we choose to question and whom we choose to blindly follow. But we must learn to take *everything* we hear and are taught and hold it up to Scripture to verify its truth or to refute it as false. No matter if it is Jim Wallis or David Barton, Brian McLaren or John MacArthur, Barack Obama or George W. Bush. Leaders must be held accountable for what they say, what they teach, and what they do. The Word of God must be our sole judge of what truth is and what is false.

Statements versus Questions

How we make arguments or enlighten people on issues is just as important as that we do it in the first place. An adage we try to remember is this: Questions lower tensions; statements raise tensions. We would all rather be asked than ordered to do something. If Nancy wants me to cook dinner, her asking me, "Honey, would you mind cooking dinner?" will go a lot further than her stating, "You're cooking dinner tonight" will ever go.

Questions are our way of exploring what is going on; statements are our definitive beliefs that we know what is going on. Questions often set the table for respectful dialogue, while statements often lead to emotional and defensive responses. If I ask a question like "Do you think Bob Smith is a heretic?" I am eliciting opinion and discussion. If I say, "Bob Smith is a heretic," I am making a strong statement. There is a huge difference between the two: one is seeking input; the other is making a judgment.

Now there are times for strong statements. Brian McLaren and Rob Bell are heretics because they deny the substitutionary atonement of the cross as part of Christian doctrine while claiming to be Christians. As watchmen, or anyone who is passionate about the truth, we will be continually tempted to call anyone we disagree with on doctrine a heretic. We must avoid that temptation! There is a time for that when a teacher crosses a very definitive line, but we must be careful about wielding the word *heretic* with every person who disagrees with something we believe. If that is the standard, then we are all heretics to someone.

In the Word of Faith Movement, some teachers have crossed a line and are teaching doctrines that are clearly refuted by the Bible. But some pastors and believers who call themselves "Word of Faith" mean something totally different than the leaders who teach false doctrine.

A listener to our show emailed me during a broadcast telling me she was offended by a post we put up on our *Stand Up For the Truth* Facebook site. She said she was offended "as a person who believes we can speak things into existence." I read her email on air and told her whoever is teaching her this is leading her down a very dangerous path. She emailed me later and asked if we could meet. Nancy and I met with her that week for about two hours. She is a very nice lady who loves God very deeply and is active in her church and in outreach to children in her community. I asked her to tell me a time she spoke something into existence, and she shared a time when they were reaching out to children with some sock puppets they had made as gifts for these poorer children. She said they had about forty puppets available but they were seeing probably eighty or more children coming to their event. So she and her friends prayed for God to provide what they needed to serve the children and she told me they ended up with enough puppets for each child.

I said, "Oh, like the story in the gospel about the loaves and the fishes," and she responded with an enthusiastic "Yes!" I pointed out to her that she did not speak anything into existence – she prayed for God's provision and He responded.

This example points to how we need to be careful with the words we use and improve our interpersonal communication between believers. If we hear something that sounds wrong or dangerous, we should first seek clarification to make sure we heard what we thought we heard. We must not give the Enemy a foothold between us as Christians.

Where this does become problematic is when a leader says or does something that is suspicious and then hides behind his entourage despite people asking for clarification. Letters, phone calls, and emails seeking clarification receive no response, leaving us to question just why no clarification comes forward. This has been the case over the years with Pastor Rick Warren, as we will discuss a little later.

One more word about standing up and defending the truth of God's Word as a watchman on the wall: You'd better have thick skin and you'd better not get too full of yourself. You will be loved one day by a person who admires your boldness, and despised the next day because you dared question a movement he is involved in. There will be longtime friends who suddenly look at you with either pity or disdain because they feel you have gone over the deep end. You will be called courageous one day and a bully the next. You will be called a divider, a Pharisee, a Sanballat, mean-spirited, and a hater. I am many things, and some of them not too good, but those that know me know I am none of these things. But it is the price you pay these days for discussing issues too long ignored by the church.

A former boss I worked for almost thirty years ago summed it up best when I told him I wanted to recommend to the board that our savings and loan institution consider selling annuities to our customers, a controversial proposal at the time. He looked at me and said, "Well, they say you can always tell who the pioneers are; they're the ones with the arrows in their backs."

No matter how loving, careful, or considerate we are as watchmen, we will get some arrows in our backs, and they may come from sources we least expect. That just comes with the territory. But God is so worth any small price we have to pay for defending His Word and His church.

We must reach the point of spiritual maturity where what others think of us pales in comparison to speaking the truth in love when their eternal souls are in jeopardy. When you speak the truth with love and grace, presenting God's Word to those who are confused or deceived, and you are hated by the world, you are in very good company with people like Jesus and Paul.

There are no neutral people in this great spiritual battle: You are either on God's side or you support His enemies. Your silence as people are being deceived places you in the camp of the Enemy.

Chapter 3

The Rise and Fall of a Nation under God

The Birth of American Christianity

Something amazing happened in 1775. A group born of immigrants from Europe smelled freedom – a freedom birthed by God and anchored in responsibility to Him and to His perfect law. Men such as George Washington, John Adams, and Thomas Jefferson started to talk treason. They and their ancestors had come to a new land called America to plant their roots and grow. They sought a new land where a man could start over, grow, and prosper. A place where a man could escape a tyrannical monarchy that wanted to control everything from their pocketbooks to how they worshipped. They thought if they distanced themselves from England, they could prosper and grow, but what they got instead was, I believe, inspiration from the Holy Spirit.

As England tried to tighten the reins on their burgeoning independence, these men and others started to whisper "independence" – a word the British Empire simply never tolerated. After many long, painstaking meetings filled with heated debate, the United States of America declared its intention to break away from England. And truly, history was made.

These men envisioned a nation unlike any in the history of mankind. A nation that recognized any rights of man came from God alone; a nation that believed that government was an impediment to worshipping God; that any time a man tried to act as an intermediary between God and another man, something was lost in the translation. Some of these men were deists, but most were solid Christians who read the Bible regularly.

The forthcoming Declaration of Independence and Constitution were modeled on the Bible and were established on the example of the servant leadership Jesus lived by. We would be a nation where government did not exist to be served, but rather to serve and represent the people it governed.

Was it a perfect form of government? No. The only perfect form of government is one where God is King and we are His subjects. But our founding fathers came closer than anyone in history to creating a government that could glorify God and keep man in his place.

Over the last fifty years, our Constitution has been mocked, dismissed, and even shredded by secular humanists and their allies. The often-misquoted *separation of church and state* exists nowhere in our founding documents. To the contrary, many of our founding fathers recognized and wrote that a democratic republic could only survive with God's moral laws as the cornerstone.

Our nation's founders were very sensitive to the relationship between government and religion. They addressed it in the First Amendment to the Constitution which reads, "Congress shall make no law respecting an establishment of religion, or prohibiting the free exercise thereof." One could argue that our nation has remained reasonably faithful to the first portion – the "establishment of religion." But the second part, "prohibiting the free exercise thereof," is clearly under increasing attack, seen in Christian children banned from saying prayers or invoking the name of Jesus when they are on school grounds, pastors being fined or arrested for sharing the gospel in public, and churches being forced to rent facilities to any organization, regardless of religious beliefs. If this is not prohibiting the free exercise of religion, then just what is?

And it is not just any or every religion being attacked; it is a persecution that seems to be directed solely at Christianity. Up until the 1960s, whenever the government or a public institution would attempt to silence Christians, the church responded in full force. But something happened in the sixties; something was birthed that would earmark this nation for a slow, suicidal walk. We began to step toward the edge of a cliff with a blindfold on, and with each passing year, we moved one step closer to falling off the cliff into the abyss. Historically, when our nation would start to show early signs of self-destruction, the Christian church would intervene and convince or shame the culture back from the cliff. But this time it was different. Not only did the church not corral the march toward suicide of this nation, but she also joined in, ceding her moral authority, and walking to the cliff alongside the nation.

This attack on Christianity has been incremental and subtle. Humanists knew that any attempt to overtly overthrow American Christianity would be met with fierce resistance, so over time they chipped away at its foundation slowly and meticulously. Rather than a full frontal assault that was sure to fail, they started to infiltrate American Christianity with spies and traitors. They borrowed a page from *Rules for Radicals* by communist Saul Alinsky. Alinsky dedicated his book to Lucifer and spells out detailed plans on how to infiltrate and subvert government and society. A key step that Alinsky identified is to infiltrate and pollute the church, elevating new thinkers as leaders. These new thinkers include people like Jim Wallis, a disciple of Saul Alinsky, progressive pastors and priests committed to the doctrine of social justice who are slowly starting to twist the true gospel, and emergent leaders like Brian McLaren, Tony Campolo, and Rob Bell, who reject the absolute truth of God's Word in favor of feelings and experience. Alinsky taught that once people like this were elevated to leadership and positions of influence, the followers would come along in lockstep.

These Christian leaders have been subtly undermining the basic tenets of Christianity and the absolute truth of the Bible. They relate to a postmodern culture that has been prepared by secular education and media to question everything and believe that no truth is absolute. To them, truth is subjective and dependent on our personal emotions and experiences.

Alinsky understood that the only way to bring down the republic was to apply pressure from several sources and that the church held the key. Once the church was effectively neutralized, everything else would fall into place. Hitler realized and accomplished this in his rise to power in Nazi Germany. When you can successfully neutralize the church, victory will soon follow.

It is a mistake to view the attacks on America and American Christianity as separate battles. Founded on Judeo-Christian beliefs and dependent on a strong Christian church, a free republic and a strong church need each other. Secularists and extreme left-wing progressives realize this, and their attacks to implement "hope and change" are a coordinated assault on both the American republic and Christianity in America.

From 2009 to 2016, an Alinsky disciple occupied the White House. President Obama claimed to be a Christian but his stances on abortion and homosexual marriage betrayed his heart. Many of the Obama appointees were anti-Christian, either atheists or secularists who believe in the goodness of man. Christian leaders who support him generally dismiss the Bible as absolute truth, no less a secular stand even though they are Christians. The Obama Administration successfully expanded abortion rights, expanded marriage to include homosexual couples, and brought the illusion of transgenderism into public education and dialogue. They opened a two-front assault on our republic and traditional, fundamental Christianity in a war that is being won because many church leaders lack the courage to speak out against these abominations that are leading people to eternal separation from God.

The mandate under Obamacare that forces health insurers, employers, and religious organizations to provide free contraceptives and abortion drugs is more than just an attack on the right of American citizens to decide if they will purchase health insurance; it is an attack on freedom of religion. It puts the federal government one step closer to mandating the religious beliefs of every American citizen.

The Era of Narcissism

The sixties were really a wonderful time to be a child in this nation. The nation was prospering economically, the boundary between socially acceptable and unacceptable behavior was well defined, and life as a whole was pretty wonderful. Admittedly, this perspective comes from a middle-class white guy, and there certainly were difficult times in this nation if you were black. Racial discrimination was still a stark reality for many minorities, but the nation took steps to correct this through civil rights legislation and a growing pressure on racism as a whole.

A song that would become popular by a group called Buffalo Springfield became iconic. One of the lines read, "There's something happening here; what it is ain't exactly clear." Social unrest started to grow as the nation escalated its war in Vietnam. College campuses began to witness violent riots, and illegal drugs were flowing into the country from greedy parasites looking to turn a profit off the minds and lives of young Americans.

An entire generation was calling for personal freedom: freedom of expression, freedom to consume any mind-altering drug they chose, sexual freedom outside the established morals, and freedom from laws or moral restraint. Individual freedom became the rallying cry of an entire generation. A slogan that was born in this era said it all and would have a profound effect on the future of this nation: "If it feels good, do it!"

Freedom! Freedom! Everywhere freedom! But this generation seemed to forget something our nation's founders knew all too well: freedom without responsibility is a mirage and would be the death of a nation and a people. Freedom without responsibility became the cry of an entire generation, and the Christian church in America seemed to start embracing it. Suddenly the Christian church in America was not there to bring proper moral balance to the cry of a wicked and perverse people. The church was to be the guardian of this nation, providing righteous, moral boundaries to keep this nation "under God." But the church started to remain silent at a time when our nation needed it the most. And it would get worse – much worse – just a few short years later.

Sadly, freedom without responsibility has become a hallmark for many Christian churches and teachers. We tout our new freedom in Christ Jesus as we should, but we have been deceived about just what this freedom in Jesus represents. To many Christians we are free from the law and obedience to God and we are free to continue sinning with no consequences. They believe we are free to behave the way we want as

Christians, rather than how God's Word teaches us we should behave. This is reflected in many studies that show Christians divorce at a rate equal to non-Christians; Christians access pornography at a rate as high as unbelievers, including up to 80 percent of pastors secretly admitting to this; and Christians are just as apt to cheat on their taxes or expense reports as unbelievers.

Jesus died to free us from sin, not from obedience. In fact, He raised the bar on obedience by telling us a lustful thought for another woman is tantamount to adultery. He died to free us from the punishment of sin for eternity, the power of sin in this lifetime, and the presence of sin when we live with Him in heaven. He did not die to free us from obedience and the consequences of sin in this lifetime. We expect the world to be full of narcissists. We should not accept that same attitude among Christians.

The Day American Christianity Began to Die

Sometimes the onset of insanity is a process. Sometimes it comes on suddenly, without warning, causing unbelievable actions and consequences. On January 22, 1973, insanity struck suddenly in this nation. In a shocking case of improper judicial restraint and moral bankruptcy, seven U. S. Supreme Court justices ruled that a woman's right to privacy trumped the life of the child she was carrying in her womb.

There are times when you just look at something and say, "Huh?" Can someone please tell me what the right to privacy has to do with ending another person's life? What could possess seven intelligent men, Supreme Court justices, to rule that a woman had a right to murder her child because of privacy? I'm sure the evil depravity of man has nothing to do with it!

I love to argue the ridiculous from an equally ridiculous point of view sometimes, so here goes. Say I catch a man outside peeking at my wife in the bedroom and I go out and kill him. Do you think there is a court in the land that wouldn't convict me of murder, or at least manslaughter? I can consume alcohol to any extent I want in the privacy of my own home. If I get in my car and run over a pedestrian and kill him, is there a court anywhere that will exonerate me if I claim a right to drink privately as a defense? "Well, Mike, that's just a ridiculous argument." I agree. It's almost as ridiculous as arguing that privacy protects a woman's right to murder her own child.

In Exodus 1, we see the first recorded account of babies being killed. As the Israelites in Egypt grew in numbers, the Egyptian king was fearful of their increasing numbers and ordered every male child of the Israelites to be killed at birth to control their population growth. But midwives who remained faithful to God refused to obey this hideous order and were blessed by God for their obedience to Him. Their obedience also led to the survival of a man crucial to the history of the world: Moses.

These Israelite women honored and obeyed God, bringing life when there existed a culture of death, and they were blessed by God. Today, with the church sitting back idly, our nation allows the murder of more than one million children every year in the name of "choice."

> *"And you took your sons and daughters whom you bore to me and sacrificed them as food to the idols. Was your prostitution not enough? You slaughtered my children and sacrificed them to idols."* (Ezekiel 16:20-21)

Our children – God's children – are being slaughtered once again, sacrificed to our own personal idol: ourselves. We kill innocent children after conceiving them in prostitution with the world and our flesh every time we have sex outside of marriage. We give in to our carnality and then compound the sin of adultery with the sin of murder. And where is the church in all of this? We are sitting on the sidelines for fear of being seen as hateful or judgmental. Our silence has cost the lives of millions.

January 22, 1973, will go down as the day that American leaders officially thumbed their noses at God and His commandments. And if we think we will escape God's wrath and judgment as a nation, we are more arrogant than we could ever imagine. God is slow to anger, but don't think for one second He doesn't get angry. Many times in the Old Testament He brought judgment and punishment down on the nation of Israel for abandoning His ways. Is His anger beginning to swell when He looks at America, a land He has blessed abundantly? Look at 9/11 and the social and economic problems we face. Is God lifting His hand of protection from this great nation? It sure looks like it, and it will get worse if we continue on with our wicked ways.

As tragic as the *Roe v. Wade* decision was, there was an even greater tragedy that was ushered in at that time. Christianity in America sold its soul. The reaction, apart from some Catholic leaders, was pretty mute. The original decision was that a woman could only abort her child in the first trimester, and the church took the bait. I could imagine some Christian leaders actually breathing a sigh of relief over the initial decision. Their rationale would go something like this:

"Well, not a great day, but it could have been a lot worse. After all, the plaintiffs stated that the outcome would make abortions 'rare, but safe.' And besides, abortions can only be performed in the first trimester. Now if they had allowed unfettered abortion at any time of pregnancy, well, we wouldn't stand for that!"

Well, guess what? The initial ruling that abortions could only be performed in the first trimester was later overturned by the very court that initially imposed that restriction. The Christian church in America abandoned what would become fifty-five million children and counting. Being light and salt to the world was replaced with moral and spiritual cowardice!

The year 1973 marked the time when American Christianity basically surrendered our moral standing within this nation. We crossed a line that should never have been crossed. We became that which we previously detested: an immoral, ungodly culture, and we have not recovered from this surrender. In fact, we continue to surrender to the very humanist culture we are called to affect. As Pogo once said, "We met the enemy and he is us."

Going Down – Quickly!

Once you step off a cliff, the fall to the ground is very quick, as fast as gravity carries you. American Christianity, once a beacon of light to this nation and the world, is falling into an abyss of darkness. And short of a miracle of God, we will never return to our once-prominent position of moral authority.

Once you sit by idly and allow fifty-five million children to be murdered, everything else becomes relatively easy. Once you have allowed evil to be seen as acceptable, you only have one way to go – down. And Christianity in America is going down at an accelerated pace.

I simply cannot understand why the outcry from Christians over the murder of fifty-five million babies is not deafening. Have we grown so arrogant, selfish, and callous as Christians that we just sit back and watch a genocide go on that makes Hitler look tame in comparison, without holding our politicians responsible? Sadly, we do because we are no better than the pagan culture we bemoan. We continue to sit by idly as mass murder by the millions happens in our nation every year. In fact, we do worse than just sit by idly; we participate in the genocide when we continue to vote for pro-death candidates because they appeal to us economically. We are, in essence, financially paying for the murder of innocent children.

We cheer in church when a couple has a child and marvel at the miracle of life, yet do nothing to stop the murder of other innocent children who should have the same right to be born. Quite frankly, the hypocrisy of this makes me sick.

For Christians who vote for progressive pro-abortion candidates, I ask you to answer this question: How many children are you willing to let die for your tax cut or for an increase in your government subsidies? One? One hundred? One thousand? One million? How many murders are you willing to participate in for your personal gain? What will you say to God when you stand before Him and He asks you to explain your vote – why you cared more about your tax cut or government benefits than the life of children He knitted into their mother's wombs? If you will not at least think about these questions, don't you dare tell me how much you love God, because I ain't buying it.

I Guess It *Is* Okay to Be Gay

I confess: I used to watch *Seinfeld*. While some of the episodes crossed a line with sexuality, I found the story of four narcissistic, self-centered New Yorkers to be humorous, well written, and sadly indicative of where we are headed as a nation and as a church.

In one episode, a reporter overhears Elaine pretending George and

Jerry are gay and she proceeds to write an article talking about them as a couple. The episode goes on with the two of them trying to squelch the lie, saying, "I'm not gay – not that there's anything wrong with that."

But there is something wrong with it: It is sin. Perhaps no worse than adultery, but it is sin nonetheless. On the issue of standing up for the truth of God's Word on homosexuality, the church has boxed itself in on this issue over the years and is now paying a price. For years, homosexuals were demonized as the *worst* of sinners. They were treated as less than human, instead of men and women struggling with sexual sin. We bashed homosexuals as evil, all the while turning our back on heterosexual adultery within Christian leadership. A Christian leader could fall because of heterosexual adultery and usually be restored later on. But if that leader, or even a rank-and-file Christian, fell due to homosexual behavior, they were finished.

The Christian church in America was accused of being homophobic haters, and sadly, there is some truth in that accusation. We must confess any hatred we have toward homosexuals, particularly Christians who struggle with that sin. As the church in America singled out homosexuals as the worst of deviants, the homosexual movement was making inroads into a culture that today accepts their behavior as normal. The media, supportive of secular culture, accused the church of being homophobic and hateful.

Most church leaders have recanted their hatred and now view homosexuality as a sexual sin no different than heterosexual sin. But, in a case of overcompensating to relieve our guilt on this issue, we have gone too far. Out of fear of ever being called homophobic or hateful again, we have chosen to not even call homosexuality a sin in many Christian churches. So we first hated the homosexual, and now we are piling on more hate by not pointing out their sin against God and offering the forgiveness and restoration of the gospel.

In 2015 the U.S. Supreme Court legalized homosexual marriage in our nation. The church again sat silently on the sidelines. But when we let fifty-five million babies be murdered because we are lazy or fear being called close minded, this approval via silence makes perfect sense. It is only a matter of time, perhaps a few short years, until churches will be forced to marry homosexuals or lose their tax-exempt status. Sadly, most will capitulate because they worship money instead of God.

Where Is the Church?

As a whole, the church seems content to sit the battle out. Our pastors have been intimidated into believing the church can play no role in selecting our government leaders. They are fearful that anything they say about how a Christian should vote will land them in hot water with the IRS.

The Alliance Defense Fund ("ADF"), an organization dedicated to defending the rights of Christian individuals and organizations, spends millions of dollars every year defending Christians and attempting to educate Christian leaders and pastors about their rights to affect the political culture of this nation. In fact, they are picking a fight with the IRS, hoping they will just try to sue a pastor or church over talking about politics from the pulpit. Every year, hundreds of pastors use their Sunday services in an election year to talk about the need for Christians to vote for pro-life, pro-marriage candidates. The pastors record their sermons and send them to the IRS, waiting for some kind of challenge.

According to the ADF, the IRS knows they would lose in court if they sued a church for preaching on politics the way ADF teaches churches what they are legally allowed to say. A pastor can point out where particular candidates stand on issues like abortion and gay marriage. He can say almost anything except whom his church members should vote for. Many pastors take advantage of this freedom. The only problem is 99 percent of them are progressive pastors who approve of issues like gay marriage and abortion. So while these wolves in sheep's clothing take advantage of the law to promote ungodly candidates, many pro-life, pro-family pastors and churches sit back idly, allowing our nation to become a modern-day Sodom and Gomorrah.

This may sound harsh, but the truth sometimes hurts. Any pastor who claims he is unaware of his freedom to discuss politics and candidates from the pulpit is either lazy or lying. Chances are he is afraid, not of the IRS, but of offending someone in his own church, afraid of criticism that might lead to a member being offended and leaving his church. I might suggest that if a church member threatens to leave your church because he supports abortion or homosexual marriage, your church should be thankful as he exits the church body. You will be a stronger, more-righteous body without him. If a Christian cannot understand that abortion and homosexuality are sins, they are probably not truly born-again believers and shouldn't be allowed to stay to pollute others.

The church must engage in the political process and the culture war, but must also never forget that this is primarily a spiritual war, fought in the heavens. But simply "hiding behind prayer" is not enough. I do not underestimate God's power or the power of prayer, but too often Christians vow they will pray but are distracted and never get there. Or we pray expecting God to do all the work as our excuse for laziness or apathy. And if we as Christians do not care enough to be engaged in the battle, just how seriously will God take our prayers?

Fifty-four percent of Roman Catholics and 40 percent of people calling themselves Bible-believing Christians voted for Barack Obama, sweeping him into office as president. Barack Obama, without question, is the most pro-abortion, pro-gay marriage president in our history. Any Christian who took ten minutes to research his voting record, or who by some fluke would have actually heard a pastor share Obama's record, would know what values he represented. But I guess that is asking just a little too much these days.

Many Christians now are complaining as the Obama Administration dismantled this nation economically, morally, and spiritually, but many of those complaining probably voted for him. But we are only getting what we asked for, folks. How is that "hope and change" working out for you Christians?

The church either *affects* the secular culture or the culture *infects* the church. Millions of murdered babies and a growing acceptance of homosexual marriage clearly show us which one of these is happening in American Christianity these days.

Which Savior Are You Voting For?

No politician, republican or democrat, conservative or progressive, can save our nation. Only God can pull us out of the sewer we are swimming in. But our vote does matter and we'd better start taking the time to research candidates and know their voting record and where they stand.

We must also check our own motives in who we vote for. Are you willing to vote for a man who will lower your taxes or protect your union rights but who supports abortion or gay marriage rights? Are your voting values those of the world or are they lined up with God's values?

Some Christians behave and speak as if the savior of this nation will be the next guy they vote for. The culture war and political involvement is important, but too often we look for human answers to spiritual problems. We must research candidates and vote for those who will restore our Christian values, but to become obsessed with one man's ability to save the nation is foolish and futile. We must fight this battle in the spiritual *and* cultural arenas. An either/or approach simply will not do.

> *If my people, who are called by my name, will humble themselves and pray and seek my face and turn from their wicked ways, then I will hear from heaven, and will forgive their sin and will heal their land.* (2 Chronicles 7:14)

There is the savior of America – *God*! Our only real power as a nation comes not from our military, economy, or ingenuity. The only source of real power that has propelled this nation to greatness is our faith in and obedience to God. Over the past fifty years we have turned our back on God and His ways, and our nation, along with American Christianity, has become a shell of its former self. Nothing will change until we repent and ask for God's forgiveness and restoration.

Losing Perspective in Economic Chaos

The presidential election in 2008 was the first election in my memory where abortion was practically ignored as an issue. When Rick Warren hosted Obama and John McCain for his candidate forum, why did he roll over and not pin down Obama on his 100-percent pro-abortion voting record? He let Obama tap-dance around the issue, admitting he was pro-abortion but refusing to ask Obama how he squared up that belief with his self-profession as a Christian. Obama said he wanted to find "common ground" on the issue with pro-life leaders. No wonder Warren let him slide, since Warren has committed to doing the same thing with Islam. Great leadership, Rick! Way to take a stand for life and Christian principles.

The reason this crucial issue is being ignored is this: running on a pro-life platform is probably a surefire way to lose an election at this time in American history. It doesn't seem to make sense when polls show nearly 60 percent of Americans consider themselves pro-life, but standing strong against abortion will probably cost you a lot of votes. Why? Because Christians who claim to be pro-life do not seem to treat it as a core voting issue. We consider ourselves pro-life, but we fall for the candidate who appeals more to our love of money or security over a candidate who stands for biblical righteousness.

This nation was founded upon God's righteous law. We are squandering it away as the nation resembles Babylon more than a shining city on a hill. Blame the atheists, Hollywood, the media, or public education if it makes you feel better. But the truth is, American Christianity was entrusted by our founding fathers to be the moral guardian of this nation. If we are honest with ourselves as Christians, we need travel no farther than the closest mirror to find the real culprits. We, the professed body of Christ in America, have failed this nation and its citizens.

Instead of affecting the secular culture, we have embraced it. This culture is a cancer and that cultural cancer is being invited into the Christian church. The church has surrendered to this cancer and it is permeating and conquering every cell in the body. The result is a slow demise at our own hands.

Chapter 4

Fighting or Surrendering to the Cultural Cancer?

God created man to live in communion with Him for eternity. Adam and Eve were to populate the earth with millions of children to live in perfect harmony with God, living in a world of perfect God-directed peace and harmony. Our world would be one without sickness, disease, poverty, injustice, or death – a world without sin.

Man chose an alternative world. He chose to know evil, following the lead of a rebellious, fallen angel who chose a similar path years or ages earlier. He chose to believe a lie over the truth. Sin entered the world and death became a part of life. Not just physical death, but also spiritual death. Man made a choice that fateful day and choices have consequences. The eternal consequence we face out of that choice is the real possibility of eternal damnation, separated from God in a place without hope of future redemption.

Physical death comes upon us in many forms. So does spiritual death. Both can be sudden or a slow march. Physical death can come about instantly at the hands of an armed criminal or a drunk driver, but most of the time it takes a slow journey where our minds and bodies slowly break down and eventually fail us. This is the fate of man in a fallen world. Every man faces physical death; it is simply unavoidable.

Spiritual death, however, can be avoided. We can live in eternity with God. However, this is not a right, it is a choice. Jesus said the path to eternal life is narrow and very few find it. Conversely, He taught that the road to destruction and eternal spiritual death is wide and many find it.

So physical death is guaranteed, but spiritual death can be avoided. American secular culture is leading millions to eternal spiritual death. America, built on the laws and values of God, is disintegrating rapidly as we turn our backs on the goodness of God to pursue lives of wealth, depravity, and greed.

The Christian church in America has traditionally stood strong, correcting any shift in American culture that drifted from God. But over the past fifty years, the church has started to look more like the very culture it opposed for hundreds of years. Secular culture promotes sexual promiscuity; the church is doing little or nothing to address sexual sin among its people. Studies show that television viewing habits among Christians vary little from those who are not Christians. Secular culture promotes abortion as a matter of choice; the church stands by idly as millions of unborn children are killed every year. The divorce rate in this nation now hovers near 50 percent; divorce among people claiming to be Christians is hovering around 50 percent as well. Secular culture accepts and even promotes homosexuality as an acceptable lifestyle; the church out of fear refuses to call homosexuality out for what it is: a sin that is dismantling God's definition of marriage.

One is hard-pressed to see any real distinction between the secular culture and the millions who claim to be Christians these days. In fact, our self-identity as Christians these days has become confused, with the word *Christian* having no clear meaning anymore. I can sit in my garage and think I am a car, but I am not. I can also sit in church and say I'm a Christian and not truly be one.

> *"Many will say to me on that day, 'Lord, Lord, did we not prophesy in your name, and in your name drive out demons and in your name perform many miracles?' Then I will tell them plainly, 'I never knew you. Away from me, you evildoers!'"* (Matthew 7:22-23)

The Great Sumo Wrestling Match

If you have ever witnessed Japanese sumo wrestlers fight, it is an amazing thing to watch. Two huge, powerful men square off in a battle of tremendous strength and leverage. They slam together with incredible power pitting the irresistible force against the immovable object. They push on each other hoping to overpower and defeat the opponent. Using this great strength and leverage, each attempts to get the other off balance. Once this is accomplished, the opponent is overpowered and falls back in defeat, knocked out of the battle circle.

Secular culture and American Christianity are like sumo wrestlers – two powerful foes attempting to vanquish and defeat the opponent. The cultural warrior is bigger, but the Christian warrior (the church) has far greater inner strength and heart with the Holy Spirit. The only problem is it seems the Christian warrior left his heart and inner strength in the training room. American Christianity is being slowly pushed right out of the battle circle, ceding ground with each passing year. Defeat seems inevitable at this point in the match. The secular sumo warrior might soon stand alone in the battle circle while its opponent, American Christianity, is on the outside looking in, wondering what happened.

Over the past two hundred years, this has been a recurring battle and the church has prevailed. We fought with our heart and inner strength, the Holy Spirit, and we were for the most part continually victorious. Every time the secular sumo wanted to do battle, we defeated him. Not this time, however. We are on the brink of defeat and we either don't know it or we don't care. See, this cultural opponent has been training vigorously. He has learned from previous defeats and each time comes at his opponent with renewed vigor and commitment.

The church has become Rocky Balboa in the third movie edition of the series. Clubber Lang, Rocky's latest challenger, was hungry and driven. Rocky, flush with victory and all its trappings, grew soft. He didn't train as hard, thinking he was invincible. All he had to do was show up and Lang would be defeated. But Lang knocked him down and out. Rocky was decimated and defeated.

Rocky, recommitting to train and fight for victory, came back later and defeated Clubber Lang, regaining the title. He trained and fought harder than he ever had and the result was victory. But that is Hollywood, not always reality.

American Christianity has been knocked to the canvas by a powerful Enemy, and the count has reached nine. One more wave of the referee's hand and the match will be over. We will have lost, and the price for this defeat will be felt for an eternity. Satan will have claimed many more eternal disciples from the ranks of lukewarm Christians and American youth.

Christianity either affects culture or culture infects Christianity. Which seems like the most likely scenario happening today? If you think the church is winning this battle, you are either incredibly naive or tremendously deceived.

Who *Is* Leading This Dance Anyway?

I admit it. My wife got me to take ballroom dance lessons. Admission number two: I enjoy dancing with my wife; maybe not quite as much as I enjoy a Milwaukee Brewers baseball game, but I do enjoy dancing with Nancy.

Being born with two left feet, and having no real dance experience, it was torture learning to dance. I would constantly try to take us in one direction while Nancy thought we were headed in another, making it look more like a wrestling match than a dance. Then one time, Nancy collaborated with our dance instructor to try to straighten out my disastrous foray into ballroom dancing.

Dale explained to me that in every dance there is a leader and a follower. Well, that much I had figured out. Dale pointed out that if a leader is strong and knows where he wants to go, the follower will have no choice but to go there. In other words, I, as the man and leader, needed to lead from a position of strength and confidence, and then Nancy would have no option but to follow my lead. The rest is pretty easy, as long as the leader knows where he wants to go and is committed to going there.

In the battle between secular culture and Christianity, one will lead and one will follow. So who seems to be leading and who is following in this all-important dance? No doubt that secular culture leads and American Christianity is following, seemingly powerless to do anything about it.

Culture is redefining marriage away from God's law and the church is following along with hardly a whimper of protest. The Supreme Court has legalized homosexual marriage, but that does not force the church to partake of it. But a growing number of churches are doing this out of fear of reprisal from a government that can tighten the financial screws if it wants to.

Abortion has brought about the murder of more than fifty-five million babies since 1973. The church doesn't notice or doesn't care, because standing up against the murder of innocent children might be seen as harsh. Well, American Christianity has been an accessory to the murder of these fifty-five million babies (a number more than eight times the number of Jews the Nazis butchered in World War II, by the way) by refusing to get seriously involved. We make Hitler seem tame by comparison.

We scream about the growing sexuality, anti-Christian rhetoric, and violence on television and keep right on watching television instead of making our voices heard. We scream about the growth of our federal government and the decreasing morality in legislation and behavior from our elected leaders. We complain that they don't listen to our wishes and how they seem to be bent on kicking God out of our society, yet we helped elect the most pro-abortion, pro-homosexual president in our history. We abandon our Christian principles because we think our guy will get us a little more money in our wallets or because we like his charm and charisma.

We virtually outsource our children's morals and values to a public education system that is a humanist organization, trying to override all the "antiquated" beliefs on morality that religion and parents have instilled. We may complain about it a little, but how many have ever attended a school-board meeting or even a parent-teacher conference to find out just what our children are being taught and by whom?

The secular culture leads, and American Christianity follows blindly. They are setting the agenda and we are just going along because we are too lazy, ignorant, or fearful to question their agenda and motives. We follow blindly wherever they wish to lead.

I am not a dominionist. I do not believe we can stop the world from going to the brink of self-annihilation before Jesus returns. I read the Bible and know that things will get a lot worse in the coming years. The *Titanic* is sinking and we cannot stop it, but we can fight for every person on that sinking cruise liner, running up with lifeboats to rescue them. We can work to help bail water, hoping we can buy a little more time to help a few more get off the sinking ship. We can care enough about people to stand up and make noise when we see the evil and depravity closing in on us as Americans.

We cannot do these things if we continue to let secular culture lead us around by the nose, intimidating and marginalizing us as Christians. But the sad truth is we have twisted and abused the Scripture that tells us to be in the world but not of the world. We have used this as an excuse to believe we have no responsibility for the state of American culture decaying into an evil thing.

Progressive Christian churches bring their favorite candidates in before elections but conservative churches crouch in fear over being seen as "political." Pro-death and pro-homosexual "Christians" get involved with social justice movements while conservative, Bible-believing Christians sit back and pick their noses.

Culture leads the dance, stepping all over our toes, and we just take it, asking for forgiveness because they step on *our* toes! American Christianity led this dance for nearly two hundred years and when the culture wanted to go in a different direction, we did not allow it to go there. But we have given up our leadership, choosing to do so out of fear, ignorance, or a desire to become followers, not leaders.

When the epitaph on this once-great nation is read, it will remember a time when America stood for God's principles and truth; a time when a Christian-led nation stood up to evil and said "no way"; a time when a strong, vibrant, moral church was the leader of this nation. On America's death certificate it should read, "Compliments of American Christianity." God forgive us.

American Christianity: Introducing the 1976 Tampa Bay Buccaneers!

The Green Bay Packers had a remarkable ride as a team in 2011. Coming off their fourth Super Bowl championship, many thought the team was set up to become the next dynasty of professional football. The team had a franchise quarterback, a strong corps of wide receivers, and a championship quality defense led by a general manager and a head coach who were quality men on and off the field. All Wisconsin was buzzing in anticipation of a miraculous year.

There was no disappointment as the Packers steamrolled virtually every opponent en route to a 15-1 regular season. Life was good in Green Bay, but there were underlying signs of problems from day one. That championship-quality defense from the previous year never looked anything like its old self. It gave up yardage at a record pace, but the offense was so prolific that the Packers managed to outscore every opponent but one.

Then the New York Giants, the eventual Super Bowl champions, came to town on a cold Sunday for a playoff game. Fans were certain the Packers would prevail and move on to the Super Bowl a few weeks later. The Packers were heavy favorites and the darlings of the media. Fans were certain that in this game the defense would show up, and even if they didn't, the offense would continue to make up for the poor defense.

Well, a funny thing happened on the way to a second consecutive Super Bowl championship for the Packers: the defense was its usual inept self, but the offense was not there to bail it out this time. The Packers were eliminated and an entire state went into a three-week state of depression.

The previous year's Super Bowl opponent, the Pittsburgh Steelers, was also primed for a repeat appearance. They were built almost opposite of the Packers, with a sterling defense and an offense that could never quite click all year. They traveled to Denver in the first round of the playoffs to face Tim Tebow and the Broncos. The offense played pretty well, more than holding up its side of the bargain. But the vaunted defense, the crown jewel of Steelers teams for decades, got "Tebowed." The Steelers, like the Packers, ended an exciting season on the scrap heap, wondering what happened in the playoffs.

Championship teams need a great offense and a great defense. They need strong, committed, principled leadership, and they need ownership that is willing to give leadership the tools they need for success. Teams with huge deficiencies on both sides of the ball, combined with poor coaching and leadership, end up more like the 1976 Tampa Bay Buccaneers, the first team in NFL history to go winless during a fourteen-game season. During the season, Coach John McKay was grilled about his offense's inability to score points. After an excruciating loss, a reporter asked McKay, "What do you think of the execution of your offense today?"

McKay never missed a beat: "I'm all in favor of it."

The 1976 Buccaneers were a hapless bunch, demoralized with each passing loss. Other teams would often comment that they felt the Bucs were defeated the moment they walked onto the field because the malaise and ineptitude were so evident even in warm-ups before the game. Well, ladies and gentlemen, may I introduce to you the latest version of the 1976 Tampa Bay Buccaneers: American Christianity. This team has become built to lose.

American Christianity was once a juggernaut, seemingly invincible. With a high-powered offense and stingy defense, and strong, principled leadership, the opponent never had a chance. Run with precision to detail and a passion never seen before, this team was built for victory from the beginning.

The owner is a perfect owner, giving leadership and the team everything it needed for success. He inspires the team and disciplines them when needed. He was with them every day, reminding them how much He cares for them, even when practices and games got difficult. No team ever had a greater owner and one so committed to the success of His team.

The leadership of the team was very solid, committed to the vision of ownership, and making sure each player knew their role and the goal of the team as a whole. But something happened. Ownership remained the same and was every bit as powerful and committed, but somewhere along the line this team developed a selfish, losing attitude. Leadership became soft and started implementing a strategic plan that conflicted with ownership. But the owner, being patient, hoped leadership would turn from its destructive patterns and once again carry out the vision of ownership.

The players became flushed with wealth and earthly success and just didn't practice or play as hard as they used to. They also didn't memorize the playbook like they once did. They developed an attitude of surrender instead of a passion for victory. They started doing things their way instead of following the proven method of success that the ownership had installed many years ago. It became all about them.

A team built for ongoing success became apathetic and lazy. It was not as committed to success as in previous years. It didn't have the confidence in the owner and leadership it once had. American Christianity had lost its passion and purpose and today is struggling to find its own identity. American Christianity these days has an ineffective, lazy offensive game plan, and we are getting nowhere against the growing secular culture. This must change.

American Christianity also needs a strong defense that refuses to allow the Enemy to gain one inch of our territory. We need to have spiritual eyes, ears, and discernment to see how the Enemy plans on attacking us. We need watchmen on the wall, warning the church of the Enemy's overt and covert attacks on the foundation of the church.

American Christianity needs to return to its once-powerful roots and purpose. It needs an offense that will take the battle to the Enemy, an offense that is aggressive and puts the pressure on the opponent. We need to take the battle to the secular culture instead of playing passively and on the defensive constantly. We do this by being involved in the culture wars. We do this by actively supporting political candidates committed publicly and privately to God's standards of morality. We do this by flexing our muscles as a church.

Every year in our community some of our churches engage in forty days of prayer for our community, and this is a very good thing to do. But our prayers must be coupled with a willingness to be God's vessels to take the battle to the Enemy. God can do anything within His divine nature, but for some reason He chooses to work through His children. We need to become willing partners with God to reclaim the culture from the Enemy. Prayer alone will just not cut it, because if we pray for our community and culture but are unwilling to get off the bench and fight for it, just how seriously will God take our prayers? God commands His people to be active in the world without succumbing to it. We are called to be *in* the world but not *of* it. This is not a call to isolation or retreat from the world, but rather a call to action and involvement with the world, being careful not to lose our spiritual perspective.

Sadly, these days, watchmen are viewed more as irritants by church leadership than they are as strong participants in the battle between good and evil. When watchmen stand up and warn of coming attacks, they are often marginalized as "divisive" or "unloving." When watchmen have the courage to confront leadership on unbiblical teachings or programs infiltrating the church, they are either dismissed or ridiculed. Every church would be served well to have a team of watchmen as part of their leadership team: men and women who are aware of dangerous doctrine or movements creeping into American Christianity; watchmen who are willing to take the time to vet programs and speakers before they are endorsed by church leadership.

A large majority of pastors complain that they are overworked and overwhelmed by the scope of their duties, and they are probably correct in that assessment. Yet they have what seems to be a martyr syndrome, preferring to remain overworked and stressed so they can show just how valuable they are to the church. They could help themselves and the church by getting off their high horse and asking for help. Start to invest in future leaders. Sit down with church members and find out what their passions and gifts are, and start to utilize these skills and passions to build a strong community of believers.

Leaders in the church must reclaim their roles as spiritual leaders. They must build a strong team within the local church, a team equipped with offensive warriors and defensive stalwarts. Stop complaining about the overwhelming scope of your duties and get your church members involved. If they don't want to be active participants in the church, ask them to move on, because you are probably better off without them if they are that self-focused.

A strong football team is comprised of an aggressive offense and a staunch defense, plus strong, principled, and committed leadership that sets the tone. It also develops depth with a strong bench willing and able to get in the game if injuries occur or if a starting player leaves the team. That is where training and educating our youth become so important. Today's reserves are tomorrow's starters and we need to begin training and equipping them to step into a starting role when the time is right.

A great team also knows its identity. It knows what it believes and is committed to its goals as a team. But because of our slide into mediocrity as a church over the past fifty years, we have what looks more like a team of misfits rather than a powerful, effective team. We are suffering from a lack of individual and corporate identity as a church.

Inept Leadership or Self-Centered Followers?

Does inept leadership create self-centered followers, or do self-centered followers create inept leadership? This is a classic "chicken or the egg" question. Are our Christian leaders the primary reason Christians have become shallow and self-centered? Or are our self-centered attitudes causing us to elevate and promote inept leaders?

Our government was formed in 1776 on the belief that the federal government would play a very limited role in the lives of its citizens. Its primary economic purpose was to do what it could to foster equal opportunity for all citizens. That's just not good enough anymore for many Americans, however. We will no longer settle for equal opportunity; we want equal outcomes.

In 2008 Christians joined the chorus of voters who elected Barack Obama as president of the United States. As a United States senator, Obama had a near-perfect record of supporting unrestricted abortion rights and homosexual marriage. He is also a big-government liberal who believes in a powerful federal government that is now trying to control every aspect of individual life. From what we eat, to the firearms we own, to mandatory government health insurance, Obama is a proponent of government controlling virtually every aspect of society, presenting real concerns for Americans who value individual liberty. His policies brought trillions of dollars of more debt that will saddle our children in the future. We got what we truly desired, and are only getting what we asked for.

In 2016 President Trump was surprisingly elected, but by that time the federal government had become so powerful and intrusive that it may never be reined in again. The passion on both sides of the political spectrum has become so vociferous that meaningful dialogue and cooperation may never return. And secular humanism has become so entrenched in the minds of many Americans that President Trump's stance on religious liberty is being met with violent resistance. Americans have been seduced into slavery and we have become comfortable within its protective walls. Notice this president has said little to nothing about reforming welfare or social security in spite of these bankrupt institutions threatening our financial future. He sadly realizes that to even suggest that Americans might have to make financial sacrifices is a sure recipe to be kicked out of office.

As a nation, we seem to have lost our adventurous spirit. We prefer a bird in the hand to the opportunity of two in the bush. The economic system built on free-enterprise capitalism propelled our nation to the status of the wealthiest nation in history and provided every citizen with the opportunity to prosper if he was willing to work hard. But equal opportunity is riskier than equal outcomes, and we don't have the stomach to be at risk anymore.

Life is full of risk. Every time you get in your car, you put your life into the hands of another driver who is rushing carelessly or who just doesn't see anything wrong with getting liquored up and driving. When we work for a company, our job is only as secure as the company's ability to turn a profit for the owner. As we grow older, our bodies begin to break down, and knees, hips, and vital organs begin to fail. Life is a daily crapshoot and the future in this life always contains the unknown lurking around every corner.

Life is also not fair. Some people enjoy good fortune or blessings; others seemingly cannot catch a break. Real control is an illusion. No matter how healthy or wealthy we are, it could all unravel tomorrow. We cannot control circumstances, only how we react to them.

We elected a leader in President Obama out of our desire to avoid risk and pain in the short haul, but the long-term devastation we will harvest is immeasurable. We have sacrificed the future of our children because of our aversion to short-term risk and pain.

In this case, inept, corrupt leadership is the consequence of those being led. Followers want what they desire more than what is right. Whether it is our choice of political candidates or leaders within the church, we seem to vacillate to those who tell us what we want to hear rather than leaders who tell us what we need to hear. Just as the presidential or congressional candidate who tickles our ears will likely get our vote over the candidate delivering a message of self-discipline and personal responsibility, likewise we want the church leaders who help us feel good about ourselves rather than the leaders who call us to a life of sacrifice, turning from our wicked ways, and seeking holiness.

It is far easier to blame others than ourselves for our circumstances. The church these days is filled with inept, unprincipled leaders who cave in to the culture rather than fight it with the truth of God's Word. Leaders who embrace a corporate mentality to church growth instead of preaching the Word of God and allowing the Holy Spirit to add to their numbers as in the book of Acts. Leaders who are compromising with the world to become popular and who think their "seeker-friendly" approach is anything but what it is – compromising with sin and admitting that deep down we are ashamed of the gospel. And an arrogance that leads us to believe our silver tongues are more powerful than the gospel itself to transform lives.

Yet we who follow our leaders seem to desire this type of leadership. We are more comfortable coming to a church that is more like a social club rather than a place where we challenge and build one another up spiritually. Many churches seem to have become places where we suppress our weeklong defeats and lukewarm faith and just put on a happy face. It seems more like a class reunion where people one-up each other with tales of phony success instead of a place where we are honest with one another. Deep down we seem to desire leaders who will let us stay in a comfortable place rather than challenging us to be honest about our spiritual shortcomings. So if we as followers want a place where we can feel good about ourselves, even at the expense of honesty, then that is the type of leader we will seek.

So I move forward believing it is self-centered followers who breed weak, compromising, and ineffective leadership. And it is killing American Christianity.

Summary

Are we fighting the poison of American culture or surrendering to it? Perhaps the best way to answer that question is with another question: Does American Christianity today look more or less like the culture than it did fifty years ago? If you believe it looks less like it, I have a bridge I would like to sell you because there is no doubt we are surrendering to the culture instead of fighting it. With each passing year, the secular culture becomes more engrained within the church, and one day it will totally consume us if we do not wake up.

Chapter 5

Satan's Pawns

There is no shortage of enemies purposefully trying to destroy American Christianity. A simple glance at the newspaper or watching a random sitcom on television indicates what we are up against. There was a time when the church would stand up and fight any effort to introduce immorality into media, government, Hollywood, or public education. As they say, those were the good ol' days. Sadly, those days are long past us as American Christianity has become a lapdog for immorality. We have the power of the Holy Spirit within us, yet we act like obedient dogs begging for scraps.

Just where and when did the church begin to take in the cancer of secular beliefs and culture? It is difficult to pinpoint an exact date because there is perhaps no single event we can point to as the beginning of the end. It has been more a death by a thousand cuts. No single cut by itself was fatal or even seemed serious at the time. But as the cuts mounted and we failed to dress and heal the wounds, an infection began to grow within the body of Christ in our nation. We have now reached the point where a few more cuts might lead to death. Let's examine some of these recent cuts that are mounting to slowly bring us to the brink of spiritual suicide. No cut by itself will appear fatal. This is more death by attrition.

Scientific Fact or Science Fiction?

Genesis teaches us God created the universe in six days. He created man in His image out of the dust of the earth and breathed life into him. Adam and Eve were created to live forever in the presence of God in a world free from sin, death, and pain.

These facts are now being presented as an antiquated myth by many in the public realm. When Darwin wrote *On the Origin of Species*, most people thought he was a crazed heretic. He was dismissed by the vast majority of people as a bitter lunatic who was angry at God for some reason. But a select few people embraced his writings as truthful genius. These people were called "scientists."

Science is defined as "the study and theoretical explanation of natural phenomena; knowledge acquired through experience," according to Webster. So science can be defined as both theory and knowledge, but there is a huge difference between those. Sadly, in these days where humanistic thought rules, science is often purposefully combining the theoretical with knowledge into humanist propaganda, a propaganda driven by arrogance to do all it can to prove God does not exist. Those scientists and scholars who dare to challenge the "fact" of evolution, noting there is actually far more irrefutable proof of some kind of "intelligent design," are shamed, shunned, and fired, like what happened to David Coppedge, a computer specialist at NASA's Jet Propulsion Laboratory. Ben Stein's documentary, *EXPELLED: No Intelligence Allowed*, points out several instances where doctors, journalists, and academics were either fired or censored by institutions favorable to evolution, including Baylor University, a Christian institution.

You will be hard-pressed to find a public school that teaches intelligent design, let alone creationism, on an equal footing with evolution. Public schools, held up as standards of learning and truth, teach evolution as fact and intelligent design as "another theory," if they teach it at all. The effects of this are more far-reaching and devastating to youth than most people imagine.

When a child is led to believe that mankind is some sort of accident or chance happening rather than human beings uniquely created in the image of God, he tends to feel insignificant. This can have a devastating effect on how the child looks at himself or views life. Life without purpose, the result of random chance, leaves one feeling empty and lost. Conversely, when a person sees themselves as the product of a loving God who values them and has a purpose for their lives, that person looks at life from a whole different perspective.

Science partnered with the medical community in the abortion debate, trying to determine when a fetus became life. Initially, science determined that viability was attained much later in the pregnancy than we now know. They jumped to premature conclusions about when life began in the womb. Bible-believing Christians, a shrinking minority in this nation, know that God determines when life begins. He told the prophet Jeremiah in Jeremiah 1:5, *"Before I formed you in the womb I knew you."*

Science does have a key role to play in religion. In the Middle Ages, scientists, including Galileo, started to suggest that the earth was not the center of the universe. Their findings pointed to the fact that the sun did not revolve around the earth as the early church taught, but that the earth revolved around the sun. These scientists were threatened with excommunication or even death if they did not recant their findings.

It turned out the church was wrong and the scientists were correct in this instance. This conflict caused many to wonder what else the church might be wrong about, and it started planting seeds of doubt as to the church's teachings on the origin of the universe and man himself.

We need to approach science and its findings with caution these days. Remember that the definition of science talks about it being both knowledge *and* theory. These days scientists are much quicker to jump to conclusions as they experiment, racing for the next big grant or publicity program. A new finding that might seem to support the "real" story of the creation of the universe sells much better than findings that prove the truth of the Bible. We should not dismiss science as totally evil, nor should we approach it as "gospel truth." As with all things, it must be held up to Scripture to discern its reported findings.

In an era where science is making huge strides, we should expect to see a great deal of new discoveries. It is important to understand that scientists are human and some will seek to skew their findings or conclusions to support their preconceived beliefs about the universe or God.

Science presents itself as a pursuit of truth. But as we know, truth is often in the eye of the beholder. Without an anchor of absolute truth to compare everything to, the pursuit of truth often becomes tweaking findings to support one's *version* of truth. Some scientists are atheists bent on proving that God does not exist, so be careful of what you accept as "scientific fact." In a world that hates God more with each passing day, it is important that we never allow a seed of doubt as to the truth of the Bible to enter our minds. Once there, it is easy to slip into doubt. Hold every "fact" that science presents against the Word of God.

Public Education or Indoctrination?

No institution has done more to discredit Christian teachings and doctrine than the public education system. For centuries, parents had educated their children at home. But public education has grown in this nation to where it has almost become a mandatory requirement for American children. With the advent of two-income families, fewer parents see homeschooling or Christian education as an option.

In today's busy culture, time has become one of our most precious commodities. As parents spend less quality time with their children, public education becomes the de facto "nanny" for their children. The average parent spends about five minutes per day in meaningful conversation with their children. The school system has their attention for seven hours every school day. Given these facts, who do you think has the greater potential influence on our children?

But who are the men and women who influence our children as teachers? I think we can safely say the majority of them are very nice people with the best of intentions. Some are Bible-believing Christians who are trying to help our children navigate very difficult times in their lives. But even the best teachers belong to a system that is definitely anti-Christian in its values and beliefs. They belong to quite possibly the most unscrupulous public organization in our nation: the National Education Association ("NEA").

With each successive school year we see the progression of an agenda that seeks to override the values of religion and even parents themselves, an agenda increasingly hostile to Christianity. This is not by happenstance. Quite to the contrary, this is the culmination of nearly one hundred years of scheming and gradual implementation of secular humanism.

The NEA is in lockstep with the globalization plans of the United Nations ("U.N.") through UNESCO. The ultimate plan is a united world of secular humanism. Quite simply, our children are being brainwashed and indoctrinated. This is not an indictment of many fine teachers in our schools; it is an indictment of a corrupt teachers' union and the U.N. that believe they are charged with overriding the archaic beliefs that parents and religion have forced on our children – these are their words, not mine.

Time and space will not permit a thorough analysis and exposure of these two anti-Christian organizations. That would be a separate book all on its own, and there are several excellent books that go into great detail on the subject of public education. We will touch base on some larger points and encourage you to research this subject on your own. Look at the very words and actions of NEA leaders and compare them to the Word of God.

The End of Education and the Beginning of Indoctrination

John Dewey is considered the father of American public education. His work and writings heavily influenced public education in its slide to indoctrination of our youth. Dewey equated individualized thinking with insanity. He believed only a type of "collective thought" could save humanity. He rejected the notion of God or any supreme creator.

In 1933, he co-authored *A Humanist Manifesto*, which called for a "new world religion" – secular humanism – where man is taught that *he* is God. Dewey called for radical social transformation of the world and mankind, believing it was the only hope for mankind. He and his comrades knew American adults would reject his ideas out of hand, so they developed a system to begin public indoctrination of their humanist agenda through the public education system.

Psychology would provide the "scientific tools" for this indoctrination. These tools were refined a few decades later by B. F. Skinner, a psychologist quoted to this very day in public classrooms. In 1953, Skinner wrote that "Operant conditioning shapes behavior as a sculptor shapes a lump of clay." This is a devious and clever twist on Scripture, which teaches us that we are the clay and God is the sculptor. Skinner effectively inserted their humanist manifesto as an acceptable replacement for God in the public school system.

A few years earlier, Skinner exposed his hand on how lumps of clay (students) were to be molded. In *Walden Two*, he wrote, "What was needed was a new conception of man, compatible with our scientific knowledge." In the previous discussion on science, we noted how science has been transformed from seeking truth to pushing theoretical knowledge upon people as "facts." Science, in partnership with humanists shaping public education, was ready to strike, bringing slow death to pure education. *The fight began to turn education into indoctrination.*

Dewey continued to teach that "all of man's experiences, in an attempt to understand and alter his environment, are continuing and variable, and therefore not subject to interpretation by any fixed or basic principles." Read that again, slowly and carefully, because this is the belief upon which not only public education but also progressive Christianity are based: there is *no* absolute truth and we depend on our feelings and circumstances over established truth. Dewey had started the emergent church without realizing it.

In 1932, John Dewey became the honorary president of the NEA. His legacy as the father of American public education was cemented in history. The NEA began a systematic march to indoctrinate every American child into a humanist agenda.

The Goals of the NEA

In 1948 the NEA released the following statement: "The idea has become established that the presentation of international peace and order may require that force be used to compel a nation to conduct its affairs within the framework of an established world system. The most modern expression of this doctrine of collective security is in the United Nations Charter."

The alliance between the NEA and the U.N. began in earnest. These two humanist organizations now dominate the landscape of American education, shaping every curriculum and transforming our children into "global citizens." Common Core is their latest experiment to control the beliefs, values, and thought processes of students, turning them into obedient little global citizens who believe whatever they are taught and do whatever they are told.

In 1956 former public school teacher and communist Dr. Bella Dodd admitted that "the Communist Party, whenever possible, wanted to use the teacher's union for political purposes." Bella went on to admit that virtually every suggestion Communists proposed was adopted by the NEA within the next year or so.

So at a time when Communists were seeking to infiltrate every level of the federal government, they also successfully infiltrated the NEA. Communists realized adults would never capitulate to their desire for total transformation from a free capital system to a state-controlled system, so they began planting seeds for future generations to slowly be indoctrinated into their socialist beliefs. They knew over time the nation would slowly be transformed from the bottom up. When you see the transformation that is taking place today as our government becomes more intrusive and more powerful, we must tip our hat to the NEA. Their plan is working to perfection.

In 1970 the Association for Supervision and Curriculum Development ("ASCD"), the official curriculum arm of the NEA, published *To Nurture Humaneness*. In it, they wrote the following: "The old order is passing... the controls of the past were sacred...social controls cannot be left to blind chance and unplanned change, usually attributed to God. Man must be the builder of new forms of social organizations and education must play a stellar role."

Right under the noses of American Christianity, a new Tower of Babel was being constructed. Belief in God was classified by the NEA as "blind chance," and the church remained silent.

Communists and their NEA allies realized that to change a nation fundamentally from being capitalist to being communist, they would need to neutralize religion. Stalin had done it and so did Hitler. Now it was beginning to happen in America. Unlike Russia and Germany, the United States would take more time to be transformed. Our strong economy, love of individual freedom, and strong Christian roots would require patience to undermine this nation when compared to nations facing economic collapse.

In 1972 NEA President Catherine Barrett boasted that "We are the biggest potential political striking force in this country, and we are determined to control the direction of American education." Think about that the next time your school district's newsletter talks about "partnering" with you as a parent.

The NEA and its big brother, Education International, are in lock-step with the United Nations. These two organizations, both definitely anti-Christian, control the entire public education system of the United States. The U.N. organization that the NEA takes its marching orders from is UNESCO. The first director general of UNESCO, Julian Huxley, wrote this back in 1948: "The general philosophy of UNESCO should be a scientific world humanism, global in extent and evolutionary in background." The public education system was charged as the catalyst to make it so.

"Scientific world humanism, global in extent." And you thought your school system reflected the values of your community. No, the true value system the NEA is interested in is global secular humanism. It is important to understand that many U.N. agencies and programs reflect the exact-same goals. Several U.N. agencies and officials are on record calling fundamentalist religious beliefs and systems the single greatest threat to the survival of the world. When you view the above information, we see the NEA shares those beliefs.

But it is not just social studies, math, and science that the NEA wants to brainwash your children with. It goes well beyond that. The NEA wants to totally take over the education of your children and actually raise your children for you. Parents just cannot be trusted with the future of our global citizens, and we certainly cannot allow religious teachings to warp the minds of our future leaders either.

In 2011 an NEA spokeswoman addressed the United Nations, encouraging mandatory worldwide sex education for girls as young as six years old. Speaking to a panel combating "homophobia and transphobia," Diane Schneider stated the following:

> "Oral sex, masturbation and orgasms need to be taught in education. The only way to combat heterosexism and gender conformity is comprehensive sex education. Gender identity expression and sexual orientation are a spectrum and those opposed to homosexuality are stuck in a binary box that religion and family create."

And you thought the NEA was partnering with you as a parent to educate your child. There is no partnership here, parents. You and your "antiquated" religious beliefs are the problem, and public education by the NEA is the solution to how you are corrupting your child's values and beliefs. Think about that the next time you go to vote and see a candidate who is endorsed by the local teachers' union or the NEA.

In the past year, some young grade-school students, purposefully confused about their gender by public education, have actually started hormonal treatments to "change" their gender under the protection and support of public school officials, without the consent of their parents! Christian parents need to understand that if you oppose the globalist, humanist vision of the NEA, you will be undermined at every turn.

This is but a brief summary of the roots, history, and agenda of the NEA. The damage this organization has done to American Christianity through its indoctrination of students is staggering and possibly irreversible. It has been more than instrumental in raising successive narcissistic generations that embrace humanism over the truth of God.

In these challenging economic times I wish every parent could send their children to Christian schools. I ask you as parents to take a step back, assess your financial situation, and prioritize where you are spending your money. Our children are our legacy and our future. They are the single-greatest investment you will make in the future of this nation. If you can afford to invest in their education by sending them to a solid Bible-teaching Christian school, it will be the best investment you ever make.

"Someone Take Care of Me, Please?" The Nanny State

On January 8, 1964, President Lyndon Johnson delivered his State of the Union Address to congress and the nation. He declared a war on poverty, asking congress to fund programs that would reduce poverty in the nation and provide a basic economic safety net for Americans. It was a noble cause, but, as usual, the best of intentions go awry when the federal government gets involved beyond its constitutional mandate. Johnson called for expansion of the federal government's role in healthcare and education, much to the delight of the NEA. Sugar daddy had arrived!

What started off as a necessary safety net for the poorest of Americans has grown into an uncontrollable beast that threatens the liberties and very fabric of our great nation. The NEA's goal of dominance in the education arena would soon be funded with billions of taxpayer dollars. This war on poverty would also plant the early seeds of an entitlement mentality that would destroy the work ethic of millions of Americans, leading to social unrest and the eventual chaos we see today in the Occupy and Black Lives Matter movements.

A recent poll of Occupy protestors, who are manifested in movements like Black Lives Matter and Antifa, show that 80 percent feel the government owes them a job, a home, and a retirement income. They also believe the government should be required to eliminate their student loan debts. This is far beyond a safety net; this is economic slavery that is destroying the free-enterprise capitalist system that made this nation the wealthiest in the history of the world.

Americans have historically thrived in a competitive economic environment requiring ingenuity and hard work. Today, we are rapidly becoming a second-class economy as fewer Americans are productive workers, and more and more are milking a welfare system that is destroying our work ethic and moral fiber as a nation.

What does this have to do with the demise of American Christianity? Everything, as this entitlement mentality has seeped into the teachings of many churches today. Many Christians have come to believe that we are owed something by God and that we have a right to dictate our needs and desires to Him. But the Word of God warns us against this mentality:

> *"Who has known the mind of the Lord? Or who has been his counselor? Who has ever given to God, that God should repay them?"* (Romans 11:34-35)

The Bible teaches us that man deserves only one thing: eternal separation from God because of our sinful nature. We have no rights, only privileges granted by an all-powerful, holy God. Each of us deserves to spend an eternity in hell after we die and to suffer in this life while we are alive on this earth. In reality, any good thing God grants us in this life should be treated as an unexpected bonus. We have no right to have an attitude of entitlement as Christians.

Not so, some say. Welcome to American Christianity in the twenty-first century. Life got you down and you feel lost? Just recite this "sinner's prayer" and everything will get better. No need for godly sorrow or true repentance, just invite Jesus into your heart. Don't know this Jesus? No problem. You just need to believe in Him, not know Him.

Having problems making ends meet financially? Would you like the blessings of a big, beautiful home or that new boat like your neighbor has? No problem. Just ask God for it. Hey, if you have enough faith, the world is at your fingertips. God wants only the best for you, and if you think His best means a life of luxury for you, just believe and you will receive.

Many Christians bemoan the fact that Americans have gained this new attitude of entitlement, but at the same time, we embrace it spiritually. When the apostle Paul was persecuted and beaten for his faith, he counted it as joy to suffer for the sake of his Lord. When we face any sort of challenge, we curl up in the fetal position and suck our thumbs, wondering how God could let this happen to us. American culture has once again infected American Christianity.

As Christians, it should be enough for us that God sent His Son who died as a sacrifice for our sins, and that we can one day live for eternity with Him in heaven. Any other blessing we receive in this lifetime is gravy. But the entitlement mentality of American culture is infecting American Christianity. We want everything and we want it now.

Islam: the Darling Religion of Satan
and American Culture

The Constitution of the United States was charged in Article 1 with protecting the right of every individual to worship and express their religious beliefs openly. Our nation, while established under Judeo-Christian law, was not created as a "Christians-only" nation. While Christianity would be the template for the nation's laws and moral issues, individual religious freedoms were cherished by our founding fathers and they set about to make sure the rights of the individuals regarding religious preference, worship, and expression would be protected.

Liberal courts and legislators have succeeded in gutting many of the religious freedoms that Christians have historically enjoyed. Recently in California a homeowner was threatened with fines and imprisonment for holding a weekly Bible study in his home because so many people were attending that the street was lined with parked cars (legally). A neighbor complained and the police responded by threatening the homeowner, insinuating that he was creating a public nuisance. The city backed down after threats of countersuits by organizations like the Alliance Defense Fund.

Jack Phillips, a Colorado man who owned a cake-baking business, found out how far this world will go if you stand on your deeply held religious principles. The Colorado Civil Rights Commission fined him tens of thousands of dollars and tried to prosecute him as a criminal for his refusal to bake a cake for a homosexual wedding. While the U.S. Supreme Court overturned his conviction, many feel the ambiguous ruling will actually encourage more such actions. In essence, the Supreme Court only chastised the Colorado commission for not at least *pretending* they cared about Jack's religious freedoms. The result of the cowardly ruling? They are again suing Phillips, hoping to shut his business down because he will not participate in a homosexual wedding ceremony by baking their cake.

Think about that: a city threatening to shut down a Bible study under the guise of it being a "public nuisance" and a Christian cake baker being forced to condone homosexual marriage when it goes against his convictions as a Christian. This is the tip of an iceberg that soon will surface and destroy the religious freedoms of Christians not only in California but also around the nation. If the Christian church in America does not stand up and resist the evil knocking at our doors, how long will it be until Christianity itself is seen as a public nuisance or even a threat to America?

After winning back the U.S. House of Representatives in the 2018 midterm elections, presumptive Speaker of the House Nancy Pelosi announced the first thing the new congress would be working on is a national "non-discrimination" bill which is code for dismantling religious freedoms guaranteed in the Constitution. The hatred of God and His people has grown so intense that it is now at the top of liberal thought.

But take consolation that religious persecution is not hitting every religion in America. There is one religion that is seemingly embraced, protected, and even promoted in our nation today: Islam.

Islam is more than a religion – it is a social, economic, and political system that is intolerant and even belligerent toward all other religions. It is the fastest-growing religion in the United States and in the world, and it is a real threat to the religious beliefs and lives of people around the world.

In her riveting book *Because They Hate*, Brigitte Gabriel shares her personal testimony as a Christian girl growing up in Lebanon. She talks about how when Muslims were in the extreme minority in Lebanon, some were her neighbors and were helpful to her family when needs arose. However, when the Muslim population grew to significance, the call for jihad went out and the nation became a breeding ground for the murder of Christians and Jews. These same friendly neighbors of the past turned into rapists and murderers.

I have read the Quran and the Hadith, Muslim "holy books," four times. I have interviewed guests who are experts on Islam, some of them former Muslims and now Christians. The truth must be told about Islam so Christians will not approach it out of fear or ignorance.

Not every Muslim is a terrorist in training. Many are nice people who make good neighbors and citizens. But some are waiting in the wings, blending into society, and patiently waiting for the call to jihad. When that happens, America will not know what hit her.

Islam is not a religion of peace. It is a religion of intolerance with the sole goal of world domination as the only acceptable religion for mankind. The Quran is a hodgepodge of stories and teachings, some of which resemble stories from the Bible, with others just plain bizarre and nonsensical. The Quran's Allah is not the God we worship as Christians. In the Quran, Jesus is a minor prophet, subject to the prophet Muhammad who wrote the Quran.

Reading and understanding the Quran can be challenging because the teachings are so contradictory. At times Allah commands love of Jews and Christians and at other times calls for their death if they do not convert to Islam. Some verses teach peace; others order Muslims to kill all unbelievers.

You will often hear Muslims and naive Christians refer to Islam as a religion of peace. They will recite a sura (verse) that seems to confirm their statement. But here is a key to understanding Islam: the Muslim rule of abrogation. It states in the Quran that if two verses conflict, as is often the case in the Quran, the later verse overrides the earlier verse. Early in the writings of the Quran, Muslims are commanded to love Jews and Christians, but the later verses teach Muslims to hate and be prepared to kill Jews and Christians when commanded to do so. So when a Muslim cites a verse in the Quran teaching Islam as a religion of peace, they are being coy and deceptive, or at the very least, ignorant of their own religion.

Islam will settle for nothing short of universal conversion or death to all "infidels." Islam teaches that good Muslims should lie to their enemies to win their confidence. This explains how Muslims have broken every peace treaty they have ever signed with Israel or any other nation.

We will discuss Chrislam, a movement to combine Islam and Christianity, later, but one more thing about the teachings of the Muslim holy books. Jesus is not the Son of God, nor did He die on the cross. He was assumed to heaven as a prophet by Allah. In the Muslim teachings of the end times, Jesus appears before Allah. Allah asks Jesus if He ever claimed to be God's son and Jesus says no. Jesus then gets angry and helps the Muslim messiah kill every Jew and Christian remaining.

Recently I watched the republican presidential debates and U. S.

Representative Ron Paul stated a nuclear Iran was no threat to Israel or the world. His logic was that with just one or two nuclear bombs, Iran would never dare attack Israel or the United States because the retaliation would destroy Iran. Now this is arguably sound logic when you view things from the world's perspective, but obviously, Ron Paul and every one of his opponents had never acquainted themselves with Muslim teachings. The sect of Muslims leading Iran believe their messiah, the Mahdi, is alive today and that he will come forward when Israel has been destroyed.

So if Iran obtains a nuclear weapon and its current regime stays in power, a nuclear attack on Israel will occur. It is just a matter of time. The Iranian regime is committed to starting a war they believe will usher in the return of their messiah. This regime is not composed of lukewarm Muslims, but of radical fanatics who believe they are charged with bringing about the end of the era where Allah will return to rule the entire world with an iron fist, killing all who do not convert to Islam.

With all the facts, testimonies, and history available to our government leaders about this religion of hatred and violence, these warnings are not only being ignored by the vast majority of our leaders and citizens, but Islam also seems to be protected and elevated in this nation. Christians are fair game for the courts; Islam is the sacred cow.

On November 5, 2009, Major Nidal Malik Hasan, an army major and psychiatrist, stormed into the Soldier Readiness area at Fort Hood, Texas, and killed thirteen people and wounded twenty-nine while yelling "Allahu Akbar" ("God is the greatest"). The reaction since that day has shown just how far our government will go to pander to and protect Islam.

Government officials were quick to discount this as the terrorist attack that it was. They downplayed and even dismissed the fact that Hasan had been in regular contact with known Muslim terrorists for years. Hasan has been portrayed as the "victim" of religious intolerance, when in reality no religious intolerance existed. Instead, it appears he was acting on orders from his spiritual leaders to commit mass murder.

Two subsequent events highlight the government's complicity in downplaying this event as a terror attack by a dedicated Muslim:

- A government spokesman started spinning this brutal attack as an incident of "workplace violence" instead of the terrorist attack it was. This is a blatant cover-up for Islam that would never be presented that way if a Christian were the shooter.

- It was later announced that the victims of this terrorist would *not* be given Purple Heart medals. The Purple Heart is given to soldiers wounded in battle. It is a symbol of gratitude given to military personnel wounded in war or wartime activities. The reason these victims would not be awarded Purple Heart commendations is this: To do so would be to show the government admitting that we are in a war with radical Muslims. This war has already been declared on the United States by Muslim leaders around the world and those living in the United States. We are seen as the "big Satan" by Muslim leaders, with Israel cited as the "little Satan." War was declared on us when Muslim terrorists flew two planes into the World Trade Center in 2001 and a third plane into the Pentagon, killing almost three thousand innocent citizens.

One brave leader, Representative Peter King of New York, has tried to take a stand and expose the agenda of radical Muslims living in the United States. He chaired House Intelligence Committee meetings, exposing verified information of Muslim terror cell groups and public statements made by Muslim clerics calling for the death of America. King has exposed solid information showing many Muslim mosques in this nation as terrorist breeding grounds. King has been labeled as a bigot for his public stance, but he continues undaunted in his efforts to warn Americans of the danger of the Muslim agenda.

Islam is completely incompatible with a society that cherishes religious freedom and democracy. Islam accepts only a theocracy, with Islam the only religion acceptable. It will accept no other religions, no competing economic or political views, and no legal system except Sharia law, which would outlaw Christianity and any other religion.

What is incredibly baffling, but consistent with the spiritual blindness of many progressives in our nation, is how Islam is considered a religion of peace by progressives, yet Christianity is so hated. Islamic law calls for potential death sentences for adulterers and homosexuals, while Christianity teaches we are to love all men and lead them to the truth of the gospel. We confront them with their sin, but we do not kill or even hate them. Islam treats women like property, while Christianity teaches they are equal to men in God's eyes. Yet Islam is the darling religion of many progressives. They are blind fools. Radical feminists and LGBTQ supporters love Islam, failing to understand that if Sharia law is ever implemented in our nation, they will be the first ones imprisoned or killed by radical Muslims.

Saudi Arabia, a nation committed to worldwide implementation of Sharia law, is the largest single funder of American colleges, literally buying American higher education. Its billions of dollars in grants is funding terrorism, brainwashing college students into believing Islam is a religion of peace, and winning the acceptance and hearts of an entire generation. Saudi Arabia, a country in which having a Bible warrants imprisonment or death, is funding American higher education. American colleges are producing the next generation of American-born terrorists that will one day bring death and chaos to our nation.

Islam is a religion of antichrist. First John 4 clearly identifies it as so. Yet Christian leaders like Rick Warren, Bill Hybels, Jim Wallis, and Brian McLaren call for dialogue and reconciliation between Christians and Muslims, hoping we can find a common ground of spirituality and beliefs. We will discuss this poisonous movement called Chrislam as we look at the internal agents of death slowly killing American Christianity.

Our responsibility as Americans is to welcome Muslims into our nation if they are here legally, and as American citizens they should have every right we enjoy as Christians. They have a right to worship as they please and build mosques, but we have a responsibility as Americans to know the dangers of Islam and to keep a close eye on what is being bred within our nation.

Our responsibility as Christians is to love all men, including Muslims who belong to an antichrist religion and need Jesus as much as anyone, but they need the truth about who Jesus really is. He is not a prophet who returns with the Muslim messiah, denying He ever claimed to be the Son of God and proceeding in anger to help kill every Christian and Jew. He is the only begotten Son of God who came to be the perfect sacrifice so that anyone who truly believes in Him could be free from the punishment and power of sin, having everlasting life with God.

It's Music to Our Ears – and Our Hearts

Music has always captured the hearts and imaginations of man. Many of the Psalms are songs giving praise and glory to God with breathtaking beauty. Music has a powerful influence, speaking to us on a subconscious level. Every once in awhile I will turn on a local radio station and listen to oldies music from the sixties and seventies I enjoyed when I was a teenager. I find that some songs I have not heard in more than thirty years are still etched in my subconscious memory and I remember every word. Music has this power. It reaches our hearts and minds and the lyrics imprint themselves in our memories.

In June of 1967, the Beatles, reaching the apex of their popularity, released a song titled "Sergeant Pepper's Lonely Hearts Club Band." One of the lines in this wildly popular song says, "I get by with a little help from my friends; I get high with a little help from my friends." This endorsement of recreational drug use encouraged millions of youth to use drugs like marijuana and LSD to "get high." Illegal drug abuse skyrocketed.

Two years later, Vice President Spiro Agnew held a press conference criticizing the negative influence that modern music was having on youth, citing the lyrics in this song. Many people dismissed Agnew's comments as paranoid behavior.

Shortly after that, Beatles members John Lennon and George Harrison began touring the nation with Maharishi Mahesh Yogi, a famous Hindu mystic, encouraging youth to combine illegal drug use with Hindu mysticism to attain "higher consciousness." Again, millions of youth blindly followed the example of their musical heroes, starting a journey down a dangerous spiritual road. Today, Hindu mysticism has a strong foothold in Christianity through many teachers of the emergent church movement, leading our youth away from the one true God.

Even today, when youth are asked whom they admire, popular musicians are often the "heroes" they identify the most. Music has a huge influence on youth, laying a foundation for their beliefs, attitudes, and behaviors. I encourage parents to take the time to know and study the musicians your children listen to and look up to. Today's popular secular music is laced with lyrics that encourage violence, drug abuse, and extreme sexuality. Many popular rap musicians sing about young girls as nothing more than sexual objects available for the pleasure of young men. Our young men grow up thinking of women as nothing more than objects of pleasure, and our young girls are being taught that unless they are sexually promiscuous, no man will ever love them. An interesting contradiction is how many women who consider themselves "feminists" actually love some of the music produced these days that demeans women, reducing them to sexual objects.

Music speaks to us in a deep way, and the music we listen to can have a lasting effect on our beliefs and behaviors. Today our youth listen to music an average of thirty hours a week, and the music they listen to is leading them down a very dark path away from God and into the arms of an Enemy bent on their eternal destruction.

News and Entertainment: "The Opiate of the Masses"?

Life in America used to be much simpler and much healthier physically, emotionally, and spiritually. Families used to spend time together and do things together. We used to spend time with our neighbors, getting to know them. When a neighbor had a project that needed to be done, families would chip in and get it done. There was a real sense of family and community. Life was good.

In the forties, television was invented. Only rich families could afford one at first, but by the sixties, virtually every household owned one. Today most households have three or four televisions along with the Internet to occupy our free time.

Our one local television station in Green Bay used to broadcast only about ten hours a day when we were young. Now we have hundreds of channels to choose from, twenty-four hours a day. The Internet, Facebook, and YouTube have become a crucial part of our lives.

When I was thirteen, my best friend found a *Playboy* magazine his father tried to hide. By today's standards it was very tame, but it filled our inquisitive minds with a lot of garbage at a very early age. Today, pornography is at our fingertips 24/7 in the privacy of our homes, compliments of the Internet. What was once a high-risk venture has become an easy and low-risk opportunity as thousands of websites are at the disposal of people anywhere and at any time.

A life of family, close friendship, hard work, and a sense of real community have been replaced with a life of instant gratification and communication that no longer has to be face to face or even involve a spoken word.

We have become obsessed with and absorbed into media. The average youth now spends nearly forty hours a week immersed in media – music, the Internet, television, and social media. And it is not only youth who are being absorbed into media. Millions of adults are also becoming addicted to social media, YouTube, and Facebook. We have become obsessed with social media, telling everyone about every minutia of our lives – where we eat, what we like, and when we are going to the bathroom.

As with everything, the Internet and media as a whole are neither a blessing nor a curse on their own, depending on how we utilize them. The Internet is a useful tool for information and opinions, and social media can connect us, albeit in a very superficial manner.

Try to go anywhere and not see someone texting, talking on their phone, or tweeting – it is virtually impossible. At a youth event a couple years ago, I watched for ten minutes as a circle of four young girls worked their smartphones furiously without saying a word to each other. Out of curiosity, I approached them and said, "Excuse me, but I couldn't help but notice that for at least the past twenty minutes you ladies have not said one word to each other, just working your smartphones. Why don't you have a conversation with one another?"

One girl said, "We are. We're talking by texting one another."

I asked why they wouldn't actually have a conversation with their voices and her response was alarming. "I might be saying something to one of my friends that I don't want the others to hear." Welcome to the whacky world of the American teen in the twenty-first century.

We utilize media, but there is a danger that media can control us. Social media is isolating people and is the easiest way to be phony, as we can present an image of what we would like to be seen as instead of the reality of who we are. Without face-to-face conversation, eye contact, and voice inflection, it is easy to be misunderstood or to get away with lies that personal interaction can see through. While the Internet can be an invaluable means of gathering information and opinion, it can also be a way for cowards to spread lies and rumors with little or no accountability. Much damage has been done to good men and women by anonymous cowards out to slander or destroy them for a variety of reasons. The Internet has become a god we worship, isolating us and creating superficial relationships that replace meaningful, personal relationships.

Posting "selfies" on our social media is all the rage, but something interesting and dangerous is starting to happen. When people post their selfie, it can actually be photoshopped to make us look more attractive than we really are. Young people are starting to get depressed when they look in a mirror and see a less-attractive version of their selfie and are starting to spend thousands of dollars on plastic surgery so they can look more like the photoshopped version of themselves on social media. We are building a world of self-illusion that is costly and dangerous instead of facing reality.

Speaking of reality, "virtual reality" is becoming the next opiate of the masses in our nation. Scientists and even the people who invented virtual reality systems are warning that the more time people spend absorbed in these programs, the more challenging it will be for them to actually distinguish reality from fantasy. The onslaught of mass shootings in our nation seems to have an increasingly common thread: the perpetrators are often people who have spent hours absorbed in first-person shooter games or virtual reality programs where *they* are actually the shooter. This just serves to devalue life even more.

No News Is Good News

With the explosion of cable television and the Internet, news is available to us instantly, 24/7. There is a positive side to this, assuming what we are watching is news and not propaganda.

News media has always been considered the "fourth estate" of government. The news media has been a watchdog, reporting news and sharing inside information that helps us keep our government in check. It has been an invaluable tool in keeping Americans informed as to the inner workings of our government. During the Watergate scandal, newspapers and television brought us the real story of a paranoid president covering up criminal activity. The media coverage and subsequent outrage of the American people led to Richard Nixon's disgraceful resignation.

But somewhere in the past forty years, media began to cross and blur lines. There had always been a definitive line between what the media would report as news and what it would state as commentary, but not anymore.

In a scene from his movie *Annie Hall*, Woody Allen is upstairs in the host's bedroom watching the New York Knicks basketball game while his date is downstairs having discussions with her friends who are professors and media moguls. His date comes upstairs, upset to find him immersing himself in a basketball game instead of engaging in conversations with the guests downstairs. (Hey, what man can't relate to that?)

Allen starts defending his action, saying he had no desire to get into a discussion with people who specialized in "dysentery." His date corrects him: "You mean *commentary*." Allen responds that he heard "commentary had combined with news to create dysentery." Sad but true these days.

To remain a free people, we must have access to accurate facts necessary to make proper judgments. We need truth, not just opinions. But secular media abandoned their commitment to truth a long time ago. Network news has become a joke; it's no longer about reporting facts, but rather is dedicated to pushing an agenda: a progressive, anti-Christian agenda.

In recent polls, 94 percent of people working in the media call themselves liberal or progressive, while only 6 percent identify themselves as conservative. This is reflected in the reporting of "news," which is actually commentary and propaganda indoctrinating naive people into a progressive, anti-Christian worldview.

When a Muslim terrorist, Major Hasan, opens fire, killing thirteen soldiers while yelling, "Allahu Akbar," the media has little to say about his ties to Muslim fanatics. This is not reported as terrorism, it's just another indiscriminate killing in America. However, when a lunatic in Norway kills dozens in a premeditated shooting spree, he is presented as a "Christian" because in one of his blogs he made a vague reference to church and Christianity.

The media in this nation is unbelievably powerful, and it has destroyed many a life by reporting half-truths and incomplete stories, advancing their destructive progressive agenda.

The "God" of Oprah Winfrey

Oprah Winfrey is the most powerful person in media today. Millions regularly watch her television shows every day and she has started her own television network. When Oprah endorses a book it is almost certain to become a best seller, and when she says someone is a great person, America listens.

Oprah was raised as a Christian but became disillusioned at a young age. She could not accept the notion of God being a God of judgment, so she started to search for God on her own terms: something that happens every day with disillusioned Christians. But Oprah was different. This nice young lady would grow into a powerful media presence who would have the ears and hearts of millions of disciples, hanging on every word she speaks, believing it as truth.

By all indications, Oprah is a kind and very generous person. She is also one of the most dangerous enemies of Christianity in America. She has now partnered with Rob Bell in a series of television shows about "seeking spirituality." She has introduced Christians to many other dangerous false prophets and teachers including Eckhart Tolle; Rhonda Byrne, author of the best-selling New Age book *The Secret*; Dr.

Mehmet Oz, whom we will discuss later; and a lady you probably never heard of – Marianne Williamson.

Marianne Williamson is energetic, charismatic, eloquent, and very dangerous. In 2008 Oprah and Williamson covered a daily one-year study over satellite radio on *A Course in Miracles*. Millions listened, including many Christians.

A Course in Miracles was written in 1975 by Columbia University Professor Helen Schucman. She claimed God spoke to her to give her new revelation and to "correct" misinterpretations in the Bible. Among the revelations Schucman reported were:

- There is no sin.

- The slain Christ has no meaning.

- The journey to the cross should be the last useless journey.

- Do not make the pathetic error of clinging to the old rugged cross.

- The name of Jesus is but a symbol as a replacement for the many names of God to which men pray.

- The recognition of God is the recognition of yourself.

- The oneness of the Creator and the creation is your wholeness, your sanity, and your limitless power.

- The atonement is the final lesson man needs to learn, for it teaches him that, never having sinned, he has no need for salvation.

Welcome to the Church of Oprah, a church that millions, including Christians, are embracing as "the new Christianity." The teachings of *A Course in Miracles* are exactly the opposite of what the Bible teaches, yet millions are embracing them as truth. Oprah is admired by Christians who are swayed by her gentle compassion. And now Rob Bell, a dangerous heretic whom American churches allowed in to influence millions of young people, partners with Oprah to help people find "true spirituality."

We have covered Oprah extensively on *Stand Up For the Truth*, sharing her theological beliefs that are leading many to destruction. In one broadcast, she adamantly insists that there is no way Jesus could be the only path to God. The book by Rhonda Byrne, *The Secret*, became a best seller when Oprah endorsed it, and many Christians, including some close friends of mine, read it and loved it. Byrne's message that if you send good thoughts into the universe that the universe will bring back good things to you speaks directly to some Christians seeking happiness in all the wrong places.

I could write an entire book on the deception of the Church of Oprah, but if you want more information, I suggest two great resources: the first is by my friend and author Warren Smith of Mountain Stream Press. As a former New Ager, Warren has written several books on the New Age movement, Oprah Winfrey, and *A Course in Miracles*. I also recommend a book by Josh McDowell and Dave Sterrett titled *'O' God: A Dialogue on Truth and Oprah's Spirituality*.

Summary

American Christianity is under constant attack by some powerful external enemies. Poor science, public education and indoctrination, an expanding socialist government, and the anti-Christian propaganda of the media combine as a powerful force, attempting to destroy Christianity in this nation. Islam has replaced Christianity as the darling of American media. This is a powerful army pounding at the walls, seeking to destroy American Christianity. But as powerful as these enemies are, they should be powerless against the church. We have the truth and the Holy Spirit on our side.

But something is happening here that is giving the Enemy a huge advantage in this battle, tilting the balance of power. There are traitors in our own camp. Some of these traitors are intentional in their mission while others are naively supporting the work of the Enemy. These naive people are being seduced, thinking they are helping the church to embrace and defeat the Enemy, when they are only contributing to the destruction of the church they claim to defend and love.

Whether they are conscious traitors or unknowing pawns is an important distinction. All of us as Christians get things wrong sometimes.

When we do, we need to be shown the error of our ways so we may repent and be restored. Many of the people we are about to discuss are unknowing pawns in the Enemy's chess game. They are ignorant and have been seduced by the lies of the Enemy. We need to expose the darkness they are advancing and confront them in their error in the hope that they will repent of the dangerous path they are leading many people down. The future of American Christianity depends on it.

Chapter 6

The Internal Pawns of the Enemy

William Wallace, the warrior who led Scotland to its freedom from the repressive rule of England and its notorious King Longshanks, surveyed the field where the battle for freedom would be fought. A mile away stood thousands of skillfully trained English infantry, cavalry, and archers – the greatest fighting force of that time.

Behind him stood a ragtag group of Scots, farmers, and shepherds who had taken all they could take. Their wives had been raped, their ancestors murdered, and their dignity stripped. Enough was enough! Freedom would be won this day, even at the cost of their own lives. Their children would be free, even at the sacrifice of their own lives.

Out of view of the English were the Scottish nobles. They were greedy thieves themselves, accepting bribes of land from Longshanks to be his proxy of oppression to the Scottish commoners. But Wallace believed he had stirred something up in them: a desire for freedom. This day Wallace believed the nobles would stand strong for the sake of their countrymen and help Scotland free itself from English tyranny.

Wallace would first set a trap for the English cavalry, destroying it in a brilliant move. Infantry forces had never defeated superior cavalry forces before that day, but Wallace had a plan. As the English cavalry charged at the waiting Scots, a fire engulfed them as the Scots fired flaming arrows into the ground they had soaked with oil the night before. The powerful English cavalry was destroyed, setting the table for a

Scottish victory that day. They attacked the English infantry, who probably figured they would never even see battle that day, as they assumed the mighty English cavalry would scatter and destroy the ragtag Scots. The battle slowly turned in favor of the Scottish rebels and Wallace's plan was working perfectly.

Wallace was ready to lead Scotland to a decisive victory. Behind a hill, invisible to the English, were the Scottish nobles with hundreds of cavalry troops. When Wallace gave the signal, they would swoop in, scattering the English infantry. Longshanks would be captured, the English army destroyed, and Scotland would earn its freedom.

The time was right. With hundreds of dead soldiers around him, William Wallace picked up and waved the banner as the sign for the Scottish nobles to attack. Victory was at hand. As Wallace frantically waved the banner, his heart was about to be broken. The Scottish nobles acknowledged the signal, but then slowly turned, leaving the battle area.

The valiant Scots were left to be slaughtered, scattered, or captured. Defeat had been snatched from the jaws of victory. Traitors in his own camp had betrayed Wallace and the Scots.

Eventually, Wallace was executed and the dream of freedom seemed a distant memory. A few months later, Robert the Bruce, one of the nobles who had betrayed Wallace, assumed leadership of the Scots. He stood in a field, opposite English royalty, preparing to pledge loyalty to the English crown on behalf of all Scotland. But something welled up in Robert the Bruce that day. Before the previous battle, his father, an evil hypocrite who only cared about power, had already arranged the betrayal by the nobles even though Robert had pledged his support to Wallace. Robert the Bruce went along, betraying his friend, out of loyalty to his earthly father.

The pain and shame from his betrayal welled up that day. Robert the Bruce had his eyes opened to what was right. He pleaded with the remaining Scots to follow him as they once followed Wallace. They responded, charging the English. Scotland would win her freedom.

We all have choices to make every day. They are often presented as an option between what is right and what is convenient. We make choices to do the right thing or the selfish thing. Robert the Bruce historically caved in to his earthly desires, choosing the selfish thing. One day he stood up and decided to do the right thing – and he changed history.

There are a growing number of "Scottish nobles" leading our churches these days: men who have become comfortable in their positions of authority and who are allowing philosophies and ideas of this world to influence them as leaders. We need more leaders like Robert the Bruce in the church these days: men who recognize the errors of their decisions and choose to make things right. Men who look deep into their own hearts and ask God to share what He sees when He looks there. Men who confess they have made bad choices and ask God for forgiveness and the strength to make things right. Men who are more interested in doing what is right than what is convenient. Men who are willing to admit they are consciously or unconsciously compromising with the world for either personal benefit or because they have been seduced by the lies of the Enemy.

American Christianity is having an identity crisis. It is struggling with how to be *in* the world but not *of* the world. It is struggling to understand the ever-changing secular culture without compromising with it. Slowly we are giving in to the Enemy because deep down we doubt the power of the gospel and its power to transform lives, so we have embarked on a new marketing campaign. Rather than confront the culture and call it out for what it is, we have decided to "relate" to it. The results have been nothing short of abysmal. Too many Christian leaders have assumed the role of the Scottish nobles, compromising with evil so we can maintain some semblance of existence, and turning our backs on the people we are charged to lead.

As Hitler came to power before World War II, he consolidated power through deception and intimidation. He approached church leaders of his day and first convinced them that they had a common enemy: the Jew. He appealed to growing anti-Semitic passions, claiming the Jews were bleeding Germany of wealth, prosperity, and identity.

He also let them know that he could not and would not tolerate disloyalty of German churches to the "noble" quest he was on to establish Germany as a world economic and military power. He intimidated them by threatening to shut them down if they spoke against the Nazi

Movement. The church leaders folded like cheap suits to maintain their livelihood and status. Among the new rules Hitler imposed on the churches were the banning of all Bibles and the mandate that only Third Reich employees could preach. He also took down every cross.

Leaders were faced with a decision to trust God or give in to pressure and fear. In spite of some brave people like Dietrich Bonhoeffer, many churches chose fear, and Hitler was effectively able to silence any resistance from most Christian churches. The results of this cowardly surrender speak for themselves. Are some Christian leaders in America today giving in to fear these days? Might we be slowly surrendering to an evil secular culture that will one day control American Christianity and gut it of its ability to lead our nation back to God?

One internal pawn of the Enemy has tremendous influence on young Christians. Young people who have been trained to question anything that claims to be absolute truth are finding a home within Christianity. They are finding a place where they can accept or reject parts of the Bible so they can customize it to their perceptions of truth and reality. Truth becomes subjective, not objective. God becomes who you want Him to be instead of who He tells us He is in the pages of Scripture. This is a powerful ally in Satan's master plan to diminish or destroy Christianity. It is subtle, yet very dangerous – and it is working.

The Emergent Church – Emerging toward What?

Brian McLaren is an intelligent, articulate writer. He is well spoken and persuasive. He is referred to as the "guru of the emergent church movement," and he is leading hordes of young Christians over a cliff like lemmings. In his book *A New Kind of Christianity*, McLaren argues that our traditional beliefs about Christianity are archaic and must change. What fundamental changes does McLaren propose to this "archaic Christianity"?

On page 66 of the book McLaren states, "The question is 'Who is Jesus and why is he important?' The versions of Jesus presented by contemporary Christian institutions could hardly be more different from one another – or from the four gospels."

I will concede the first part of McLaren's argument that the different versions of Jesus presented in some Christian institutions these days are all over the map. Jesus is portrayed as judgmental by some, non-judgmental by others; strong by some and weak by others; a destroyer of the law by some and a completer of the law by others. To some He is a harsh taskmaster requiring sacrifice and that we turn our backs on any good thing this world offers; to others He is our own personal genie just waiting to grant any wish if we just have enough faith. So, Mr. McLaren, I concede the point: much of American Christianity is distorting the character and nature of the Son of God. But this does not warrant a call for a new kind of Christianity. This calls for greater reading of the Word and discernment by the Holy Spirit.

McLaren goes on in later writings to talk about confusion within the Gospels themselves, suggesting that the apostles themselves might have been confused about who Jesus really was and what He taught. This casts doubt on the authority of Scripture.

McLaren later goes into a lengthy diatribe about how the church has sold out the gospel by putting a Greco-Roman spin on it. Again, this is an attempt to undermine the Scriptures as absolute truth. When you read the Bible in its entirety and study it in the original written languages, you find a beautiful consistency from beginning to end. Are there certain teachings we may not completely understand? Certainly, because none of us will have a complete understanding of God until we stand before Him in all His revealed glory. But McLaren and many other emergers seek to undermine the absolute truth of the written Word, convincing naive Christians to trust in their own feelings rather than in the Word of God. This is going where no man should dare go and will lead many to eternal destruction.

What McLaren is doing is subtly but effectively stating that Christians must doubt the written Word of God and that we cannot rely on the written Scriptures as our source of absolute truth. Instead, we must rely on our personal feelings, beliefs, and experiences. Welcome to a core teaching of the emergent church: Feelings trump facts; emotions trump truth. Your personal beliefs about God are more important than what was written down by men in the Bible.

But McLaren is only warming up, folks. On page 72, he poses the following "dilemma":

> "How should followers of Jesus relate to people of other religions? We wake up each day in a world whose very future is threatened by interreligious fear, hatred, and violence. Many of us wonder if there is a way to have both a deep identity in Christ and an irenic, charitable, neighborly attitude toward people of other faiths. So we ask: Is Jesus the only way? The only way to what? How can a belief in the uniqueness and universality of Christ be held without implying the religious supremacy and exclusivity of the Christian religion?"

It can't, Brian. Christianity is superior to any other religion because it is truth! It is an exclusive club, not because we are special, but because of the sacrifice of Jesus on the cross. Christianity is superior because of Jesus, God in the flesh, who took our sins upon Himself. He died for our sins and rose from the dead. Did Buddha or Muhammad do this? No other religion is remotely similar in its beliefs and none can be held up as equal, an no other religious is true. True Christians will spend eternity with God and those who are not will spend eternity separated from Him. This fact, and any fact for that matter, drives emergers nuts. They cannot stand anything that presents itself as absolute truth. McLaren is planting early seeds of his universalism beliefs and planting seeds of doubts in naive Christians who admire his "open-minded" attitude. They are music to the ears of a generation raised early on to doubt anything that claims to be absolute.

Ready for more intellectual babble? On page 156 of *A New Kind of Christianity*, McLaren shares his method of learning:

> "My background was in the liberal arts. My training taught me to read for scenes and plots, not doctrines; for protagonists and antagonists, not absolute and objective truths; for character development and conflict resolution, not raw material to be processed into a system of beliefs."

Looking for scenes, not doctrines; not looking for or accepting the concept of absolute truth; not seeking raw material to be processed into a system of beliefs. Welcome to the cancer that is emergent church theology. But in the infamous words of every infomercial, Wait! There's more!

> "There will be no new kind of Christian faith without a
> new approach to the Bible, because we've gotten ourselves
> into a mess with the Bible. First, we are in a scientific mess.
> Fundamentalism again and again paints itself into a corner
> by requiring that the Bible be treated as a divinely dictated
> science textbook providing us true information in all areas
> of life, including when and how the earth was created."

Boiling all this down, McLaren believes that we cannot trust the Word of God. McLaren also shows his incredibly weak theological understanding of God when he writes this about God on page 269:

> "I find a character named God who sends a flood that
> destroys all humanity except for Noah's family, but that's
> almost trivial compared to a deity who tortures the greater
> part of humanity forever in infinite eternal torment."

God is now a cruel torturer instead of a righteous God who cannot tolerate unforgiven sin. McLaren insinuates it's God's fault that many will face eternal damnation, not our fault. McLaren, of course, believes a loving God would never judge anyone, so he is setting up his shallow followers for this argument later.

Heard enough on Brian McLaren? Bear with me a little longer. McLaren goes on to argue that we have to stop looking at Christianity as good and every other religion as evil. McLaren later calls the cross "false advertising for God." He argues that substitutionary atonement on the cross is a false teaching – that God would never punish one person for another's sins. Hey Brian, think about something for a moment . . . Jesus, being God, took the punishment for our sins on Himself – the ultimate in sacrificial love. God didn't punish a "third party"; He took our sins upon Himself, in human form, to bring us into a righteous relationship with Him.

Who Listens to McLaren Anyway?

This is not some obscure writer out of the mainstream of Christian thought. Brian McLaren teaches at "Christian" institutions, is admired by thousands of youth pastors, and has a cult-like following of hundreds of thousands of youth, youth pastors, and well-respected Christian leaders and pastors.

A close friend of mine and a Bible-believing Christian approached his church leadership a few years back asking permission to bring Christian teachers in who are well versed on the Judeo-Christian roots upon which our nation was founded. His idea was rejected out of hand, but a different speaker was presented as an alternative: Brian McLaren. This local megachurch saw Brian McLaren as a godly leader and teacher who could relate to young adults and youth. I am willing to bet the pastoral team never took the time to study McLaren's theology before suggesting the invitation, pointing to how careless and lazy many church leaders have become.

In Revelation 2 and 3, God writes letters to the churches with the last one penned to the church in Laodicea. Many biblical scholars believe the church of Laodicea is representative of the last church before the end of the age because it is the final church letter, symbolizing what Christianity will look like just before the return of Jesus. Laodicea comes from two Greek words meaning "people" and "opinions or judgments." So the church of Laodicea is the church of the opinions of the people. Today, much of what we call Christianity fits nicely into this description of the Laodicean church. Our opinions about God seem to matter more than what God says about Himself in the Bible. We replace the clear judgments and teachings of God with our own subjective interpretations.

It is important to understand that the emergent church movement is not a stand-alone entity. It is closely affiliated with movements like social justice, New Ageism, and Christian universalism. McLaren is one of many public spokesmen for the heresies and false teachings infecting Christianity these days.

McLaren is an eloquent, persuasive speaker and writer, and this is a real danger to a generation of Christians who place emotions above facts. He has infected American Christianity in a profound way, leading it to potential destruction. But he is hardly alone.

Red Letter Christians

Doctrine is what defines a movement or its religious beliefs. It is the groundwork for the purpose and teachings of the movement or religion: what its people believe and what they profess as truth. What a doctrinal statement says, or fails to say, gives us critical information on its beliefs and goals.

Doctrine for churches and ministries is usually expressed in what is called a "Statement of Faith." We hopefully read and explore this before we enter a church or search the Internet for teaching and commentaries. It defines the beliefs of the organization so we can ascertain their goals and motives. Red Letter Christians has no statement of faith on their site, a testament to their "God is who you think He is" belief system.

This lack of doctrinal beliefs nicely summarizes emergent theology: it stands for nothing and is pretty much open to anything the follower feels or thinks might be truth. In my opinion, emergent theology is worse than atheism because at least atheists believe in something and are not ashamed to admit it. But try pinning down an emergent leader on any sort of hard doctrine, and you usually hear a fluffy response that sounds more like a romance novel than real truth.

Jim Wallis and Tony Campolo are the brainchildren behind Red Letter Christians. Their purpose has been stated as helping Christians understand that we cannot possibly understand the entire Bible unless we read and study it through the lens of Jesus' words, thus the name "Red Letter Christians." Now, on the surface that does not seem to be an objectionable statement, but when you dig into their teachings and opinions you see a more nefarious purpose.

A basic cry of those in the movement is if Jesus didn't talk about it, it probably isn't all that important. In other words, don't fret about all the confusing stuff in the Old Testament or the Epistles, just focus on what Jesus did or did not say. That's all that really matters. This points to their weak theological wisdom about the Word of God.

It's as if they are saying Jesus overrode all the teachings of the Old

Testament. This, of course, is refuted by Jesus Himself in Matthew 5:17-18: *"Do not think that I have come to abolish the Law or the Prophets; I have not come to abolish them but to fulfill them. For truly I tell you, until heaven and earth disappear, not the smallest letter, nor the least stroke of a pen, will by any means disappear from the Law until everything is accomplished."*

In the opinion of many, the real agenda of Red Letter Christians, just like Wallis's other brainchild, Sojourners, is not a spiritual agenda but a political one. It has far less to do with the truth of God then it does with promoting a socialist utopia of justice. It promotes a sort of "Christian Communism," where having equal outcomes is more important than equal opportunities because the free-enterprise system of capitalism is just too harsh, with winners and losers.

The list of contributors and recommended authors is a real who's-who list of progressive activists including Jim Wallis, Tony Campolo, Shane Claiborne, Dorothy Day, Gabe Lyons, Lynne Hybels, Brian McLaren, Jay Bakker, and Rob Bell. There seems to be a common bond with all of them: a distaste for absolute truth and fundamental Christianity.

Apparently, anything goes with Red Letter Christians, as long as you feel good about it. No mention of sin, just a call for justice and peace. A common argument put forth by many Red Letter Christians is that homosexuality is not a sin because Jesus never overtly called it a sin. When one counters with the fact that Paul called it a sin, a common question you get in rebuttal is, "Well, who do you follow, Jesus or Paul?" This speaks to their shallow understanding of the Bible and culture when Jesus walked the earth.

Homosexuality was a sin under the law, the law Jesus did not abolish, by the way, and it was punishable by death. Every Jew knew this, so it was probably a very limited occurrence given the severe sentence. Jesus did not have to preach on it as a sin, just like He did not have to call out rape or adultery as sins – every Jew knew it.

Paul, on the other hand, was the apostle to the Gentiles, mainly Greeks. Greek culture not only allowed, but also often celebrated homosexuality. Historically, kings and conquerors were given young boys as sexual slaves to reward them and to teach the young boys the art of servitude

– disgusting, certainly, but acceptable and even commendable in Greek culture. Paul had to admonish new Greek Christians, reminding them that homosexuality is a sin and that the habitually sexually immoral person would not inherit the kingdom of heaven.

Red Letter Christian founders, Jim Wallis and Tony Campolo, are highly respected among many Christian leaders, churches, and colleges. Their books are often used by naive youth leaders to "instruct" youth on this new form of Christianity. Tony Campolo has made some controversial statements throughout the years that cause one to question just what this new form of Christianity looks like.

"We cannot allow our theologies to separate us" (speaking on the relations between Muslims and Christians, "On Evangelicals and Interfaith Cooperation," an interview with Tony Campolo by Shane Claiborne). "It seems to me that when we listen to the Muslim mystics as they talk about Jesus and their love for Jesus, I must say, it's a lot closer to New Testament Christianity than a lot of the Christians that I hear. In other words, if we are looking for common ground, can we find it in mystical spirituality, even if we cannot theologically agree? Can we pray together in such a way that we connect with a God that transcends our theological differences?"

This is also from Tony Campolo in *Speaking My Mind*, pages 149-150:

> "Beyond these models of reconciliation, a theology of mysticism provides some hope for common ground between Christians and Islam. Both religions have within their histories examples of ecstatic union with God."

Okay, stop the presses for a moment. These quotes show Tony Campolo trying to find common ground between Islam and Christianity. This is called Chrislam and we will explore that in this chapter. I have read the Quran and the Hadith four times and have consulted with former Muslims. A couple facts must interrupt Tony's lovefest:

First, Allah is not YHWH. This is abundantly clear if you read the first few suras of the Quran. Allah denies any sort of trinity and is a liar. God cannot lie, as it is against His nature. Lying is Allah's nature and he encourages Muslims to do the same, and let's remember who Jesus said in John 8:44 is *"a liar and the father of lies."*

Second, let's address this "love for Jesus" Campolo says Muslims have. Well, Muslims do acknowledge Jesus – but as a minor prophet named Isa, and the teachings of Muhammad accuse Jesus of being a liar. The commonality Campolo and others seek is biblically impossible. The Quran denies that Jesus is a deity, the Son of God. In 1 John 4:1-3, Islam fits in here as being biblically identified as a religion of antichrist:

> *Dear friends, do not believe every spirit, but test the spir-*
> *its to see whether they are from God, because many false*
> *prophets have gone out into the world. This is how you can*
> *recognize the Spirit of God: Every spirit that acknowledges*
> *that Jesus Christ has come in the flesh is from God, but every*
> *spirit that does not acknowledge Jesus is not from God. This*
> *is the spirit of the antichrist, which you have heard is coming*
> *and even now is already in the world.*

So Tony Campolo and other Christian leaders are promoting common dialogue and beliefs between Christianity and a religion of antichrist. That's what passes for Christian leadership and influence these days.

Campolo has many other quotes about reaching for "Christ-consciousness" – a fancy word for saying God is in everyone, a New Age philosophy. Campolo also appears to be a universalist, thinking all people go to heaven: "going to heaven is like going to Philadelphia...There are many ways...it doesn't make any difference how we go there. We all end up in the same place" (from his book *Carpe Diem: Seize the Day*).

Campolo also admits he struggles with the thought of homosexuality being a sin, but at least up to now, he does not endorse homosexual marriage, although his wife does. Give him time and he will be further "enlightened," I'm sure.

Earlier this year I received a call right after we covered the emergent church on an episode of *Stand Up For the Truth*. A woman asked if I was familiar with a book titled *The Irresistible Revolution*. I told her I was familiar with this book, written by Shane Claiborne and endorsed by Jim Wallis. She told me her son came home from youth group with the book, given to him by his youth leader. The leader gave every member of his group the book, telling them this book would be their "Bible study" for the coming months.

This is happening regularly in our churches. The Word of God is being replaced by writings of emergers and social justice proponents, and our youth are learning a false gospel supported by many of our Christian leaders. I cannot urge you strongly enough to meet with your church leadership and find out what your children are being taught in their youth group. If your youth leader is teaching them directly from the Bible, thank him and help him any way you can. If the youth leader is peddling garbage like *The Irresistible Revolution*, demand that this ceases and if it does not, leave the church for one that teaches the Word of God.

Red Letter Christianity is not serious Christianity at all. It is an incomplete, twisted gospel that is leading many gullible Christian youth astray with its message of love and acceptance. There is no call for repentance and no real acknowledgment of the existence of sin in our lives. It's like a bad chick flick, full of fluff with no real content or story.

Social Justice

Wallis and Campolo are also leaders in the social justice movement that is making inroads into every denomination of Christianity. The social justice movement, while claiming to be a Christian movement, is nothing of the kind. Appealing more to the human perception of justice rather than God's definition of it, this movement is damaging Christianity from within, weakening it to the external assault of Satan's army.

Jim Wallis, as noted earlier, is nothing but a political hack. He has continually supported communist regimes around the world, dating back to when he was a chapter leader for Students for a Democratic Society in the late sixties. He is a disciple of Saul Alinsky and has successfully hoodwinked Christians into supporting pro-abortion and pro-gay marriage candidates, including Barack Obama and Hillary Clinton. In fact, I believe Wallis was the key person responsible for Obama's election. A majority of Catholics and a high percentage of evangelical Christians voted for Obama, and Jim Wallis was the catalyst.

The social justice movement is a loose organization that includes some dangerous teachings that the leaders have convinced people are biblically based. Liberation theology and black liberation theology teach that Jesus hated rich people and that the rich must be overthrown before Jesus can return. In fact, Jim Wallis is close friends with Pastor Jeremiah Wright, Obama's former chief spiritual advisor prior to Wallis, and the same Jeremiah Wright who prayed God would damn America rather than bless and restore her.

The social justice movement that is infiltrating mainstream Christianity might sound noble on the surface. It calls for helping the poor through better housing and transportation, rehabilitation instead of incarceration for non-violent criminals, and for Christians to be more generous financially. It is *how* they call for this financial sharing that is a concern. They are proponents of forced wealth redistribution through higher taxes. This takes the voluntary giving of Christians, where we can choose which organizations to help, and gives that power to a federal government that has proven to be hateful of Christianity.

Jim Wallis is a staunch supporter of the Occupy Movement and racist movements like Black Lives Matter and the Southern Poverty Law Center that support chaos. This fits perfectly into Saul Alinsky's game plan in *Rules for Radicals*, the handbook of the social justice movement. Alinsky was a proud communist and atheist who dedicated his book to Lucifer. Now why would a "Christian" like Jim Wallis be an avid disciple of a man who was an atheist and who dedicated a book to Lucifer?

The social justice movement's crown jewel is *Sojourners* magazine. Claiming again to be Christians, Sojourners is nothing but an interfaith movement that disgraces the gospel, replacing it with a man-made gospel of communism and humanism. A frequent offer for new subscribers is a poster of Gandhi. The website refers to climate change, economic inequality, and national borders as sins, but does not call abortion or homosexuality sin.

As its chief editor, Wallis has a team of progressives as editors and regular contributors, including Tony Campolo, Brian McLaren, and Lynne Hybels, wife of Pastor Bill Hybels. They are anti-Israel and a shill for the Palestinian cause: these same Palestinians who partner with Syria and Iran to launch thousands of rockets into Israel every year, killing innocent children.

Wallis and Sojourners also have a sugar daddy in George Soros.

Soros is a billionaire atheist who hates Christianity and America. He invests millions of dollars every year into organizations bent on destroying Christianity and America as a nation. He has openly stated that America is the last obstacle to a one-world government that he believes is necessary for the survival of mankind. In 2010 when it was reported that Soros was funding Wallis and Sojourners, Wallis publicly and adamantly denied it. When documents confirmed that indeed Soros had sent Wallis and Sojourners nearly $1 million, Wallis deflected, stating he could not be expected to keep track of "every little contribution."

The social justice movement twists the gospel to claim that Jesus cared more about the condition of this world than He did for the eternal souls of men. They promote blatant humanism and communism, along with a pattern of speaking highly of candidates who support homosexual marriage and abortion.

Wallis applauded the Arab Spring as a great day for democracy, but has remained silent as Christians in Egypt are murdered, churches are burned, and the Muslim Brotherhood that initially controlled Egypt announced they would disregard Egypt's peace treaty with Israel. Wallis also signed on to the "A Common Word Between Us and You" heresy we will discuss later.

I have spoken with Jim Wallis. He is not stupid. He is smart and eloquent and knows exactly what he is doing. Combined with the social justice movement's close sister, the emergent church movement, they are out to destroy traditional Christianity and replace it with a religion of universalism based on humanism.

Jim Wallis is the perfect leader for the social justice movement because he is as phony as the movement is. Any person with a modicum of common sense can see through the flowery rhetoric of this anti-Christian movement, yet it continues to make inroads into Christian churches of all denominations.

Rob Bell

Rob Bell, now former pastor of Mars Hill Bible Church in Michigan, had been touted as the next wave of Christian leadership by many in the emergent movement. He is charismatic and articulate, but biblically shallow. He has produced countless *Nooma* videos that are entertaining Christian youth in youth groups around the world. Youth leaders seem to worship the ground he walks on, claiming he reaches the heart and soul of the younger generation. Teachers like John MacArthur ask if he fits the mold of the false prophets Jesus, Paul, and Peter warned us about. Let's take a peek at the man who has a hold on our youth with his glitter and rock-and-roll personality.

Bell was raised an evangelical and graduated from Wheaton College, for whatever that is worth these days. He claims to be "evangelical and orthodox to the bone," but his teachings seem to refute that claim. Historic evangelicalism has affirmed the authority, inerrancy, and sufficiency of Scripture as God-breathed. How do Bell's beliefs line up?

Rob Bell authored a best-selling book, *Love Wins*. In it, per the emergent handbook, he asks a lot of questions but provides few if any answers. He questions if hell really exists. Would a loving God really send someone to hell? Conceding that even if the existence of hell might be possible, Bell goes on to question hell as an eternal place of suffering and separation from God.

Questions can be important. They can help you grow deeper in your knowledge of the truth, and they can help us wrestle with difficult questions of doctrine. But how Bell asks the question is just as important as the question itself. "Has God created billions of people over thousands of years only to select a few to go to heaven and everyone else to suffer forever in hell? Is this acceptable to God? How is this 'good news'?" This frames the question in a very misleading way, claiming it has to be good news for *everyone*, not just those who choose Jesus.

Bell goes on to write: "A staggering number of people have been taught that a select few Christians will spend forever in a peaceful, joyous place called heaven, while the rest of humanity spends forever in torment and punishment in hell with no chance for anything better.... This is misguided and toxic and ultimately subverts the contagious spread of Jesus' message of love, peace, forgiveness, and joy that our world desperately needs to hear."

Sorry Rob, but Jesus says the path to eternal life is narrow but the road to destruction is wide and many find it. But is hell a future reality or a just a present state? Is it an earthly reality or one that exists elsewhere and for eternity? According to Rob Bell, hell appears to be more about what we *do to each other in this lifetime* than what happens when we reject Jesus Christ as Savior and Lord. Bell reads Jesus' warnings of divine punishment as addressing only the temporal, rather than both the temporal and the eternal. These warnings were for the religious leaders of the day, and had very little to do with some other reality or some other time, he argues (pp. 82-83). Instead, hell is "a word that refers to the big, wide, terrible evil that comes from the secrets hidden deep within our hearts all the way to the massive, society-wide collapse and chaos that comes when we fail to live in God's world God's way" (p. 95). In other words, hell is here and now in this life, not a place of eternal punishment.

You also find very broad statements offered as fact. "At the center of the Christian tradition since the first church has been the insistence that history is not tragic, hell is not forever, and love, in the end, wins."

Scripture clearly points to hell as a place of eternal damnation, so I am not sure what Bell means when he talks about Christian tradition. The New Testament is the beginning of Christianity, and Jesus clearly taught of a literal, eternal hell. Bell cites the Greek word *aion*, a small word that is central to his arguments. While this word is commonly translated as "eternal" or "everlasting," Bell argues that it can also mean "age" or "period of time." Using this approach, he briefly argues from the parable of the sheep and the goats (Matthew 25:31-46) that eternal punishment isn't eternal, but rather an intense period of pruning.

But if we are going to accept that definition of the word, we must be consistent in its interpretation. That same word is used in John 3:16. So if we assume that these words primarily mean "age" or "period of time," what happens when we apply that definition to John 3:16 where it is also used? For God so loved the world that He sent His only Son so that whosoever believes in Him will not perish but have life for a *limited period of time*? You can't have it both ways, Rob.

Citing 1 Timothy 2:4, where Paul states that God desires all people to be saved and to come to the knowledge of the truth, Bell reflects and asks, "How great is God? Great enough to achieve what God sets out to do, or kind of great, medium great, great most of the time, but in this, the fate of billions of people, not totally great; sort of great; a little great." A God who would allow people to go to hell is not a great God, according to Bell, and the traditional belief that He would is "devastating ... psychologically crushing ... terrifying and traumatizing and unbearable" (pp. 136-37). Rob Bell almost seems to be attributing evil intentions and actions to God.

If *Love Wins* accurately represents Bell's views on heaven and hell, it reveals him as a proponent of a kind of Christian universalism. "As soon as the door is opened to Muslims, Hindus, Buddhists, and Baptists from Cleveland, many Christians become very uneasy, saying that then Jesus doesn't matter anymore, the cross is irrelevant, it doesn't matter what you believe, and so forth."

This is just not true of the Christians I know. They desire for all people from all religions to have their eyes and hearts opened to the saving gospel. But God will not come to us on our terms. We must come to Him on His terms – acceptance of Jesus as the Son of God, Savior, and Lord of everything. No other scenario will do.

So there are the beliefs about salvation, heaven, and hell from the man your children adore – the man your youth pastor might be holding up as cool and relevant. And do not think for one minute that Rob Bell could never be influencing your children or the youth pastor who is teaching them. Bell's *Nooma* videos are still popular and widely used in many churches, even though Bell has now partnered with the "Church of Oprah Winfrey" to promote false teachings about God, and has officially denied the Christian doctrine of substitutionary atonement for our sins through the death and resurrection of Jesus Christ.

Respectfully confront your pastor and ask that he get involved with what the church's youth are being taught in youth group and learn more about the people his youth leader looks up to. Do not assume your children are being taught the absolute truth of the Bible in youth group. There is a good chance they are subtly learning that the Word of God is more subjective than absolute.

Christian Universalism

Christian universalism is the position that all of mankind will ultimately be saved through Jesus, whether we repent of sin and place our faith in Him as the Son of God or not. It claims that God's qualities of love, sovereignty, and justice require that all people be saved and that eternal punishment is a false doctrine. It claims that the saving work of the cross does not save us from eternal damnation, it saves us from sin.

There are two slightly differing belief camps in Christian universalism. The first teaches that unrepentant sinners will be *punished proportionately in a future state*, according to the degree of sin committed in the current life. Christian universalists generally hold to the belief that this punishment is moral and not physical and that there is no hell. In essence, unrepentant sinners will carry a burden with them in heaven. The second camp teaches that *all the punishment for sin occurs in this life* and that God's discipline in our lives is for the purpose of purifying us. In eternity, there will be a loss of reward for those who did not trust in Christ in this lifetime.

So one camp generally believes they will carry a burden in heaven; the other believes that we will lose some blessings in heaven. But both camps maintain that everyone, regardless of their faith or religious beliefs, will be in heaven with God. It is unthinkable to them that a loving God would ever condemn anyone to eternal punishment.

Some Christian universalists claim to hold many of the basic beliefs of traditional Christianity: the Trinity, the deity of Christ and the Holy Spirit, and salvation by grace alone. Some hold to the inerrancy of Scripture but believe it has been maligned by man as history progressed.

Others deny the teaching of the Trinity, claiming the belief of Arianism, where God is a divine entity, but Jesus was created by Him. Many also claim God has taken various forms throughout history and has revealed Himself through other religions like Hinduism and Islam.

Many profess a belief that Jesus is the Son of the living God, but we must examine their belief closely because of the belief of Arianism, where Jesus is the *created* Son of God, not a member of the Trinity. The slippery and subtle nuances of their language make this appealing to a generation that is biblically illiterate and is seeking acceptance over exclusion in religious beliefs.

Many Christian universalists affirm the physical resurrection of Jesus, but some claim He did not rise from the dead physically, but instead that He was assumed into heaven to dwell with God. If the physical resurrection of Jesus is denied, as it seems it is, then anyone who holds to that position is indeed a non-Christian, since they are denying one of the essential doctrines of Christianity.

Many deny that the Holy Spirit is God. The Holy Spirit is viewed as a part of human existence – the spirit within every man that desires to connect with his Creator. It is a human spirit of each man, not God Himself.

Many Christian universalists believe in a "second-chance" theology at work where people who have rejected Jesus in this life can come to faith in the next life. Some believe it is a reincarnation while others believe along the lines of what Rob Bell suggests – that eventually all humans are reconciled to God after a brief separation.

Christian universalism is very attractive to the current generation of young people. It falls much more in line with a loving God then a God of justice and judgment. While you will not find many emergent Christians who admit it, when you read the entirety of their writings and beliefs, many are Christian universalists. That is one reason their teaching is so appealing to a biblically illiterate generation of Christians: their teachings feed our sinful flesh.

There is a very deep danger in how this false teaching is infecting American Christianity. It seeks to eliminate the judgmental nature of God. God is a holy God who cannot tolerate sin. Heaven will be a place that is void of the very presence of sin according to Scripture. When we eliminate the righteous judgment of God, we diminish His holy, perfect character. We reduce Him to something lower than He is, and God will not be mocked or subject to our human understanding or desires. This teaching also removes the fear of the Lord. We are instructed to have a healthy fear of falling into the hands of an angry God. He does judge and He will condemn many to eternal hell. This is a healthy fear that helps us in our Christian walk. When we no longer fear the wrath of an angry God, we in essence worship a false god. True Christians should see God as our loving Father, one who protects and cherishes us. But we are never to lose our reverent fear of Him if we turn away from Him.

Be watchful and have your ears open when discussing the Christian faith with young people and new Christians. Ask probing questions, drilling beneath the surface. Christian universalist beliefs are taking hold of many younger Christians and we need to be prepared to recognize and refute them with the Word of God.

Chrislam: Sleeping with the Enemy?

Sometimes an external and internal enemy can be one in the same. Chrislam, a bait thrown out by Muslim leaders and swallowed by many Christian leaders and pastors, is such an enemy.

Chrislam is an unofficial term for a movement that seeks dialogue and common beliefs between Christianity and Islam. It is a dangerous topic to approach, as televangelist Jack Van Impe discovered in 2011. He ended a longtime partnership with the Trinity Broadcasting Network ("TBN") when he prepared to air a show on the network explaining Chrislam and naming names of Christian leaders and pastors embracing it, including Rick Warren, "America's Pastor." Jack, you should have called me first. No person we discuss on *Stand Up For the Truth* leads to more backlash than Rick Warren and the path he is on. More on him later, but back to Chrislam.

We are warned in the book of Revelation of a false prophet representing a false, unified religion that will work with the Antichrist to gain world domination. The apostles and Jesus warned that in the final days there would be many false teachers.

In 2007, 138 Muslim leaders sent an open letter to Christian leaders. They were concerned about escalating rhetoric that, quite frankly, was occurring as Muslim terrorism became more prevalent throughout the world. This open letter was titled "A Common Word Between Us and You." It asked for interfaith dialogue, claiming the two great monotheistic religions shared two basic principles of doctrine: Love of the one God and love of our neighbor. These Muslim leaders were appealing to Christian leaders to find common ground to bring peace to the world through dialogue.

What is the purpose of dialogue? To find a basis for common beliefs and goals. You are willing to compromise and give up some things to reach agreement and common purpose. If this attempt was to have Christian and Muslim leaders discuss ways we could reduce the tension between the religions and respect each other as human beings, I wouldn't have a problem with it. However, since it is an attempt to find common dialogue and *beliefs* between us, it is wrong and dangerous.

Second Corinthians 6:14-17 says, *Do not be yoked together with unbelievers. For what do righteousness and wickedness have in common? Or what fellowship can light have with darkness? What harmony is there between Christ and Belial? Or what does a believer have in common with an unbeliever? What agreement is there between the temple of God and idols? For we are the temple of the living God. As God has said: "I will live with them and walk among them, and I will be their God, and they will be my people." Therefore, "Come out from them and be separate, says the Lord. Touch no unclean thing, and I will receive you."*

The Scriptures are clear: We are not to mingle God with the god of unbelievers. We are to have no part in religious syncretism with those who are not Christians. The "A Common Word Between Us and You" letter was a call to base all future interfaith dialogue between Christians and Muslims upon what these Muslim clerics believe is the common ground between the faiths. The letter states:

The basis for this peace and understanding already exists. It is part of the very foundational principles of both faiths: love of the One God, and love of the neighbour. These principles are found over and over again in the sacred texts of Islam and Christianity. The Unity of God, the necessity of love for Him, and the necessity of love of the neighbour is thus the common ground between Islam and Christianity.

Thus in obedience to the Holy Qur'an, we as Muslims invite Christians to come together with us on the basis of what is common to us, which is also what is most essential to our faith and practice: the Two Commandments of love.

So let our differences not cause hatred and strife between us. Let us vie with each other only in righteousness and good works. Let us respect each other, be fair, just and kind to one another and live in sincere peace, harmony and mutual goodwill.

How beautiful, yet how deceptive. If one takes the time to study Islam and its holy books, you can see right through this deception. Islam allows for peaceful coexistence with other religions *only* when it fits the Muslim agenda of leading to the destruction of the opposing religion. In other words, when you are in the minority, smile upon the infidel, but never love him in your heart. This is the historic pattern of Islam around the world: speak peace until you are in a position to make war.

The Quran does not teach Islam as a religion of peace. In several verses good Muslims are commanded to kill Jews and Christians.

Muslims are taught Jesus is *not* the Son of God. He did not die on the cross and He was a secondary prophet to Muhammad. The Muslim Hadith teaches Jesus was taken to heaven by Allah and will return in the last days with the Muslim messiah, the Mahdi, to kill Christians and Jews.

Muslims believe that as Abraham's first son, Ishmael was due Abraham's inheritance and birthright. God specifically said Isaac received the birthright and inheritance. Read God's prophecy over Ishmael in Genesis 16:12: *"He will be a wild donkey of a man; his hand will be against everyone and everyone's hand against him, and he will live in hostility toward all his brothers."*

Has this prophecy come true? Of course it has; it is in God's written Word. Muslims kill non-Muslims and they kill one another. Shiite and Sunni Muslims are constantly killing one another, as the war in Iraq clearly shows. Islam's only real goal is this: The whole world submissive to Allah, with death to all those who refuse.

Having said that, I want to point out a recurring deception used to try to spiritually link Islam and Christianity, and that is calling Islam an "Abrahamic Faith." Ishmael was the first in the line of what would become Arabic nomadic tribes. He had nothing to do with establishing Islam, which would not appear until thousands of years later. So Ishmael was the beginning of nomadic Arab nations, and centuries later Muhammad would gather those nations under the false religion of Islam.

An increasing number of deceived Christian leaders still call Islam an Abrahamic faith, and this is leading millions into deception and potentially eternal damnation as they equate the false god Allah with the one true God of the Bible.

The "Christian" Response

Four scholars at Yale Divinity School's Center for Faith and Culture chose to respond to "A Common Word Between Us and You" with a full-page advertisement in the *New York Times* that was published on November 18, 2007. They titled this response, "Loving God and Neighbor Together: A Christian Response to A Common Word Between Us and You." It was endorsed by over 100 Christian theologians, pastors, and scholars, among whom were Rick Warren, Brian McLaren, Bill Hybels, Richard Mouw, Robert Schuller, and Jim Wallis. The letter was one of Christian repentance and delight – repentance for wrongs committed by Christians against Muslims, and delight for the efforts of the Islamic scholars to find this common ground between the faiths. It read, "As members of the worldwide Christian community, we were deeply encouraged and challenged by the recent historic open letter signed by 138 leading Muslim scholars, clerics, and intellectuals from around the world." These Christian leaders agree with the common ground between these two faiths. The response continued:

> What is common between us lies not in something marginal, nor in something merely important to each. It lies, rather, in something absolutely central to both: love of God and love of neighbor. Surprisingly for many Christians, your letter considers the dual command of love to be the foundational principle not just of the Christian faith, but of Islam as well. That so much common ground exists—common ground in some of the fundamentals of faith—gives hope that undeniable differences and even the very real external pressures that bear down upon us can not overshadow the common ground upon which we stand together.

You may want to read that several times. These Christian leaders just said that the very foundational beliefs of Islam and Christianity are identical. And since these people seem to value world peace over the Word of God, that should not be a surprise. The letter incorrectly presumes that Muslims and Christians worship the same God and, in fact, gives gravitas to the Muslim faith, an anti-Christ religion according to the Bible. Yet Bill Hybels and Rick Warren signed on to spiritual compromise and surrender.

The letter concludes with further agreement that this common ground ought to be the basis for further interfaith dialogue. It concludes with the promise that these leaders will continue to labor towards the goal set by these Muslim clerics.

> "Let this common ground"—the dual common ground of love of God and of neighbor—"be the basis of all future interfaith dialogue between us," your courageous letter urges. Indeed, in the generosity with which the letter is written you embody what you call for. We most heartily agree. Abandoning all "hatred and strife," we must engage in interfaith dialogue as those who seek each other's good, for the one God unceasingly seeks our good. Indeed, together with you we believe that we need to move beyond "a polite ecumenical dialogue between selected religious leaders" and work diligently together to reshape relations between our communities and our nations so that they genuinely reflect our common love for God and for one another.

> If we fail to make every effort to make peace and come together in harmony you correctly remind us that "our eternal souls" are at stake as well.

> We are persuaded that our next step should be for our leaders at every level to meet and begin the earnest work of determining how God would have us fulfill the requirement that we love God and one another. It is with humility and hope that we receive your generous letter, and we commit ourselves to labor together in heart, soul, mind and strength for the objectives you so appropriately propose.

Congratulations to our wonderful leaders! They just equated Islam, a religion of antichrist, with Christianity. Shockingly, the documents take for granted that the God of Christianity is the god of Islam. Nowhere in this document would one come to believe that the God of the Bible is different than Allah of Islam.

Allah denies the Trinity. Allah tells people to lie. Allah says that Jesus is not God's Son. Muhammad writes in the Hadith that Allah told him that when the Muslim messiah appears, Jesus (Isa) comes with him, denying he ever claimed to be the Son of God. In anger, Jesus breaks every cross and helps the Mahdi kill every Jew and Christian.

Yet Rick Warren, Jim Wallis, Brian McLaren, Richard Mouw, and Bill Hybels, along with many other respected Christian leaders, endorse this deception. With any modicum of biblical wisdom or discernment they would be able to see through this deception. They are either incredibly naive or deceivers themselves – God alone knows and will make that judgment.

I hope they are simply deceived. But if so, how could they be so naive? Simply put, they were dealing with an Enemy much smarter than them. They were hungry, starving fish that took the bait of a crafty, experienced fisherman.

The Great Deception of "A Common Word Between Us and You"

The Muslim clerics stated that the common foundations between the two religions are:

- Belief in the one true God.

- The command to love our neighbor.

Both religions are monotheistic, believing in one God. But if the illustrious leaders who bought in to this deception had given five minutes of thought, or had bothered to read the Quran, they would have known that Muslims worship a false god. Strike one!

The command to love our neighbor was taught as crucial for Christians by Jesus. He listed it as the second greatest commandment, behind loving God with all our heart, mind, and strength. However, the command is *not* a foundation of our Christian faith; it is a command. The *foundation* of the Christian faith is belief in the one true God, YHWH, and the belief that Jesus Christ is His only begotten Son and the only way to righteous standing with God and eternal salvation. This foundation is denied by Islam as heresy and is used to refer to Christians as infidels.

Nowhere in the Bible does Jesus tell us to find common ground with other faiths; we are to remain separate from them in religious matters. Nowhere do the apostles engage in dialogue or in seeking common ground on which to pursue God together with false religions.

This unbelievable surrender to Islam by these leaders shows their lack of understanding of this antichrist religion. They fail to realize that Muslims must reject the authority of the Bible, deny the triune God, and deny the deity of Jesus Christ.

These leaders have in essence sold out Christianity for public acclaim or the appearance of being loving and caring. Quite frankly, they are a disgrace to Christianity and need to repent of their actions. Some of the original Christians who signed on to this abomination have repented and recanted their support. Those who have not owe every Christian they lead or influence an apology. But most importantly, I pray that God will show them the error of their ways and that they will repent for their own sake.

Summary

There are many more internal pawns of the Enemy within the walls of American Christianity. Many Christian universities and seminaries are a shell of what they once were, abandoning doctrine and sound biblical teaching for emergent, post-modern theology. The adoption of homosexuality as acceptable behavior by a growing number of churches, a church more concerned with image rather than substance, and growing biblical illiteracy are chief among the internal subversives.

We must not fail to understand that these movements are not separate, stand-alone entities. They are intricately interwoven with leaders of each movement tied in with leaders of other movements. Leaders like Brian McLaren, Rob Bell, Tony Campolo, Bill and Lynne Hybels, Rick Warren, and Jim Wallis are a network of leaders supporting and interacting with one another to advance a larger movement than any one of their individual entities represents on its own. This "octopus" is getting its tentacles into every denomination of Christianity and will soon be in position to squeeze the life out of American Christianity.

Any entity – a business, an army, a ministry, or a church – will only go as far as leadership is able and willing to take it. Leadership is crucial to the direction and success of any organization, and next, we will explore the condition of leadership in American Christianity.

Chapter 7

The Demise of Christian Leadership

A word about our pastors as we take a look at leadership within American Christianity:

I meet with local pastors regularly and have known many of them for twenty years. The vast majority of them are kind, hardworking, wonderful men of God, and they work long hours with low salaries. Some are forced to have their wives hold jobs to help support their families while their wives also play a critical role within the church. This can cause tremendous stress on the pastor and his family. These pastors care deeply about the people they lead, often giving up a lot of their personal time to meet with members of the church when needs arise.

Pastors are forced to wear many hats: preacher, teacher, friend, marriage counselor, parental advisor, financial manager, and often janitor, and that's by no means the total extent of their duties. They work countless hours, preparing a weekly sermon that must sadly be a near-perfect balance. Too soft and some will not feel fed; too strong and some will feel he is being awfully harsh, not understanding what they are going through in their lives.

Tragically, pastors are often held hostage by the financial condition of the church they lead. Consciously or unconsciously, this puts a lot of pressure on them. They are forced into the role of performer too often, having to be entertaining when delivering a message (the gospel) that shouldn't need to be entertaining.

Our pastors need our prayers, our financial support, and our help. Somewhere over the past few decades, churchgoers started embracing an attitude that pastors worked for us. They were "hired" to run the church and run it at our beck and call. We simply show up on Sunday like we were going to lunch, expecting to be served. We the people *are* the church. We must take ownership in our part of the body of Christ and stop expecting the pastor to carry the load on his own.

Pastors are under tremendous pressure these days, and members and elders need to step up and help them. Many are on the verge of physical and emotional burnout and are often tempted to quit, to find a secular job where they can work more manageable hours and support their families.

Pastors alone are not the problem. A dysfunctional church system and self-centered followers are the real problem. These godly men carry too heavy a burden with pressures from those they serve and their elders. This must change.

Defining Leadership

Leadership is difficult. It requires courage, commitment, passion, and wisdom. It also requires a servant's heart and humility. Leaders are often placed on pedestals by those who follow them that are much higher than we deserve. And when people continually look up to you and tell you how wonderful you are, pride begins to lurk around every corner.

I have been blessed to serve and lead here at Q90 FM for more than sixteen years. Our board took a chance on me as I had no radio experience when they hired me. They figured that the station had plenty of people who knew radio, and that I possessed a heart and skill set that would serve our listeners well. I hope I can always live up to their faith and expectations. About ten years ago, a listener stopped in and thanked me for the role I play in this ministry. She told me she was blessed when she watched me interact with youth at concerts and felt that I had helped bring the ministry to a new level serving the Christian community.

I thanked her, somewhat embarrassed by the praise, and when she left, I returned to my office. And then it happened . . . I began to believe my own deceptive heart. I started thinking to myself, "Man, I am doing a pretty good job. The ministry is growing and financially we are becoming more secure. Boy, I am good!"

Then I learned that God is the Master of all things, even "instant messaging." I heard an immediate soft voice whisper to me, "Mike, I love you, but if you don't think I can take any drunk, homeless person off the street and make him a better leader than you, then you don't really know me." I had been given a piece of dessert, humble pie, and it didn't taste very good at all. Pride is the most dangerous enemy of any leader, not insubordinate followers or external challenges. Pride can undo a lifetime of accomplishment the moment it becomes entrenched in our ego.

Leadership is tough, and we as leaders are often the greatest obstacle to becoming truly great leaders. We become puffed up, we start to coast by living on past laurels and accomplishments, and we believe we are infallible and should never be questioned. In a "what have you done for me lately" world, there is no time to coast, and the day we feel we should never be questioned or challenged as leaders we become gods in our own minds.

Leadership also requires an understanding of, and commitment to, the core principles and values of the organization you lead. It is not enough to simply agree with them; it is crucial that you commit to not wavering from them. Ten years ago, the team at Q90 FM underwent a painful assessment of what our core values as Christians in this ministry should be, and one we decided on after a lot of prayer was relational honesty. We decided that if we really loved one another and were committed to the Christian organization and God that we serve, relational honesty must be a core principle.

We have learned to be honest and, when necessary, argue. We have learned to get beyond the superficial and challenge one another when our words or actions seem to contradict biblical teachings. It has not always been easy, but it has been beneficial.

Eight years ago as I sat in my office, a couple team members wanted a word with me, and of course I obliged. They proceeded to tell me that I was not enforcing my own rules on operational procedures. My first reaction as a leader was to deflect and deny, but I just listened. Their message was basically that I was impeding them by not following procedure, making their jobs more difficult.

Those who know me know I can be stubborn and defensive at times, and that I am not good with details. As they finished confronting me, they awaited my reaction. They had just told their boss to shape up! I purposefully milked the tension for a moment, and then looked at them and said, "Thank you. I needed to hear that. I know I stink at basic procedures sometimes. Will you please help me?"

The entire ministry has rallied around me. While not enabling me, they recognized that minute detail is a weakness for me, and they have put in systems to make up for that weakness. They have freed me to do what I do best as a leader, and the ministry has been blessed. I am not holding myself up as a perfect leader by any stretch, and those who work with me will tell you I am far from a perfect leader. But one area in which I do lead well is giving those I lead freedom to challenge me whenever they think I might be straying from the Word of God in any decision, word, or action that comes out of me. In fact, I insist that they do this. It has been a blessing to me knowing those I lead are watching the example I set and are there to hold me accountable for my words, actions, and leadership. It has made me a better leader.

Leaders lead, but they must also be accountable to those they lead. If not, they foster a potentially poisonous work environment. Leaders are ultimately accountable for the performance of the organization and the people they lead. Leaders establish the framework for values, principles, and expectations.

American Christianity is suffering from a lack of real leaders who lead like Jesus taught us to lead. He scolded the Pharisees for not doing what they taught others: hypocritical leadership. He scolded them for adding more burdens upon the people while not carrying those burdens themselves: selfish and arrogant leadership. He rebuked them because they knew the letter of the law, but not the heart of the law: a lack of discerning, wise leadership.

Leaders are the ones ultimately held responsible for the performance of the organization. If you look at American Christianity as an organization, how would you rate its performance over the past fifty years? Is it a stronger or weaker church because of its leadership over the past fifty years? Is it impacting the culture for better or worse? Is it an organization that is truly transforming lives?

Surrounding Leaders with the Right People

In the mid-1990s I was charged with taking a start-up organization and leading it to viability. It was a unique organization that would provide newly available, even unheard-of, services to employers. One of the charges was to build a team that would serve customers twenty-four hours a day in a traditional nine-to-five industry. Needless to say, there were challenges.

We would be hiring about twenty new employees, so we posted job positions in the local newspaper and were flooded with applications. I interviewed probably close to one hundred people over the course of two years. Inevitably, some of the hiring decisions would come down to hiring a person with a college degree *or* hiring a person with practical experience and working knowledge.

In theory, the person with the impressive college degree would probably have more upside, while the person without the degree but with practical experience was probably the safer bet, with the thought being that the person with a verifiable track record was more of a known quantity. So at times I hired the college graduate and other times I hired the better-known quantity. What I eventually found out was that *who* I hired would not matter if I hired them into a dysfunctional system.

If an organization knows its mission and is dedicated as a team to fulfilling that mission, that is a great starting point. If the organization has effective systems in place and proper accountability for goals, corporate performance, and individual performance, the odds are much greater that the person hired will succeed. If the organization lacks in any of these areas, even the best of hires will ultimately fail or at least turn out to be mediocre in performance, and the organization will suffer. In other words, an organization's values, principles, mission, and systems are more important factors than the individual we hire, assuming an acceptable level of competency and character is present in the employee.

Character, values, principles, and commitment matter far more than an individual's qualifications, especially in a Christian organization. Leaders who understand and fully embrace the values and principles of an organization are best suited to lead that organization. When we hire people that agree with those values and principles, the odds are much higher that it will be a successful hire.

Crucial Characteristics Needed for Christian Leadership – Values, Principles, Character, and Commitment

Values, principles, character, and commitment are vastly more important in leaders than potential, charisma, or charm. But how do we define these necessary qualities for a Christian leader? I would propose the following as a starting point for any Christian organization:

Values

- Honesty, no matter what the cost
- Love, as God defines love
- Wisdom to discern truth by God's standards, not man's standards
- Spiritual integrity and mutual accountability

Principles

- Non-compromising with sin or human culture
- No shortcuts for immediate gain at the sacrifice of long-term success
- Always doing the right thing, even if it is painful
- Willing to be held accountable by those we lead and serve

Character

- Doing the biblically correct thing when no one is watching
- Consistent behavior at work, home, or when alone

- Looking at yourself first when issues or conflict occur

- Never saying something about someone you would not say if they were present

<u>Commitment</u>

- True kingdom focus (Matthew 6:33)

- Commitment to developing strong leaders

- Commitment to developing disciples, not just members of the organization

- A willingness to release team members who are continuous problems

So how does this relate specifically to the church and its leadership? Do we overlook values, principles, character, and commitment in favor of the educational level of a person we elevate as a leader? A degree in religious studies or thirty years of experience does not make a good pastor; biblical values, principles, character, and commitment do. Without these foundations, a leader will fail eventually.

Dysfunctional Leadership Systems

Staying on my pesky urge to ask hypothetical questions, I offered this scenario to twelve pastors I know well a few years ago: "If you as a pastor feel God is telling the church to do 'A,' and the elders feel God is leading them to do 'B,' who wins?" Remarkably, I got the same initial answer from all of them: "We would meet and pray together about it." I countered with, "So you do that, but the conflicting messages remain. Who wins?" Only one of the twelve could cite how the conflict would be handled.

Christian leadership needs to be thoughtful, wise, discerning, and above reproach whenever possible. It must also be well organized and purposeful, with duties and accountability clearly spelled out. And leaders must be appointed not by their human credentials, but by their spiritual credentials. Pastors and ministry leaders must have a clear understanding of where their authority begins and ends. They must clearly know what decisions they are empowered to make and when they need to consult those they are accountable to.

I sit on several boards for Christian non-profit organizations. Recently the executive director of one of them offered the name of a new potential board member for our consideration. I asked why he felt this person would be a positive addition, and his response centered on the fact that he was a CPA and was knowledgeable on fundraising techniques. When I asked about his spiritual qualifications, the executive director said he didn't know.

This is a sad situation that happens way too frequently within Christian organizations and the church. Human qualifications are often elevated above spiritual qualifications when we consider people for leadership. A local church recently hired a pastor whom it had to dismiss just six months later because they discovered spiritual flaws in his character once he assumed a position of leadership. They also discovered this man would fall to pieces when conflict arose.

How should a church decide on who the elders should be? The amount of their tithes? Their position and qualifications in the corporate world? Or should we seek elder and leader qualifications as outlined in the Scriptures? Of course we will all answer that the Scriptures should determine the qualifications of church elders, but do we practice it? Leadership sets the tone for the entire organization; however, even the best, most biblically solid leaders will still fail if they are surrounded and suffocated by a dysfunctional system.

Dysfunctional systems lead to dysfunctional leadership. And dysfunctional leadership is a disaster waiting to happen in a church. When church leaders do not anticipate conflict and consider how it should be handled biblically, we find ourselves one day facing a crisis, one that could have been averted by prior planning and discussion.

The State of Christian Leadership Today

Generally, it's a mess. When people like Rob Bell, Brian McLaren, and Joel Osteen are held up as leaders, we are in deep trouble. When pastors like Jim Wallis, Bill Hybels, and Rick Warren seek compromise and common ground with an antichrist religion, has leadership sold out to the world? When the size of a church means more than the spiritual depth of the church, American Christianity is one step away from spiritual adultery.

In fairness to these leaders, as we discussed earlier, they are primarily by-products of our own fleshly desires as Christians. We seem to want leaders who tickle our ears or make us feel good about ourselves more than we want the truth. The truth can hurt, and our tolerance for pain as Americans and Christians is at an all-time low.

When watchmen stand up and question the teachings and activities of Christian leaders, we are told we are not to question God's "anointed." In the Old Testament, the Israelites had fallen under the same spell, being led by false teachers and false prophets into compromise and apostasy. How did God respond?

> *"Among the prophets of Samaria I saw this repulsive thing: They prophesied by Baal and led my people Israel astray. And among the prophets of Jerusalem I have seen something horrible: They commit adultery and live a lie. They strengthen the hands of evildoers, so that not one of them turns from his wickedness. They are like Sodom to me; the people of Jerusalem are like Gomorrah."*

> *Therefore this is what the LORD Almighty says concerning the prophets: "I will make them eat bitter food and drink poisoned water, because from the prophets of Jerusalem ungodliness has spread throughout the land."*

> *This is what the LORD Almighty says: "Do not listen to what the prophets are prophesying to you; they fill you with false hopes. They speak visions from their own minds, not from the mouth of the LORD." (Jeremiah 23:13-16)*

A question for you: Does American Christianity look more or less like Sodom and Gomorrah under the leadership of those currently leading the church? Are we strengthening the hands of evildoers or disarming them? Is the trend more toward God and His Word or away from it?

Christian leadership in America is in a state of crisis and we seem to be lacking in strong, principled leadership at a time when we need it most. When any organization is in crisis, strong, principled leadership is necessary to navigate difficult times and get the organization back on track. But as we will see, just the opposite is happening in American Christianity. Instead of steering us away from rough waters, many of our leaders seem committed to taking the ship right into a hurricane.

A Hypothetical Situation?

As I have shared, I love to ask hypothetical questions of pastors and leaders. Today's hypothetical questions often become tomorrow's real questions, so I find value in discussing them.

Nearly seven years ago a Bible-teaching church in Michigan became the center in the fight for homosexual rights. The video shot hit YouTube and was broadcast by Fox News. The church choir had just completed a song and the elderly pastor ambled up to the pulpit to deliver his sermon message. But before he could, four homosexual activists created a chaotic scene. Two of them started passing out fliers and screaming, "It's okay to be gay!" while at the same time two females starting kissing passionately at the front of the church. The pastor and congregation sat back, stunned and speechless. One elderly gentleman tried to gently convince the demonstrators to leave, but they continued for several minutes until they finally left peacefully.

I asked my pastor and several other pastors what they would do if that happened in their church. None of them could answer the question. I suggested they might want to consult with the elders of the church so they would be able to handle the situation in a biblical way if it happened in their church. Trust me, it will occur more and more, folks, as the government and the LGBTQ community seek to discredit Christian churches.

This will be a difficult situation if it arises. Do we physically remove them from the church? Or just pray for them as they rant? The important thing is that the church leaders know ahead of time how to react if these types of disturbances occur. Failure to act decisively and biblically will create a lot of confusion and lingering problems.

I asked a pastor another hypothetical question a couple months ago. And yes, this is hypothetical, folks. I proposed a fictitious scenario where my wife meets with him, telling him I am having an affair. So the pastor meets with me and I admit to the affair but insist on continuing the behavior. Would he kick me out of the church? He answered, "No." I said he was crazy, that I should be kicked out of the church if I did not repent after talking with church leadership, and that it should be done publicly as Paul states, to warn the rest of the church. Would our church be stronger or weaker with an admitted adulterer in its midst? It would be weaker.

Defining the Mission of the Church

Leaders and organizations love to throw around vision and mission statements, looking for a silver bullet to solve the problems of the organization. But Christian churches do not need new vision and mission statements because Jesus gave them their vision and mission in Matthew 28:19-20: *"Therefore go and make disciples of all nations, baptizing them in the name of the Father and of the Son and of the Holy Spirit, and teaching them to obey everything I have commanded you. And surely I am with you always, to the very end of the age."* Seems like a pretty clear vision and mission statement to me. Go make disciples. Christian leaders and pastors need to stop improving on Jesus' perfect mission statement. When you tinker with perfection, nothing good can result from it.

Now, developing a strong plan to carry out that vision or mission statement is a different story. *How* will we make disciples? What does a true disciple even look like? How can we truly invest in the spiritual growth of our church members? These are much tougher questions to answer for leadership than just getting our heads together to develop a fluffy, meaningless vision or mission statement.

Many churches in America are spiritually bipolar. They aren't sure if they want to increase numbers of members or increase the depth of spirituality, making true disciples. Now certainly any church would want to accomplish both simultaneously, but that is a very difficult thing to accomplish without the Holy Spirit. How do most churches act? Well, ask a pastor to tell you about his church and the first thing he will probably share is how many people attend – a nod to the superior importance placed on numbers over spiritual depth.

The church in Acts gathered regularly, listened to the teaching of the apostles, prayed, ministered to one another, and shared all God was doing. Great signs and wonders were experienced, *and the Lord added to their number daily those who were being saved* (Acts 2:42-47). Wow! The *Lord* added to their numbers, not culturally relevant messages or cool praise and worship bands, but the *Lord*! Might the Word of God just be trying to tell us something here? When our goal is to increase numbers, any warm body will do. The early church was more intent on true discipleship and fellowship than it was on reaching into the community for new members.

There were no marketing plans, no evangelism committees, and no pastors spending days trying to make the sermon sound just right. They met, prayed, shared, and praised God. A simple formula for success has been replaced by a modern marketing plan that leads to dismal failure. Oh, you may counter that your church has hundreds or thousands attending every week, but what is the level of spiritual depth and maturity? You probably don't know. Granted, that is a difficult thing to measure, as most Christians are great salespeople, telling you they are doing great. But most struggle just to get through the week, hoping to get a little Jesus on Sunday with enough gas in the tank to make it through another week.

There is nothing wrong with having a large congregation; however, bigger numbers do not necessarily mean a better church. The power of any church congregation comes from a passionate love of God. When we gather in unison to worship and praise Him, learn from His Word, and challenge one another to a deeper intimacy with Him, the Holy Spirit will begin to add to our numbers. But when we seek to add to our numbers out of human ambition or plans, are we weakening the church?

Bigger Is Better – and a Ticket to Fame

When numbers become more important than raising real disciples and developing more Christian leaders, we get ourselves into serious trouble. When nickels and noses become the benchmark for success, Satan is laughing and God is brokenhearted.

But that is what appears to be happening in American Christianity. The megachurch has become the standard of success. Can a church have huge numbers and still be truly successful? Certainly, but it is a difficult balancing act as large numbers plant a desire for larger numbers. Large collections and tithes breed a desire to bring in even more so we can "do more work for God." God doesn't need our money, He wants our hearts. When He truly has our hearts, He accomplishes great things through us regardless of our financial status.

Why is it that virtually every Christian pastor viewed as a leader these days pastors a megachurch? Steven Furtick, T. D. Jakes, Andy Stanley, Rick Warren, and Joel Osteen all pastor huge churches. Seems you're not a leader if you don't pastor a megachurch. There certainly are exceptions, but it seems bigger is better, and bigger automatically elevates you to national leadership and the acclaim that comes with it.

Now there is nothing wrong with leading a megachurch, but it can be a trap. Suddenly, you get the feeling you are King Midas and everything you touch turns to gold. You are held up as a model pastor and leader and you hit the national speakers' tour, and maybe you even have your own national television show! Ask Jim Bakker, Ted Haggard, and Jimmy Swaggart how that worked for them.

Leaders and teachers will be held to a higher accountability and standard by God when we stand before Him. And leadership, with all its trappings, is waiting to snare us and drag us down. Many of the leaders in American Christianity might be headed down the path of Bakker, Haggard, and Swaggart because the Enemy has his eyes on Christian leaders, setting subtle but effective traps for leaders in the church. Any of us can step into those traps when we become filled with our own self-importance and success. That trap, invisible to the all-important leader, has two characteristics: arrogance and power.

The people I am about to comment on are recognized leaders in American Christianity. I do not think they are evil men. Quite to the contrary, I am pretty sure they are wonderful husbands and fathers, and men who love God and believe they are doing the right things.

They are men who very much want to grow Christianity in America. It is not their heart or even their motives that I question, rather, it is their methods . . . methods that embrace secular culture and humanism in favor of biblical principles and wisdom. They may be blindly leading American Christianity to the brink of spiritual apostasy, and the lemmings are only all-too happy to follow them right off the cliff.

If these men are to blame for what is happening to American Christianity, others must share in that blame. Are their elders and mentors holding them accountable to the Word of God? Or do they fear that if they do, the leaders will pack up and move to the church across town, taking many members and dollars with them?

And what about those of us who follow these leaders? Are we more enamored with their eloquently worded sermons that get us excited than what they are teaching in those sermons? Are we excited that we attend the biggest church in our community even if the Word of God is not being preached in its entirety? Has the charismatic, charming pastor replaced God on the throne of our lives?

Leaders and followers are a direct reflection of each other. They form a symbiotic relationship, feeding off and needing one another. Is this symbiotic relationship spiritually destroying American Christianity?

Leading Christians, but to Where?

I can guarantee that some of you will bristle at some of the thoughts, opinions, and facts I am about to share. None of us wants to think poorly of our leaders or wants to think they are deceived. I am not asking you to be judge or jury on their faith or even their motives. A day might come when we do have to judge them harshly, but if we must, we should remember that their ultimate place in eternity can only rightly be judged by God. God never gives up on us and we should never give up on anyone else. We seek to restore, not condemn, when we see a brother faltering. I encourage you once again to do your own research and be a good Berean, searching the Scriptures on all issues. The Word of God is the only source for absolute truth, so learn it and hide it in your heart.

If you start to feel anger or even hatred well up in you as we share what these leaders are up to, we must first look at ourselves as the people who follow them and have elevated them into leadership positions. They lead because we allow them to, and the fact is we seem to desire mushy, soft leadership these days that tells us what we want to hear, not what we need to hear.

Anointed or Appointed Leaders?

On *Stand Up For the Truth* we question everything except the Word of God. I find with each show I am forced to question my own level of dedication to God, as still too often I wander into sin. We question movements like Word of Faith, Signs and Wonders, Chrislam, and the emergent church. And we question Christian leaders like Rick Warren, Bill Hybels, Andy Stanley, and Joel Osteen. No subject or person should be above question or reproach.

When we question the words or actions of popular Christian leaders, we get this frequent question from those who are their followers: "Who are you to question God's anointed?" In 1 Chronicles 16:22 God does warn us about harming His anointed prophets, so we should be very careful when we question or accuse leaders. But exactly how do we know if a leader is anointed by God or appointed by men?

In Romans 13:1 Paul writes this: *Let everyone be subject to the governing authorities, for there is no authority except that which God has established.* Yet several times in Scripture we see examples of God's people disobeying man's authority because it conflicted with God's teachings. In Acts 5:29 the high priest forbade the apostles from teaching the gospel, but they responded by saying, *"We must obey God rather than human beings!"*

So how can we be sure if a leader is anointed by God or is appointed by men? Or appointed by themselves? And even if God allows or anoints a leader, do we automatically obey and never question them? God ordained Saul as king and later rejected him because of his wicked ways. *But Samuel replied: "Does the LORD delight in burnt offerings and sacrifices as much as in obeying the LORD? To obey is better than sacrifice, and to heed is better than the fat of rams. For rebellion is like the sin of divination, and arrogance like the evil of idolatry. Because you have rejected the word of the LORD, he has rejected you as king"* (1 Samuel 15:22-23).

Saul was rejected because he disobeyed the word of God. If "anointed" leaders these days are disobedient or teach a questionable gospel or messages inconsistent with God's Word, do we just blindly follow? Or do we question them and confront them when necessary? Is our allegiance to earthly leaders or to God?

A Balanced Approach to Leadership

Every one of our leaders will make mistakes, saying something the wrong way, or perhaps teaching something that might contradict God's Word. Leaders will fall for slick presentations like "A Common Word Between Us and You" because they have a heart for people and want to build bridges of peace. Every one of us will get things wrong sometimes.

When our leaders do teach something that appears to contradict the Bible, they should be confronted in love and given an opportunity to clear the air. Did they simply misspeak? Did we fail to clearly hear what they were trying to say? Did they have a temporary lapse in judgment and fall for a slick presentation? Did they get wrapped up in the excitement of bringing in a well-known speaker and not check his teachings and affiliations? If any of these happen, the leaders need to be treated with love and grace, given an opportunity to explain their words or actions, and if appropriate, apologize and repent for their mistake.

But what do we do when the questionable statements or teachings become a pattern? What if the leader says one thing with his mouth but his words are belied by his actions? What if there is a pattern of bringing in speakers or leaders who conflict with the teachings of the Bible? At what point does grace no longer apply and is replaced with a tough rebuke?

These are important questions we must wrestle with as Christians. God has abundant grace for us and we should always extend abundant grace to others. But at some point, when a pattern emerges of questionable teachings and affiliations that conflict with Scripture, a strong rebuke might be in order.

But too often when a Christian leader is publicly questioned these days, people who follow that leader throw out the warning that we must not question "God's anointed ones." Well, how do we know if a leader is anointed by God or anointed by men, or maybe even self-anointed? If I proclaim that I have been anointed by God to do a radio talk show, does that exempt me from being held accountable for what I say on air? If a ministry leader claims to be anointed by God, should he go unquestioned if the ministry is suddenly faced with financial problems or personal scandal?

Have we become so shallow that we are looking to men as pure and righteous instead of to the only truly righteous one, God? When Todd Bentley has an affair and divorces his wife while leading a ministry, should we just blindly accept it because he is "anointed"? When some Word of Faith preachers teach that our words can overpower the will of God, or that men have the power to speak things into existence, do we just accept it as fact because they claim an anointing? Should we hold Barack Obama accountable to his claim as a born-again Christian while he pushed for easier access to abortions and was successful in legalizing homosexual marriage? What about George W. Bush when he proclaimed that Muslims and Christians worship the same God?

Leaders are to be respected, but they should never be above account- ability and reproach. The day we give leaders a pass from accountability and rebuke when they cross a line we are in serious trouble. But that is what is happening more and more in our nation and within American Christianity.

Chapter 8

Hybels, Warren, and Osteen – Is This Really Where We Want to Go?

B ill Hybels, Rick Warren, and Joel Osteen are among the most powerful and visible leaders in American Christianity today. Warren and Osteen lead huge churches and have a tremendous national influence. And while Hybels has resigned over sexual misconduct allegations, his influence remains intact through the Willow Creek Global Leadership Summit that he introduced to American Christianity that has done enormous damage in how American Christians perceive doctrine and leadership. All these leaders have millions of Christians who look up to them for teaching, guidance, and mentorship. They have charm, charisma, and an appearance of humility.

I have no doubt that each of them is a nice man. I do not doubt their love of God, and I do not question that each of them is doing what he *thinks* is right. This shows how deceptive Satan can be when church leadership is not held accountable to the Word of God. What I do question are their methods and perhaps some of their motives, and how they have led millions into spiritual adultery against God.

I do not sit in eternal judgment of these or any other men, and neither should you. But just like Jesus and Paul, we are to respectfully question our leaders and, when necessary, rebuke them. As we review some of our prominent Christian leaders, we sit not as the ultimate judge, but as a grand jury to decide if enough evidence exists to warrant further investigation.

Bill Hybels

Pastor Bill Hybels was the leader of Willow Creek Community Church in Barrington, Illinois, until he and his entire board resigned over sexual scandals that were initially covered up. Willow Creek has a total of seven campuses and has a network of hundreds of churches under its Willow Creek Association ("WCA"). While it does not seem to have any direct authority over these churches, WCA is a resource for pastors and churches and helps plant churches, several of which are in our own area in northeast Wisconsin.

Their website shows a doctrinal statement that is solid and I have never heard anyone complain about anything seriously wrong with any sermon Pastor Hybels has given. So what's the issue? There are some events that have taken place that cause some watchmen concern.

Homosexuality

In 2011 Willow Creek announced they had severed a long-standing relationship with Exodus International. Exodus is a leading Christian organization that helps homosexuals leave the lifestyle and find hope in Jesus Christ. This decision came after a series of meetings between Willow Creek leadership and gay activist organizations who claimed that Willow Creek was anti-gay.

The now-former president of Exodus International, Alan Chambers, responded with an open letter on August 10, 2011, expressing his sadness at the decision. He disclosed at a meeting between Willow Creek and Exodus leaders that the church's leaders stated that they didn't want to help people overcome homosexuality because that wasn't possible.

Is this a denial of the power of the gospel, stating that sexual sinners cannot be released from the bondage of sexual sin by the power of God? Willow Creek leaders went on to say they wanted to tell people that abstinence was the only option for unmarried people and that the church would provide a comfortable place to abstain. Is this the right way to handle the temptation and sin of homosexuality?

In fairness to Hybels and Willow Creek, they continue to teach that marriage is biblically defined as between one man and one woman, and that all others are to practice sexual abstinence. But it is sad if Willow Creek leadership is denying the power of God to release people from the bondages of sexual sin. Thousands have been released by the power of God through Exodus International and through several other Christian organizations presenting the gospel and salvation of Jesus Christ.

If it is true that Willow Creek leadership now believes that sexual sin is not "curable" by the power of the gospel and the Holy Spirit, is this sending a very dangerous message to Christians and the unsaved alike? Are we giving up on the power of God, settling for human answers and understanding? If that is the message, is that what American Christianity should stand for? Is this leading or compromising with the culture?

Lynne Hybels

Could this shift in policy and teaching have anything to do with Lynne Hybels, Bill's wife, becoming very active in the social justice movement? Lynne Hybels is a contributing editor for *Sojourners* magazine, the leading "social justice" organization in the nation. We covered their dangerous theology earlier, but it is a good time to remind you that Sojourners and Jim Wallis refuse to classify homosexuality or abortion as sins. Is it appropriate to ask if Willow Creek is embracing the social justice movement with all its deception and false teaching?

Lynne Hybels is a Palestinian activist, partnering with others to discredit the nation of Israel and label them the aggressors in the conflict, in spite of the fact that Palestinian forces continue to fire hundreds of rockets a day into Israel, killing innocent children. She has criticized the occupation by Israel of lands they have held since the latest attacks on their nation by their Muslim neighbors. She partners with Tony Campolo and others to spread propaganda supporting a two-state solution and the division of Jerusalem in the hopes of bringing about peace. We know through biblical prophecy that this would be no real peace. The "Christ at the Checkpoint" events paint Palestinians as the victims and Israelis as the occupiers in this conflict. Are there Palestinian victims in this conflict, some of whom are Christians? No doubt. But history and

Scripture are clear who the aggressors are: radical Muslims and those seeking to destroy Israel. The land currently occupied was promised to Israel by God in Genesis, and the fact is Israel did not seek to conquer these lands; they were attacked several times and have now decided to no longer trade land for peace as they have in the past, but to no avail.

The area is of strategic defensive value, providing a buffer between Israel and her enemies who are sworn to destroy her and kill every Jew. These neighboring Muslim nations have attacked Israel repeatedly since 1948, yet Lynne Hybels and her friends are undermining public opinion in America toward Israel by confirming the propaganda of Muslim leaders around the world. They have been successful in getting many evangelical and mainline Protestants to isolate Israel in the Christian community.

Is this an issue we should be concerned with as Christians? Is Lynne Hybels' role as a contributing editor for Sojourners, an organization that refuses to acknowledge homosexuality as a sin, behind Willow Creek's confusing stance on homosexuality?

Willow Creek's Global Leadership Summit

"When God wants to begin a new work in the world, He almost always starts by speaking into the heart of one person. Drawing up the courage to listen, obey, and share the vision with others, these are the people we call leaders." This statement on the Willow Creek website explains why since its inception in 1992, Willow Creek has brought in religious, social, and world leaders to be held up as examples of effective leadership.

American Christianity needs real leaders these days. The church is in crisis and leadership is crucial to getting us through these difficult times. But just what kind of leaders is Willow Creek bringing into this worldwide Summit conference that millions of Christians attend in person or via satellite? The list of speakers who have, at best, questionable views compared to traditional Christianity is extensive, so we will concentrate on a select few. In fairness, there have been many solid Christians presented as leaders also. But I question why we feel the need to hold up leaders who are Christians yet openly support anti-Christian beliefs or even non-Christians at an event teaching leadership to millions of Christians. Remember the word *obey* from the Hybels' statement about leaders and ask yourself if the leaders discussed are obeying God's Word.

Bill Clinton

As president of the United States, Bill Clinton met an intern in 1995 named Monica Lewinsky. He started a sexual relationship with her, which he repeatedly denied publicly. He lied under oath about the affair and was impeached by the congress in 1998.

Shortly after his impeachment where he lied under oath and was reprimanded, Bill Clinton spoke at the Global Leadership Summit in 2000. He had disgraced the office of the presidency with his sexual affair and perjury. Clinton's actions also spawned a significant increase in sexual activity by teens when he claimed oral sex was not really sex. Is this the type of leader we want Christians to emulate? Should he have been deemed worthy by Willow Creek leadership to be held up as a great leader for Christians?

Rob Bell

In 2000 Rob Bell was also touted as a great leader at the Summit. The up-and-coming evangelical pastor was hailed as an example of what God is doing. Ten years later Bell would write a book where he questioned the existence and permanence of hell, a direct contradiction to Scripture and the words of Jesus Himself. Today he spreads apostasy, leading many into dangerous theological confusion.

Rick Warren

We will cover Rick Warren in-depth later. America's Pastor is seeking compromise and common theology with Islam and bringing in Muslims and New Age believers to teach holistic health to Christians.

Bono

U2 rock sensation Bono presented at the Global Leadership Summit in 2009. He has done a lot of good in humanitarian fronts but his Christianity is highly suspect. On the website of *Relevant* magazine, a progressive Christian periodical, was posted an article by Tara Cobble about what she witnessed at a Bono concert: "About five songs into their set, Bono stopped the show and strapped on a headband with a message on it: COEXIST. He began to sing, 'Jesus, Jew, Muhammad – all true' repeatedly."

Bono has made several statements denying traditional Christian beliefs, including "God's Spirit moves through us and the world at a pace that can never be constricted by any one religious paradigm," and "Be wary of people who think theirs is the only way. Unilateralism before God is dangerous."

Bono does talk about Jesus Christ as the Son of God in other interviews, but there is clearly a belief in universalism. Do universalist religious beliefs qualify as an example of great leadership to Christians according to Willow Creek leadership?

Tony Blair

The former prime minister of England certainly knows what it means to lead. But where is he leading people these days? Blair touts the legalization of homosexual marriage as an important accomplishment of his administration. Since leaving office he has founded the Tony Blair Faith Foundation. One of the goals of the foundation is religious syncretism, bringing all faiths together for the common good of humanity and the earth.

On his website, Blair brags of how as prime minister he successfully advocated for adoption of the United Nations Millennium Development Goals because he "believes they represent the world's values." The U.N. Millennium Development Goals are, simply put, a movement toward a one-world government and religion. The U.N., through its sub-organizations like UNESCO, has already succeeded in promoting a global curriculum adopted in many American school systems – an education platform that seeks to mold children into global citizens and lead them away from what they call "antiquated beliefs set in place by parents and religion."

Should a man who brags about getting homosexual marriage legalized in the country he led be held up as an example to Christians of what a successful leader should look like? What about a man who is working toward religious syncretism?

Cory Booker

Cory Booker was the mayor of Newark, New Jersey, who at the time blasted New Jersey Governor Chris Christie for his refusal to sign homosexual marriage into law. Booker has been outspoken in his promotion of gay marriage, stating, "Marriage equality is not a choice, it is a right." He also refused to conduct traditional marriages between a man and a woman in city hall to protest what he sees as inequality in marriage.

He was also the lead democratic attack dog who lied about and tried to destroy Judge Brett Kavanaugh during his senate confirmation hearing. Does a Christian leader stoop to the level of lies and hatred that Booker stooped to just to win a political argument? Booker, Willow Creek's example of a leader, was so passionate about his support for abortion that he was willing to lie and seek to destroy a nominee who was personally pro-life. Willow Creek knew of this man's stances on homosexuality and abortion but still presented him to hundreds of thousands of naive Christians as a great leader.

We start to see a pattern emerging where leaders who support gay marriage are continually brought in by Willow Creek and touted as examples of great leaders. Is Willow Creek preparing to embrace homosexual marriage as acceptable in God's eyes? Are these examples of leaders we should ask Christians to emulate?

Howard Schultz

Howard Schultz, CEO of Starbucks, was slated as the lead speaker at Willow Creek in 2011. In his biography he talks about the need for leaders to "stand on their principles." Well, apparently Mr. Schultz didn't read his own biography because he decided to cancel his appearance as keynote speaker when 728 people signed an online petition suggesting they would boycott Starbucks if Schultz spoke at an "anti-gay" church.

This story is fascinating on several fronts. First, that 728 online protestors could cause this man of "principle" to back out of an agreement to speak shows the power of the radical homosexual lobby in this nation.

Second, it shows the quandary many churches are in these days because Willow Creek does clearly state the biblical belief that homosexual relations are wrong, yet they continue to invite people in who endorse homosexuality, including Howard Schultz and Starbucks, holding them up as leadership examples for Christians. Starbucks recently came out in enthusiastic support of the movement to legalize homosexual marriage in the state of Washington and is pouring a lot of money and time into making sure homosexual marriage is legalized there.

The question must once again be asked: Why would Willow Creek leadership insist on bringing in leaders with clearly antibiblical positions, holding them up as examples of model leaders to Christians? Willow Creek is a highly respected megachurch and Bill Hybels is still a highly respected pastor among evangelical Christians. The Willow Creek Association influences thousands of churches around the world with its teaching resources and has influenced millions through its Global Leadership Summit.

Is confusion a quality we want to see from leaders? Hybels and Willow Creek seem to be uncertain about how to handle the homosexual issue. They don't condone it, but they certainly don't condemn it either. Their leadership reportedly told Exodus International that they don't believe homosexuality can be cured. Do they deny the power of the gospel and the Holy Spirit?

Lynne Hybels is extremely active in the social justice movement, partnering with Jim Wallis and Tony Campolo in activities damaging to Israel and in promoting an unbiblical social justice movement. She is a contributing editor to *Sojourners* magazine, clearly an organization promoting syncretism among the religions of the world.

A friend of mine recently visited Willow Creek Church and said he could not find one cross in the church. Many emergent and seeker-friendly churches employ this tactic to appear more welcoming, since the cross is seen as offensive by many. Should this be an additional concern?

Several other people Willow Creek has elevated as leaders whom Christians should emulate refer to Islam as an Abrahamic faith, which is a dangerous lie being spread to try to equate Islam with biblical Christianity.

Rick Warren, "America's Pastor"

Rick Warren pastors at Saddleback Church, a megachurch in California. His books, *The Purpose Driven Life* and *The Purpose Driven Church*, have sold millions of copies and are used by thousands of pastors and Christians as blueprints to successful church life.

Saddleback's statement of faith seems to be solid and Rick Warren seems to teach that salvation comes through Jesus as the Son of God. Thousands of pastors subscribe to Warren's daily emails and receive teaching ideas and daily devotionals. To say he is an influential leader in American Christianity is an understatement of epic proportions.

But there is a disturbing pattern in what Rick Warren has been doing over the past five years and whom he partners with. To begin to assess his motives and methods we must first learn about the man he was mentored by years ago.

Rick Warren's Mentor

To have a better understanding for what drives Rick Warren, we need to look at who influenced him as a young Christian leader. Rick Warren and his wife spent years taking in everything they could from another leader in Christianity who is no longer on the stage: Robert Schuller of Crystal Cathedral fame. Below is a transcript from the *Berean Call* radio show with T. (Tom) A. McMahon and Dave Hunt. This will give you a pretty solid indication of the man Rick Warren learned his theology from:

> **Dave**: I'll never forget being on a panel with Walter Martin. This was in Denver, and this was at a cult conference. On the panel, I mentioned – I think somebody asked something about Robert Schuller, and I mentioned that Robert Schuller had gone to Lee's Summit, Missouri, Unity School of Christianity, one of the worst cults out there. They deny everything in the Bible; they're into yoga and hypnosis and the New Age. They deny the gospel of Jesus Christ. That Robert Schuller went there not to correct them, but to commend them and to share his church growth principles with this horrible cult. And in the question-and-answer time,

one of them asked, "Well, what's the function of a minister in this New Age in which we're all a part?" We quoted this in *The Seduction of Christianity*, as you recall. And Robert Schuller, he didn't skip a beat, he didn't deny he was part of the New Age. He said, "Well, what we have to do is positivize religion." And he said, "Now, that's easy for you, being unity ministers in training. You're already very positive, but you understand I deal with people you would call 'fundamentalists,' and they use terms like 'sin' and 'guilt,' 'repentance,' and 'redemption.' What we have to do is positivize this." Walter Martin was sitting next to me and he said, "Dave, I don't want to hear you say that again about Robert Schuller because I went to him privately about this." I mean, he had – Robert Schuller, for example, had dedicated a Unity Temple in Warren, Michigan.

Tom: Right.

Dave: In spite of the Baptist pastor writing to him and telling him how horrible Unity is and he shouldn't do it and so forth. Anyway, Walter Martin said, "Dave, I don't want to hear you say that again about Robert Schuller, because I've gone to him personally about this in private, and he's agreed that he's not going to be involved with Unity anymore. Now he understands how bad it is."

"Well," I said to Walter, "okay, if that's what he says." A few months later, I'm driving in my car, and I turn on the Bible Answer Man. It's Walter Martin telling how Robert Schuller is back with Unity, speaking at their functions and so forth, and Walter Martin says, "And now he won't return my phone calls and he won't answer my letters." So this is an experience that we've had. You talk to someone in private, but it doesn't benefit people out there who have been publicly taught things.

There is a growing pattern among some Christian leaders to speak out of both sides of their mouth these days. Messages seem to be tailored to specific audiences, lacking a cohesive message of the saving gospel of Jesus Christ. Truth has taken a back seat to being culturally relevant, and the hard truth of the gospel is being replaced with a more "positive message." Robert Schuller was one of the early pioneers of this positive message, and Rick Warren was one of his greatest disciples. In Schuller's own words:

> "And there's Rick Warren, a pastor who today is phenom-enal. He came to our institute time after time. And in *Christianity Today*, his wife was quoted as saying, 'When we came to that institute, we were blown away.' How God has blessed him. And today Rick Warren is blessing mil-lions of people." (Robert Schuller at Crystal Cathedral, April 4, 2004)

Robert Schuller long ago was exposed as a universalist and a New Age proponent, and Rick Warren was mentored by him. This is important to remember as we look at Warren and what he is doing within the confines of Christianity these days.

Warren has been called "America's Pastor," and he conducted the prayer for President Obama's inauguration in January 2009. When I first heard that President Obama had selected Warren for his inaugural prayer, I thought that perhaps Warren would be light and salt to the world as millions watched on television. Obama was hailed as a savior to our nation by those who elected him and I thought this would be an opportunity for a strong Christian witness to many who are not Christians.

The prayer started off solid. It was thoughtful, respectful, and referred to God. Many had wondered building up with all the speculation about Obama's true religion if Warren would mention the name of Jesus. Well, he did, and so much more: "I humbly ask this in the name of the one who changed my life – Yeshua, Isa (Quranic term for Jesus), Jesus (Hey-sous, as in the Spanish way of saying Jesus), Jesus – who taught us to pray."

Rick Warren had just prayed not only in the name of Jesus but also in the name of the counterfeit Jesus of Islam. I was stunned and felt betrayed as a Christian. As we covered earlier, Isa is not Jesus. Isa is not recognized as the Son of God in Islam, Isa did not die on the cross for our salvation, and Isa returns in Muslim prophecy to renounce that he is the Son of God and helps kill every Jew and Christian who does not convert to Islam.

Is Rick Warren ashamed of Jesus and His gospel? *"What good is it for someone to gain the whole world, and yet lose or forfeit their very self? Whoever is ashamed of me and my words, the Son of Man will be ashamed of them when he comes in his glory and in the glory of the Father and of the holy angels"* (Luke 9:25-26).

Rick Warren did a lot of damage that day. He wrongly placed Islam, a religion of antichrist, on an equal footing with Christianity. He promoted, or at least did not refute, a lie that millions of Americans and many Christians believe: Allah and YHWH are the same. The same lie that President Bush pronounced just a few years earlier.

Just one year earlier, Rick Warren was signing on to an abomination we covered earlier, the infamous "A Common Word Between Us and You" document. He either bought the deception of these Muslim clerics or he really believes these two religions are equal. Shouldn't this raise serious questions about Rick Warren's true beliefs or his status as America's Pastor?

Compromising with the Enemy?

Islam is a spiritual enemy of Christianity. I know that sounds harsh, but it is true. That does not give us license to hate Muslims or deny them their rights as citizens, but we must understand that Islam is in direct conflict with Christianity and that the Muslim faith mandates worldwide dominance and implementation of Sharia law. No dedicated Muslim can wish otherwise, just like any dedicated Christian must hope that every human being one day comes to know Jesus Christ as Lord and Savior.

First John 4 clearly shows that Islam is a religion of antichrist by their denial of Jesus Christ as the Son of God who came in the flesh. No thinking Christian could possibly think that there is common ground to be found between the two religions. Or could they? By signing on to the "Common Word" deception were Warren and the others simply naive or being deceptive with an ulterior agenda? Could Rick Warren actually be at the center of a movement toward a one-world religion?

Look, we all make mistakes. Several Christian leaders who initially signed the "Common Word" deception have since recanted, admitting they were swept up in the emotion of seeking peace with Muslims. Anyone can make a mistake. So all Hybels, Wallis, and Warren had to do was admit they were tricked in a moment of weakness and they would have been forgiven. But Rick Warren didn't apologize; he doubled down.

In 2009 Warren spoke to eight thousand Muslim leaders at the forty-sixth annual conference of the Islamic Society of North America ("ISNA"). The ISNA has been charged by many with having links to foreign terrorist organizations, including the Muslim Brotherhood. Below is a report with information received through the Freedom of Information Act as reported by Steven Emerson:

> The Islamic Society of North America's (ISNA) roots in the Muslim Brotherhood have been strengthened by newly declassified FBI memos and from a second, highly unlikely source.
>
> The records, recently obtained by the Investigative Project on Terrorism through Freedom of Information Act requests, show that FBI agents investigated a parent organization to ISNA, the North American Islamic Trust (NAIT), during the mid-1980s.
>
> The FBI investigation concluded that the Muslim Brotherhood members who founded U.S.-based groups had risen to "leadership roles within NAIT and its related organizations," including ISNA, "which means they are in a position to direct the activities and support of Muslims in the U.S. for the Islamic Revolution." The FBI memo also said that: "Within the organizational structure of NAIT, there have been numerous groups and individuals identified as being a part of a covert network of revolutionaries who have clearly indicated there (sic) support for the Islamic

Revolution as advocated by the AYATOLLAH KHOMEINI
and his government as well as other fanatical Islamic Shiite
fundamentalist leaders in the Middle East. This faction of
Muslims has declared war on the United States, Israel and
any other country they deem as an enemy of Islam. The
common bond between these various organizations is both
religious and political with the underlying common goal
being to further the holy war (Islamic Jihad)."

The FBI memos date back to 1987-88. Dozens of pages of the released
files are redacted in their entirety. But others contradict ISNA claims
that it "never was, and is not now, affiliated with or influenced by
any international organizations including the Muslim Brotherhood."
Furthermore, ISNA still considers NAIT an affiliated organization.
ISNA's president is an ex-officio NAIT board member and Muzammil
Siddiqi, NAIT's chairman, serves on ISNA's governing board.

NAIT holds the deeds to more than a quarter of the mosques in the
United States and continues to build on that volume.[1]

When Warren spoke, he shared the platform with Siraj Wahhaj,
an unindicted co-conspirator in the 1993 bombing of the Word Trade
Center, a precursor to the 9/11 attacks. Warren was the only Christian
invited to speak and he was warmly received. Among Warren's quotes
from his presentation was this one: "I will tell you that I am not interested in interfaith dialogue. I am interested in interfaith projects. There
is a big difference. Talk is very cheap. You can talk and talk and talk
and never get anything done. Love is something you do. It is something
we do together."

Now you may believe that it is admirable to cooperate with other
religions in doing good works. But allow me to ask two questions: First,
what is our mission as Christians? To do good works? Or to share the
gospel of salvation? Which is considered the Great Commission? Good
works, while admirable, are a method to share the gospel. They are a
means to an end, helping us be in a position to share the message of
eternal life and salvation. But if I feed a man for thirty years and never

---

1   Steven Emerson, "New Disclosures Tighten ISNA-Muslim Brotherhood Bonds," *IPT News,*
     www.investigativeproject.org/730/new-disclosures-tighten-isna-muslim-brotherhood-bonds
     (July 22, 2008).

share the gospel and he is not saved, what have I really accomplished in light of eternity? Works are an expression of our faith and our mission to share the gospel.

Second question: When we do these interfaith projects, which faith gets to share their message with those being helped, assuming evangelism takes place? Quite frankly, the answer is probably moot because I don't believe these interfaith projects that Christians get wrapped up in are for the purpose of sharing our faith. I think they are just a way for us to feel good about ourselves, thinking we are accomplishing something great.

In fact, I think interfaith projects are cowardly. They alleviate the responsibility in our own minds of actually sharing the gospel of salvation. Please do not misunderstand what I say next because I do believe we have a responsibility as Christians to help the poor and needy. But I submit to you that in the context of eternity, it is relatively meaningless. If we feed a man but fail to be God's instrument to lead him to eternal salvation, what has really been accomplished? One can argue the only thing we have accomplished is that we have fed him and loved him right into hell.

We certainly should try to learn how to live with Muslims and not approach Islam out of fear or ignorance. But to agree with them that Allah and YHWH are the same and promise to not share the gospel with them? This is nothing short of a betrayal of Christianity and hatred, not love, for Muslims – people who need to know who Jesus really is and find salvation in Him. What about Jesus' command to *go and make disciples of all nations*? What about 1 John 4, proving the fact that Islam is a religion of antichrist because Islam denies that Jesus is the Son of God? Welcome to leadership in American Christianity.

So Rick Warren signs on to the "Common Word" travesty, and then doubles down by speaking to a Muslim organization accused of supporting terrorist organizations. What could be next? Plenty.

Tony Blair's Faith Foundation

Tony Blair, who also presented at Willow Creek's Global Leadership Summit, is at the front of a movement to embrace the United Nations

Millennium Development Goals that many think are leading to a one-world religion and a one-world government. In cooperation with the United Nations, Blair's organization encourages interfaith dialogue and cooperation in hopes of solving the problems of poverty, discrimination, and global warming.

Through its subsidiary, UNESCO, the United Nations has successfully presented and is implementing a global school curriculum around the world and in many communities within the United States. Our children are being educated by organizations like the National Education Association which is populated with secular humanists who have stated that they must undo the damage parents and religion are doing to the children.

Blair is busy building spiritual bridges between Catholics, Evangelicals, Muslims, Buddhists, and Hindus. Rick Warren is on Tony Blair's board. Warren is also a member of the Council on Foreign Relations, a somewhat secretive organization that has its fingers everywhere. Many would never believe that Rick Warren would ever intentionally try to equate Islam and Christianity. After all, he is America's Pastor and leads a megachurch! Why, he's even been on *Larry King Live*!

More Confusion on the "Gay" Thing

In April 2009, Rick Warren appeared on *Larry King Live*. He apologized for his support of Proposition 8 in California, the referendum calling for state law to legally recognize marriage as between one man and one woman. Proposition 8 passed, but has been overturned by the extremely liberal Ninth Circuit Court of Appeals in California. And in 2015 the U.S. Supreme Court legalized and mandated that all states accept homosexual marriage.

Not only did Rick Warren apologize for his support, he also went on to deny ever publicly supporting Proposition 8. Well Rick, if you didn't support it, why the need to apologize to the homosexual community? Rick Warren is trying to have things both ways, because he *did* publicly support Proposition 8. Below is a transcript of Warren's statement to his congregation two weeks before the election:

The election's coming just in a couple of weeks, and I hope

you're praying about your vote. One of the propositions, of course, that I want to mention is Proposition 8, which is the proposition that had to be instituted because the courts threw out the will of the people. And a court of four guys actually voted to change a definition of marriage that has been going for 5,000 years.

Now let me say this really clearly: we support Proposition 8 – and if you believe what the Bible says about marriage, you need to support Proposition 8. I never support a candidate, but on moral issues I come out very clear.

This is one thing, friends, that all politicians tend to agree on. Both Barack Obama and John McCain, I flat-out asked both of them: what is your definition of marriage? And they both said the same thing – it is the traditional, historic, universal definition of marriage: one man and one woman, for life. And every culture for 5,000 years, and every religion for 5,000 years, has said the definition of marriage is between one man and a woman.

Now here's an interesting thing. There are about two percent of Americans [who] are homosexual or gay/lesbian people. We should not let two percent of the population determine to change a definition of marriage that has been supported by every single culture and every single religion for 5,000 years.

This is not even just a Christian issue – it's a humanitarian and human issue that God created marriage for the purpose of family, love, and procreation.

So I urge you to support Proposition 8, and pass that word on. I'm going to be sending out a note to pastors on what I believe about this. But everybody knows what I believe about it. They heard me at the Civil Forum when I asked both Obama and McCain on their views.

So Warren initially supported Proposition 8 in California, but since then has apologized to the homosexual community for something he said he never did. Is this the type of leadership we should look for in American Christianity? Do we want leaders who lie and pander for the sake of being popular or being seen as compassionate? Who or what got to Warren? I don't know. Does he now privately support gay marriage? Given his PEACE Plan, closely tied with the U.N. Millennium Development Goals, and his close ties to Tony Blair, I believe that day will soon come.

"The Daniel Plan"

Rick Warren, by his own admission, was getting fat. He decided he had to do something to get his weight under control, helping his body and mind become a better temple of the Holy Spirit. Physical and emotional health is very important and we should all strive to have strong minds and bodies. But what price are we willing to pay for this effort? Apparently, Rick Warren was willing to pay a very high price.

In challenging his congregation, and now the millions of pastors and Christians following him to join in this quest for fitness, Rick Warren exposed them to some unusual, to say the least, experts he had recruited to teach The Daniel Plan. When discipline to exercise more and eat less would have sufficed, Warren decided to call in some big guns, and those guns might be pointed right at the spiritual condition of Christians whom Warren leads.

Dr. Mehmet Oz

Oprah Winfrey is a leader in the New Age Movement and sadly one of the most influential "Christians" in the world, and she calls Dr. Oz her favorite doctor. He was raised as a Muslim and has been influenced by the mysticism of Sufi Muslims. He subscribes to the ideas of cultist mystic Emanuel Swedenborg: "As I came into contact with Swedenborg's many writings, I began to understand Swedenborg's profound insights and how they applied directly to my life."

Swedenborg believed he could pass between the life to come and the present. He claimed he had conversations with spirits of the dead as well as angels. Swedenborg wrote that the last judgment of man occurred in 1757, though it was only visible in the spirit realm which he visited frequently. He claimed that the second coming of Christ occurred, not to all men as the Bible teaches, but to Swedenborg personally in the spirit world.

In his book *Life On Other Planets*, Swedenborg claimed he spoke with spirits from Jupiter, Mercury, Mars, Saturn, Venus, and the moon. He also denied the Trinity and salvation through faith.

Swedenborg's followers started a church called "New Church." In a 2008 edition of their magazine, *New Church Life*, Dr. Oz wrote an article exposing that his spiritual beliefs are connected to Swedenborg's theology. In an article he wrote titled "Mehmet Oz Finds His Teacher," Oz shared his spiritual journey and awakening. I have just a few excerpts due to its length, but the entire article is available for viewing at *www. newchurch.org/get-answers/ connection-magazine/science-and-religion/ mehmet-oz-finds-his-teacher*.

> I was raised a secular Moslem. I hungered for a scientific rationale to help me reconcile my newly found insights into our bodies and the deeper spiritual longings that we all possess. Help came in the form of an eighteenth-century Swedish philosopher (Swedenborg).

> Soon after I met Lisa (his wife), she introduced me to insights into heaven and hell that challenged my status quo. Swedenborg, I later learned, was a scientist and theologian whose great and defining quest was to find the nature of the relationship between the body and the spirit. In his mid-fifties he came into an altered state of awareness in which he experienced a simultaneous dual consciousness of this life and the afterlife. I began to understand his profound insights and how they applied directly to my life.

> His emphasis on overcoming the delusion of the self and on the profound interdependence of all things in both the spiritual and natural worlds aligns so closely with Buddhist

thought that the Zen Master D. T. Suzuki referred to him as "the Buddha of the North."

According to Swedenborg, heaven and hell are not merely places but spiritual states. We do not "go there" when we die. We are already there. I have always had trouble with the idea of a selective redemption. How could a compassionate God condemn his children for nothing more than being born into the "wrong faith"? How could an all-loving God choose to extend that love to only a select few? Swedenborg taught that God loves us all, and the various religions allow us to approach him in the way best suited to our needs. He argued that we are all born for heaven, and that it is what we love that determines our fate, not what we profess to believe. Further, Swedenborg claimed that God never judges us.

Angels as described by Swedenborg aren't a separate species but people who are regenerate – literally, reborn humans.

Is this Rick Warren's belief also? Does Warren also believe in this universal salvation view that is so contrary to the Bible? When a pastor parades someone in front of the church as a teacher, can we assume that the beliefs taught are consistent with the pastor? I think that should be a fair conclusion. The teacher should be properly vetted to be as certain as possible that what he teaches is consistent with the teachings of the church. If the teacher strays and teaches something that conflicts, a disclaimer should be made afterwards. There has been no disclaimer made by Warren to Dr. Oz's beliefs.

Dr. Oz is also a proponent of transcendental meditation and Reiki meditation, and his wife is a Reiki master. What is Reiki? Let's hear it from their own website, *www.reiki.org*:

"The word Reiki is made of two Japanese words – Rei which means

'God's Wisdom or the Higher Power' and Ki which is 'life force energy.' So Reiki is actually 'spiritually guided life force energy.' . . . Reiki is a simple, natural and safe method of spiritual healing . . . While Reiki is spiritual in nature, it is not a religion. It has no dogma, and there is nothing you must believe in order to learn and use Reiki."

Note the definition of being "spiritual in nature" and having "no dogma." This is a free-form spirituality – the kind that Satan just loves.

Dr. Daniel Amen

Another of The Daniel Plan doctors and teachers, Dr. Amen has done some breakthrough research on how the brain works. Based on some of his beliefs, I wish he hadn't.

> "I teamed with Drs. Dharma Singh Khalsa and Nisha Money to study the impact of meditation on the brain. We chose a simple 12-minute form of meditation, Kriya Kirtan, that is easy for busy people to practice. It is based on the five primal sounds: Saa, Taa, Naa, Maa, (aa being the fifth sound)." Now call me a conspiracy nut, but do you see any sounds in this mantra that when connected give you pause for concern?

What about this Kriya Kirtan meditation Dr. Amen promotes? Well, let's go to the official website of Kriya Kirtan meditation to find out:

> "Kundalini yoga as taught by Yogi Bhajan is a scientific technology for happiness. It extends the brain to imagine Infinity in its totality, and then it is a gradual process to work for that experience. Every movement is scientifically originated, organized and projected. This is a discipline in which there is nothing but success. When practicing Kundalini Yoga, your inner power is awakened to unite with the Universal life force, empowering you with aware-ness beyond the ordinary. This awakened state gives you the capacity to expand your perspective and experience each day with increasing inspiration and joy."

But wait, there's more! The site goes on to explain the benefit of "identifying and connecting with your inner divinity." There are also mantras and chants to bring physical healings, wealth, and increased memorization.

Dr. Amen has also teamed up to create a six-part series for improved sexuality using ancient Hindu mantras and teachings.

The Daniel Plan Summary

What could Rick Warren be thinking? Or was he thinking at all, bringing in these men to teach physical and spiritual health to Christians? Is this a case of being naive or is there a real agenda? Warren is either a careless pastor, not vetting teachers he brings in and endorses, or he is a willing participant to introduce Buddhist, Hindu, and New Age teachings into Christianity. Since he has not refuted any of the views of these teachers, we must assume he endorses their beliefs. Pastors, if this does not lead you to take a closer look at this man many of you follow and emulate, I'm not sure what will.

PEACE Plan of Saddleback Church

Who doesn't want peace? Not me, if it compromises the gospel and sharing it with the lost. And Rick Warren's ill-advised PEACE Plan will compromise the gospel and our ability to share it with lost people, no matter how good his intentions are.

One cannot escape how similar Warren's PEACE Plan goals line up with the United Nations Millennium Development Goals. If you are a fan of the United Nations and think it is an organization that is interested in anything short of global humanism and universalism, I strongly suggest you research the historical facts and statements made by U.N. leaders and in their various charter organizations like UNESCO, the global governance organization that is implementing a global education curriculum for all students. See if you can find anything remotely Christian in their beliefs and goals.

U.N. Millennium Development Goals and PEACE Plan Goals

- End poverty and hunger

- Promote reconciliation

- Universal education

- Equip servant leaders

- Gender equality

- Assist the poor

- Child health

- Care for the sick

- Maternal health

- Educate the next generation

- Combat HIV/AIDS

- Environmental sustainability

- Global partnerships

"Promote reconciliation" replaced the former goal of "Planting churches" in Warren's original plan. Does this say anything about the ultimate plans and purposes? What are we reconciling and toward what purpose? Is the goal to develop a watered-down religion that all people can agree on?

There are strong similarities between the Millennium Development Goals and the PEACE Plan goals, and both are strong social justice agendas. Now, taken on their own, none of the PEACE Plan goals are wrong. But we must step back and analyze the partners involved and the current state of affairs when Christianity partners with the secular world to solve problems.

The mission of disciples of Jesus was given in Matthew 28:19-20: *"Therefore go make disciples of all nations, baptizing them in the name*

*of the Father and of the Son and of the Holy Spirit, and teaching them
to obey everything I have commanded you."*

This is the calling of all Christians. We are to share the gospel of
salvation with the lost. Feeding the poor, caring for the sick, and educating children are a *means* to this end. Again, if we stop short at helping
the poor but are not God's instruments in leading them to Him, what
have we really accomplished in light of eternity except loving them
into hell? This is a problem for the PEACE Plan and every other multi-
religious collaboration effort: as men and women of various religions
interact with those in need, which religion shares their version of the
truth? Christianity? Islam? Hinduism?

The United Nations, which partners with Warren in the implementation of the PEACE Plan, has been proven to be an anti-Christian organization. They promote human secularism and earth worship through
every program they offer. They seek world control and have made it
clear in many publications that they see religious fundamentalism as
an obstacle to world peace.

The PEACE Plan is an ill-advised program that will waste billions
of dollars with no real effect on the eternal souls of men. By partnering with the United Nations, it has ceased to be a means to spread the
gospel and has become the greatest effort of secular social justice in
the history of the world.

There is an excellent, in-depth article on the PEACE Plan at *https://
www.crossroadto.com*. It goes into great detail about the people and
organizations involved in this program.

Summary on Rick Warren

Here is a summary of information to consider on Rick Warren's activities and associations:

- Mentored by universalist Robert Schuller of the Crystal
  Cathedral

- Equated the Muslim Isa with Jesus at the Obama inauguration prayer

- Signed on to the deception of the "A Common Word Between Us and You" document

- Was a welcome guest at the Islamic Society of North America, an organization with ties to terrorist groups

- Agreed to not evangelize Muslims

- Was a board member in Tony Blair's global spiritualization organization

- Sent contradictory messages on Christian acceptability of homosexual marriage

- Brought in New Age teachers who promote Hindu and Buddhist meditation and follow cult leaders like Emmanuel Swedenborg to teach holistic health to Christians

- Implemented the PEACE Plan which compromises with the world and will spend millions on social justice programs, consistent with U.N. Millennial Development Goals

Controversy continues to swirl around Warren and his reaching out to Muslims. Muslim leaders whom Warren partners with have openly stated that they embrace Warren because of his promise to not evangelize Muslims. Saddleback's Interfaith Outreach Pastor Abraham Meulenberg teaches the concept of "Kingdom Circles" around the world. Kingdom Circles theology teaches that all members of any religion can be saved without professing Jesus Christ as the Son of God. Does this sound like solid Christian theology or more like New Age gibberish?

Rick Warren and Saddleback Church have hired a nationally known public relations firm to handle and respond to media inquiries. Just what does a Christian church need with a public relations firm? I guess standing on the truth of God's Word just won't cut it anymore. These days we seem to desire the wisdom of the world to make sure our message is sent in just the right way and to make sure we can deflect any questions or criticisms. Is Saddleback a church of God or a corporation? Is this the future of American Christianity?

If you sat on a grand jury, do you see enough evidence to warrant further investigation into Rick Warren's activities, affiliations, and motives? I can tell you from personal experience that no leader elicits more criticism or passionate defense than Rick Warren. He is held in almost god-like status by many pastors and Christians; however, he must be examined as any other leader, regardless of how big his church or influence is.

Joel Osteen

We have all gone to a place that offers a huge buffet dinner. There is salad, fruit, meat, vegetables, and a huge table of fattening desserts. When parents take their children to a buffet place for dinner, the children want to sprint to the dessert table and load up on cookies, cake, and ice cream. But good parents will first make sure they eat food with proper nutrition before filling up on fattening desserts.

We need fruit to give us healthy sugars and fiber for our bodies. We need vegetables for necessary vitamins and minerals. We need meat for iron and protein; and every once in awhile it is perfectly fine to indulge in some dessert. But if we overindulge on the desserts and ignore the fruit, vegetables, and meat, we will become obese and very unhealthy.

Christianity is a buffet. Hebrews tells us about the "milk" – *the elementary truths of God's Word*, which include faith in God, the death and resurrection of Jesus, the forgiveness of sins, and the resurrection of the dead. It tells us that solid food (meat and vegetables) is righteousness, and this includes the pursuit of holiness. The dessert is whatever blessings God chooses to give us to bless others in this lifetime – health, wealth, and prosperity – when we deserve none of these because of our sinful nature.

When I picture walking into this Christian buffet setting, I see Joel Osteen at the dessert table inviting us to partake of all things sweet. He is luring many over as they bypass the nutritional foods in favor of the dessert bar. Joel Osteen is to Christianity what cream puffs and chocolate éclairs are to the body: they taste good, but you'd better not overindulge on them.

Joel Osteen is attractive, charismatic, and likable. He is the embodiment of what seems to define success in leaders of American Christianity these days – a lot of words without saying anything substantive; a leadership that is focused on numbers, not spiritual depth; and a willingness to compromise core Christian values and beliefs when convenient.

Osteen's sermons appear on national television every week on Christian and secular outlets. Granted, his syrupy message of love without obligation might be effective in reaching the lost initially, especially those who feel unworthy of God's love, but once these seeds start to sprout, they will wither and die quickly because Osteen does nothing to help them develop significant roots in their faith. I watch him every week just to see his latest teachings and I have yet to feel challenged even once by anything he has taught. His message is constant: God loves you and wants the best for your life – health, wealth, prosperity, and a life free of pressure or stress. If only Paul, Peter, and John had been able to listen to Osteen, maybe their lives would have been much easier.

Joel Osteen missed his calling; he should have been a politician. His ability to dodge tough questions and stay on message is admirable – I only wish it were biblical. He's had many opportunities to shine the light of the gospel into the world as he is interviewed on worldwide television. But his seeming inability to take a firm stand on any biblical teachings makes him an ineffective, even destructive, leader, as he continues to push an incomplete and dangerous gospel.

In an interview with Larry King, Osteen covered a lot of topics with his usual style of half-answers and questionable theology:

> KING: But you're not fire and brimstone, right? You're not pound the decks and hell and damnation?

> OSTEEN: No. That's not me. It's never been me. I've always been an encourager at heart. And when I took over from my father he came from the Southern Baptist background and back 40, 50 years ago there was a lot more of that. But, you know, I just – I don't believe in that. I don't believe – maybe it was for a time. But I don't have it in my heart to condemn people. I'm there to encourage them. I see myself more as a coach, as a motivator to help them experience the life God has for us.

KING: But don't you think if people don't believe as you
believe, they're somehow condemned?

OSTEEN: You know, I think that happens in our society.
But I try not to do that. I tell people all the time, preached
a couple Sundays about it. I'm for everybody. You may not
agree with me, but to me it's not my job to try to straighten
everybody out. The Gospel is called the good news. My
message is a message of hope, that God's for you. You can
live a good life no matter what's happened to you. And so
I don't know. I know there is condemnation but I don't feel
that's my place.

He preached a "couple Sundays" on sin and hell? Perhaps the collection was smaller on those Sundays as Osteen saw that his congregation
found the message too harsh. "I'm for everybody"? How about being
for Jesus Christ and the true gospel of salvation?

KING: There's a lot of books about improving yourself.

OSTEEN: Yeah. I don't know. I think coming from the
Christian base, and I think the fact that I don't know, it's
a book of encouragement and inspiration. And to me it
seems like there's so much pulling us down in our society
today. There's so much negative. Most of my book is about
how you can live a good life today in spite of all that. So I
think that had a big part of it.

KING: But it doesn't quote a lot of biblical passages until
the back of the book, right?

OSTEEN: It doesn't do a whole lot of it. My message, I
wanted to reach the mainstream. We've reached the church
audience. So I just try to, what I do is just try to teach practical principles. I may not bring the scripture in until the
end of my sermon and I might feel bad about that. Here's
the thought. I talked yesterday about living to give. That's
what a life should be about. I brought in at the end about

some of the scriptures that talk about that. But same principal in the book.

Read between the lines: The Bible and the gospel are too negative and
negativity doesn't sell.

> KING: Because we've had ministers on who said, your
> record don't count. You either believe in Christ or you
> don't. If you believe in Christ, you are, you are going to
> heaven. And if you don't no matter what you've done in
> your life, you ain't.
>
> OSTEEN: Yeah, I don't know. There's probably a balance
> between. I believe you have to know Christ. But I think
> that if you know Christ, if you're a believer in God, you're
> going to have some good works. I think it's a cop-out to say
> I'm a Christian but I don't ever do anything ...
>
> KING: What if you're Jewish or Muslim, you don't accept
> Christ at all?
>
> OSTEEN: You know, I'm very careful about saying who
> would and wouldn't go to heaven. I don't know ...
>
> KING: If you believe you have to believe in Christ? They're
> wrong, aren't they?
>
> OSTEEN: Well, I don't know if I believe they're wrong. I
> believe here's what the Bible teaches and from the Christian
> faith this is what I believe. But I just think that only God
> will judge a person's heart. I spent a lot of time in India
> with my father. I don't know all about their religion. But I
> know they love God. And I don't know. I've seen their sin-
> cerity. So I don't know. I know for me, and what the Bible
> teaches, I want to have a relationship with Jesus.

So, Osteen has an opportunity to explain the gospel, and what is the
response of one of America's top pastors? "I don't know." Every time
Osteen speaks truth – "you have to know Christ," "If you're a believer in
God, you're going to have some good works," and King questions him

on it, Osteen waffles. Why not quote John 14:6? John 3:16? John 15:5? James 2:14-17? The answer is because Osteen is more concerned with appearing non-judgmental or being liked than he is with standing up for the gospel. After all, quoting what the Bible says about salvation, and pointing out that YHWH is the only true God and all others are false, does not help him sell books.

KING: What is the prosperity gospel?

OSTEEN: I think the prosperity gospel in general is – well I don't know. I hear it too. I don't know. I think what some-times you see is it's just all about money. That's not what I believe. It's the attitude of your heart, and so you know, we believe – but I do believe this, that God wants us to be blessed. He wants us to be able to send our kids to college, excel in our careers. But prosperity to me, Larry, is not just money, it's having health. What good is money if you don't have health?

KING: Also many in the Christian belief are wary of too much material, aren't they?

OSTEEN: Yeah, I think some of them are. But to me, you know, I hope people get blessed if they can handle it right. Because it takes money to do good. You know to do things for people. To spread the good news. So I think it's all a matter of your heart.

Osteen doesn't know what the prosperity gospel is? He preaches it vir-tually all the time. And he goes on to preach it to King right after he says he doesn't know about it. And on the point that it takes money to do good, how much money did Paul and Peter have? How much money did Paul spend in marketing plans and social justice programs to "relate" with people?

KING: Don't you ever doubt?

OSTEEN: No. I don't – I wouldn't say that I do. I guess I do and I don't think about it too much.

Talk about living in contradiction! "I don't [doubt] . . . I wouldn't say that I do . . . I guess I do."

KING: Do you ever involve politics in the sermons?

OSTEEN: Never do.

KING: How about issues that the church has feelings about? Abortion? Same-sex marriages?

OSTEEN: Yeah. You know what, Larry? I don't go there. I just ...

KING: You have thoughts, though.

OSTEEN: I have thoughts. I just, you know, I don't think that a same-sex marriage is the way God intended it to be. I don't think abortion is the best. I think there are other, you know, a better way to live your life. But I'm not going to condemn those people. I tell them all the time our church is open for everybody.

Of course, a strong biblical answer here would have meant taking a tough stand that might be unpopular. Gay marriage and abortion aren't God's "best"? No, they are abominations to God because His innocent children are slaughtered and marriage is demeaned to fit sinful human desires.

Is Joel Osteen selling out the Christian faith for personal gain? He has a huge platform to spread the good news of the Bible but he would rather sell books and be loved and admired. Is this where we want our leaders to take us?

KING: You don't call them sinners?

OSTEEN: I don't.

KING: Is that a word you don't use?

OSTEEN: I don't use it. I never thought about it. But I probably don't. But most people already know what they're doing wrong. When I get them to church I want to tell

them that you can change. There can be a difference in
your life. So I don't go down the road of condemning.

Hey Joel, breaking news for you: Sin is the disease that man is dying
from, now and for eternity. Sinners need to repent and accept the forgiveness, grace, and mercy of God available to us because of the painful
sacrifice by the Son of God.

Joel Osteen is like a cancer doctor refusing to properly diagnose
and treat cancer in his patients. Any physician who did that would be
sued for malpractice and lose his license forever. Joel Osteen is guilty of
spiritual malpractice and I pray he will be convicted by the Holy Spirit
to see the error of his ways.

Osteen also weighed in on the controversy surrounding the faith of
2012 presidential candidate Mitt Romney, who is a Mormon. Here is an
excerpt from his interview on Fox News with Chris Wallace:

> Wallace: And what about Mitt Romney? And I've got to ask
> you the question, because it is a question whether it should
> be or not in this campaign, is a Mormon a true Christian?
>
> Osteen: Well, in my mind they are. Mitt Romney has said
> that he believes in Christ as his savior, and that's what I
> believe, so, you know, I'm not the one to judge the little
> details of it. So, I believe they are. And so, you know, Mitt
> Romney seems like a man of character and integrity to me,
> and I don't think he would – anything would stop me from
> voting for him if that's what I felt like.
>
> Wallace: So, for instance, when people start talking about
> Joseph Smith, the founder of the church, and the golden
> tablets in upstate New York, and God assumes the shape of
> a man, do you not get hung up on those theological issues?
>
> Osteen: I probably don't get hung up in them because I
> haven't really studied them or thought about them.

So let's analyze Osteen's response:

- Romney and Osteen both believe in Jesus as savior (note
  the absence of the word "Lord").

- Osteen admits he has not studied Mormonism. Some shepherd of the flock.

- Osteen says he is not the one to judge if Mormons are Christians or not. Perhaps, but is God qualified to make that judgment? I certainly hope your answer is yes.

What do Mormons believe? The Mormon religion, whose followers are known as Mormons and Latter-Day Saints ("LDS"), was founded less than two hundred years ago by a man named Joseph Smith. He claimed to have received a personal visit from God the Father and Jesus Christ who told him that all churches and their creeds were an abomination. Joseph Smith then set out to begin a new religion that claims to be the "only true church on earth."

Mormons believe that there are four sources of divinely inspired words:

- The Bible "as far as it is translated correctly." Which verses are considered incorrectly translated is not always made clear.

- *The Book of Mormon*, which was "translated" by Smith and published in 1830. Smith claimed it is the "most correct book" on earth and that a person can get closer to God by following its precepts more than any other book.

- *The Doctrine and Covenants*, containing a collection of modern revelations regarding the "Church of Jesus Christ as it has been restored."

- *The Pearl of the Great Price*, which is considered by Mormons to "clarify" doctrines and teachings that were lost from the Bible, while adding its own information about the earth's creation.

Mormons believe that God was not always the Supreme Being of the universe, but attained that status through righteous living and persistent effort. They believe God the Father has a body of flesh and bones as tangible as man's. Brigham Young taught that Adam was God and the father of Jesus Christ, though this teaching has now been abandoned by modern Mormon leaders.

But Mormon leaders have taught that Jesus' incarnation was the result of a physical relationship between God the Father and Mary. Mormons believe Jesus is *a god*, but that any human can also become a god, and that salvation can be earned by a combination of faith and good works.

Mormons do tend to be good, moral people, but it is clear they are not Christians. To refer to Jesus as *a god* distorts His nature. He is the only begotten Son of God, and He is God (John 1:1). To infer that we can all become gods is not a Christian belief. And to teach that God has not always been the all-powerful, omniscient God who created all things is heresy. If that is true, then who created God?

Osteen simply does what Osteen always does: deflect tough questions and show he is an empty suit. Unfortunately, this empty suit has millions of followers who think he represents Christian doctrines and teachings.

In many ways Joel Osteen embodies the state of Christian leadership these days: soft-peddling or denying sin; suggesting all gods are the same; more concerned with health and wealth in this life instead of our eternal spiritual destination; and afraid to call out false religions and beliefs. Is Joel Osteen a coward, ashamed of the gospel, and more worried about his public image than the truth of the gospel?

Summary

Bill Hybels, Rick Warren, and Joel Osteen. Welcome to leadership in American Christianity. Are we witnessing the future of the church? A future of religious syncretism, the discounting of sin, a social justice gospel, and truth sacrificed for numbers, popularity, and power? This is a "church" committing adultery against God. A future that redefines love as total acceptance of any behavior; a future where what we feel trumps cold hard facts; a future where we can pick and choose which characteristics of God we choose to believe, discounting the rest?

This future is here, right now in its infant stages. Sadly, it may have unstoppable momentum, fueled by biblically illiterate and lazy Christians who find it easier to listen to a twenty-minute sermon to select our theology instead of taking time out of our busy, selfish lives to read what God teaches us about Himself, sin, and salvation. And the next generation of leaders is appearing on stage to carry the torch forward. Mentored by these men and others like McLaren, Wallis, and Campolo, this next generation of leaders is preparing to take us to greater depths of depravity. Men like Rob Bell and Steven Furtick are ready and willing to lead us further from the truth of Scripture and deeper into the spiritual abyss.

American Christianity is on life support and continues to suck in all the cancer she can absorb, and the body is starting to shut down. Vital organs are starting to fail, the blood is poisoned, and we are gasping for air. We are preparing to pull our own plug, bringing this slow march toward suicide to its completion.

Our leaders are leading us to where we already chose to go deep down in our hearts. They have tickled ears that asked to be tickled; they have closed eyes that desired to be closed. While they are responsible for much of this slow death march, it is we who follow them who must share at least equal blame.

> So all the elders of Israel gathered and came to Samuel at Ramah. They said to him, "You are old, and your sons do not follow your ways; now appoint a king to lead us, such as all the other nations have."
>
> But when they said, "Give us a king to lead us," this displeased Samuel; so he prayed to the LORD. And the LORD told him: "Listen to all that the people are saying to you; it is not you they have rejected, but they have rejected me as their king. As they have done from the day I brought them up out of Egypt until this day, forsaking me and serving other gods, so they are doing to you. Now listen to them; but warn them solemnly and let them know what the king who will reign over them will claim as his rights." (1 Samuel 8:4-9)

History is repeating itself. Just as the Jews rejected God as King in favor of a man, we are repeating this mistake in American Christianity. We are rejecting the knowledge of God in His Word out of laziness or selfishness. We are choosing "kings" to be our leaders instead of God Himself. These kings will tell us what to believe and what to do. These kings claim they are approved by God because of how many people follow them! And many pastors listen to them and try to be just like them because maybe their churches will grow and they'll be able to have a megachurch of their own one day!

Surely these kings would not lead us astray, because they have been trained in Christian seminaries, so they must be a lot smarter and wiser then we are. They have charm and charisma and are kind, loving, and accepting. They make us feel so good about ourselves. They are our leaders, so shouldn't we just follow where they lead us?

How did that work for the Israelites? About as well as it will work for us. Welcome to our future, American Christians. Enjoy it because we asked for it, and just like in 1 Samuel 8, God is allowing it. Is He hardening our hearts like He did to Pharaoh? Are we feeling His wrath spoken of by Paul in Romans 1?

> *For although they knew God, they neither glorified him as God nor gave thanks to him, but their thinking became futile and their foolish hearts were darkened. Although they claimed to be wise, they became fools and exchanged the glory of the immortal God for images made to look like a mortal human being and birds and animals and reptiles.*

> *Therefore God gave them over in the sinful desires of their hearts to sexual impurity for the degrading of their bodies with one another. They exchanged the truth of God for a lie, and worshiped and served created things rather than the Creator—who is forever praised. Amen.*

> *Because of this, God gave them over to shameful lusts. Even their women exchanged natural sexual relations for unnatural ones. In the same way the men also abandoned natural relations with women and were inflamed with lust for one another. Men committed shameful acts with other men, and received in themselves the due penalty for their error.*

> *Furthermore, just as they did not think it worthwhile to retain the knowledge of God, so God gave them over to a*

depraved mind, so that they do what ought not to be done. They have become filled with every kind of wickedness, evil, greed and depravity. (Romans 1:21-29)

Chapter 9

A Move of the Spirit –
but Which Spirit?

Signs and Wonders Movement

*"And afterward, I will pour out my Spirit on all people.
Your sons and daughters will prophesy, your old men will
dream dreams, your young men will see visions. Even on my
servants, both men and women, I will pour out my Spirit in
those days. I will show wonders in the heavens and on the
earth, blood and fire and billows of smoke." – Joel 2:28-30*

*"At that time if anyone says to you, 'Look, here is the
Messiah!' or, 'There he is!' do not believe it. For false
messiahs and false prophets will appear and perform
great signs and wonders to deceive, if possible, even the
elect." – Matthew 24:23-24*

*The coming of the lawless one will be in accordance with
how Satan works. He will use all sorts of displays of power
through signs and wonders that serve the lie, and all the
ways that wickedness deceives those who are perishing. They
perish because they refused to love the truth and so be saved.
For this reason God sends them a powerful delusion so that
they will believe the lie and so that all will be condemned
who have not believed the truth but have delighted in wickedness. – 2 Thessalonians 2:9-12*

Okay, strap on your seatbelts and reconcile these three passages! God says in Joel that in the final days He will pour out His Spirit with great signs and wonders, yet Jesus and Paul warn us of incredible false miracles, signs, and wonders, not of God, but of the Enemy.

What these verses say is this: Test the spirits and discern! There will apparently be real signs and wonders from God, but also a lot of false, deceptive signs and wonders from Satan that will deceive many. No movement we discuss on *Stand Up For the Truth* brings stronger emotions and opinions than the Signs and Wonders Movement.

God created the universe and all that is in it, sustaining it by His might, and He has the power to suspend natural laws in order to fulfill any purpose He desires. Miracles were a huge part of the ministries of Moses, Elijah, and Elisha, and of course, Jesus and the apostles. Today, many people still seek to experience miraculous signs and wonders, and some go to great lengths to experience what they believe are signs and wonders from God.

Some want confirmation of the truth of God, and there is nothing initially wrong with that. In fact, God willingly gave signs to Moses (Exodus 4:1-9), and in John 2:23 it says, *Many people saw the signs he was performing and believed in his name.* However, there comes a time when enough miracles have been presented and the truth should be known.

Jesus visited the Samaritans *and because of his words many more became believers* (John 4:41). However, just a few verses later, Jesus rebukes the Galileans: *"Unless you people see miraculous signs and wonders, . . . you will never believe"* (John 4:48). So to continue to seek signs, wonders, and miracles in the pursuit of knowing God can be an insult to Him.

Signs and wonders appeal to us on a deep emotional level. While we are creatures of deep emotion and passion, these passions and emotions can have a dangerous hold on us when we allow them to override facts. When we desire something strongly enough, our emotions can fool us. That is why God gave us His Word, so we could measure every thought, word, action, and feeling against His absolute truth.

Some people seem to almost develop an addiction to witnessing signs, wonders, and miracles. The danger in this is that God becomes a "high" in our lives. Grounded Christians should not need continuous signs, wonders, and miracles – just knowing He is God and we are His children should be sufficient. Now some might argue that this brings them continually closer to God, but there is a real danger in becoming addicted to signs and wonders. The danger is that Satan is also capable of demonstrating his power through signs and wonders.

> *Then the devil took him* [Jesus] *to the holy city and had him stand on the highest point of the temple. "If you are the Son of God," he said, "throw yourself down. For it is written: "He will command his angels concerning you, and they will lift you up in their hands, so that you will not strike your foot against a stone." Jesus answered him, "It is also written: 'Do not put the Lord your God to the test.'"*

> *Again, the devil took him to a very high mountain and showed him all the kingdoms of the world and their splendor. "All this I will give you," he said, "if you will bow down and worship me."* (Matthew 4:5-9)

The devil transported Jesus from the desert to the top of the temple to a mountain so high they could see all the world's kingdoms. That, my friends, is a sign and wonder, but not one from God. And therein lies a serious problem in the Signs and Wonders Movement: both God and Satan can perform them. So when people claim to see angel feathers or gold dust, or claim they were transported to another place, how can we tell with 100-percent accuracy that it is God, not Satan, performing the "miracle"?

People I have spoken with who claim to experience incredible signs and wonders always report a euphoria accompanying the sighting. In such an emotional state, how can we be certain our emotions have not overwhelmed our common sense and biblical discernment? We must remember that Satan is a great counterfeiter who will make his signs and wonders seem just like God's.

A recent phenomenon over the past several years is the claim of people that they see "angel orbs." Coincidentally, this has started to surface with the development of digital photography, and can easily be manufactured by dust particles seen by these high-tech cameras. But angel orbs are really nothing new. Early Christian Gnostics and Jewish Kabbalah teachers talked constantly about seeing angel orbs. The New Age and occult sciences have taught about the sighting of these orbs for centuries. Nowhere in the Bible is there anything remotely suggesting that God sends His angels as orbs. Some point to Ezekiel, but a study of this book clearly refutes the suggestion that Ezekiel saw angel orbs.

Another claim of some in this movement is being "drunk in the spirit." They fall down and slur their words like a man who has consumed a quart of brandy, yet claim this is a manifestation from God. *But the fruit of the Spirit is love, joy, peace, forbearance, kindness, goodness, faithfulness, gentleness and **self-control*** (Galatians 5:22-23, emphasis added). Does being drunk in the spirit, falling down, and slurring words equate to *self-control*?

When we are looking for the next great thrill of a sign or wonder, could our minds be open to suggestions? Open to suggestions from an Enemy looking to speak to us when we want to believe we are hearing from God? This sets us up for tremendous deception because Satan is very clever and devious and can twist Scripture ever so slightly to advance his agenda to deceive us.

Sadly, sensuality seems to be replacing genuine spirituality in much of Christianity these days. More and more Christians are seeking greater depths of sensuality in everything they feel and encounter. This sensuality can overwhelm our common sense and send us in pursuit of dangerous passions, like a dog in heat. We become obsessed with the sensuality and will pursue it at all costs, even at the expense of sound doctrine.

There is no doubt that many of the signs and wonders proclaimed by someone like Todd Bentley are bizarre and not found anywhere in the Word of God. But a defense that is put up by some, including a few listeners of *Stand Up For the Truth*, is "Just because God has never done it in the past doesn't mean He cannot do it now." Very true, as God can do anything within His nature and character and that is what makes this issue so difficult to discuss rationally at times. Emotion runs high on both sides of this issue and we must approach it with great wisdom and discernment.

But what I often find in defenders of this movement is at times curious to say the least. They will call skeptics close minded and not open to the possibility of God doing "something new." However, I challenge them that perhaps they are the ones who are close minded because they seem to automatically think every new sign and wonder is from God instead of the Enemy. When Jesus talked about the final days before His return, He warned us *once* of wars, rumors of war, and pestilence. Yet He warned us *four times* about dangerous false prophets, false teachers, and false Christs. When God warns us of something four times, I think He is serious about the point He is trying to make. But in the pursuit of sensuality over truth, we often are led by our emotions and passions instead of discernment and the Word of God. We dive headlong into something we may not understand and just assume it is from God because we are Christians.

Now in fairness, many defenders of the Signs and Wonders Movement recognize, as one supporter puts it, that whenever signs and wonders appear, there are three camps at work: the Holy Spirit, the fraudulent, and the people who get swept up in the emotion of the event and fake it. In essence, there is my caution on getting wrapped up in this movement. It is so easy to get caught up in our emotions that sound judgment and discernment can be abandoned.

Back in 1996, three years before I committed my life to Jesus, I was in the Dallas Fort Worth International Airport, waiting to catch a plane home after a business trip. A woman was in the chair next to me and I could tell she was really struggling with an emotional issue. I asked if she was all right and she shared what was causing her a great deal of emotional grief. After about an hour of discussion she gave me a book that she said I just had to read, after asking me if I was a religious person. The book was the best-selling *Conversations With God* by Neale Donald Walsch. At this time my eyes were not truly open to who God was and for the need to become born again in the Holy Spirit. I thought I was good to go since I was raised in the Catholic Church and still attended church a whopping two times a year.

I read the book on the trip to Green Bay and found Walsch's "conversations" with God to be intriguing and heartwarming. Walsch talked about how God is in everyone and everyone is in God; about how Jesus,

Buddha, and Mohammad were all God's sons; and that we are all gods if we just realize the divinity within us. Without the Holy Spirit of God, I actually found the book to be interesting and beautiful. Maybe all I was taught about God and Jesus was wrong. Maybe we all can become God if we would just put aside our archaic beliefs.

Fortunately, I forgot about the book within a few days, returning to my job and the pursuit of worldly happiness. But for a few short days, I was caught up in the emotion of bliss, harmony, and peace. Had I received a dream or vision that seemed to confirm the heresy I was flirting with, I could have easily fallen for the lies of the Enemy and been the worst of heathens to this day. I thank God that He loved and protected my mind and heart even when I hated Him.

Emotions and feelings are often our worst enemy. They deceive us and they encourage us to believe in what we feel instead of what are the facts. Satan will play on them and, disguised as an angel of light, can trick us and lead us astray.

There are many outrageous teachers and leaders in the Signs and Wonders Movement, but one is most worthy of study and critique. There is one man who seems to embody what many in the movement believe. Beliefs that we can be taught to transport our bodies and minds to and from heaven anytime we desire. Beliefs that God has "angels of wealth" waiting at our beck and call to provide whatever we desire. Beliefs that angels will appear to us anytime we call them, serving as our spiritual guides and mentors.

Todd Bentley

While there are many Signs and Wonders teachers like Benny Hinn and Rick Joyner, Todd Bentley is among the most outrageous. Bentley was born on January 10, 1976, and raised in Gibsons, British Columbia, in Canada. According to public records, at age fifteen, he was convicted of sexually assaulting a seven-year-old boy. He struggled with alcohol and drug addictions, and at age seventeen was hospitalized after an overdose of amphetamines and hallucinogenic drugs. At age eighteen, he claims he committed his life to Jesus Christ.

In 1998 the Fresh Fire Ministry group asked him to give his testimony at one of their weekly meetings and soon after he became the leader of the group, traveling worldwide on religious crusades. In 2008 Bentley was invited by Stephen Strader, pastor of Ignited Church in Lakeland, Florida, to lead a weeklong revival. An event of powerful light flashes with rock music and colorful light shows attracted up to ten thousand people each night and became a media phenomenon. Bentley's ministry was unique indeed, as he often physically abused attendees by kicking and punching and knocking them over, claiming God told him to do it. At these events Bentley would pray for miraculous healings from God and then claimed miraculous healings did occur, but to my knowledge none have been confirmed independently.

Bentley announced a legal separation from his wife in 2008 due to an "unhealthy relationship" with a female member of his staff, and stepped down from active ministry for a short period of time. He initially submitted to restoration at the hands of church leaders, but in November 2008 the restoration oversight team at Fresh Fire announced he was no longer submitting to the process. Three short months later Bentley married the object of the unhealthy relationship, staff member Jessa Hasbrook. He agreed to come under the restorative hand of Rick Joyner, a key figure in the Signs and Wonders and New Apostolic Reformation movements. After only a few short months, Joyner claimed Bentley had been restored, so he resumed leading a ministry.

We all make mistakes and God can forgive and restore anyone. But many Christians feel Bentley's apologies were shallow at best, and that Joyner's decision to restore him was premature to say the least. Let's look at some of Bentley's "experiences" and teachings, holding them up against Scripture to discern if this is a movement of the Holy Spirit or of a different source.

Bentley's events try to call down angels from heaven – angels that he thinks carry very specific blessings to those who seek them in the supernatural realm.

> "So when I need a financial breakthrough I don't just pray and ask God for my financial breakthrough. I go into intercession and become a partner with the angels by petitioning the Father of the angels that are assigned to getting me

money: 'Father, give me the angels in heaven right now that are assigned to get me money and wealth'" (from a 2003 article titled "Angelic Hosts").

"In my ministry, I teach my disciples, 'Power first, then the Word. Go in and prophesy first, or demonstrate the power of God first in some way'" (from *The Reality of the Supernatural World* by Todd Bentley).

"We can preach the Gospel all day long, but that won't win souls. That won't win the hearts of the people" (from *Kingdom Rising: Making the Kingdom Real in Your Life* by Todd Bentley).

Bentley alleges that angels give him advice about all sorts of things, from finances to healing. An angel named "Healing Revival" worked with Bentley in many past healings. "When He comes," said Bentley, "I get ...the ability to diagnose people's sicknesses with my left hand. I get very accurate details from God. ...And whenever this angel shows up the miracles go off the charts."

Bentley claims that six angels operated on him during one of his heavenly visits. He saw "a pillar of fire" rise through the roof of a church and when "God" told him to "get into the pillar," he did and landed on an operating table in heaven. Six angels tied him down and began surgery. "They pick this thing up ...and they stuck it in me right here on my neck and it didn't hurt ...everything inside of me popped out onto the table, my heart, my liver – like everything. ...The angels start taking these white boxes ...and they start stuffing these things inside of me."

More quotes from Todd Bentley:

In the middle of the service ...in walks Emma. ...She floated a couple of inches off the floor ...emitting brilliant light and colors. Emma carried these bags and began pulling gold out of them. Then, as she walked up and down the aisles of the church, she began putting gold dust on people. "God, what is happening?" I asked. The Lord answered: "She is releasing the gold, which is both the revelation and the financial breakthrough that I am bringing into this church."

I went into a trance-like state and I saw ...the angel of finance ...In that trance I experienced one of heaven's realities and then that experience became a reality here on earth ...I found myself in a treasure room in heaven. The only item in this room was gold coins, and I began stuffing those coins into my pockets until they were falling out.

Bentley held up a letter at one of his events claiming proof of a thirteenth resurrection from the dead because of his ministry, but when pressed to release names or proof he came up empty then, and again time after time.

At another event Bentley called his first wife and three children up on the stage with him. He said his family was "prophetic proof" that God was ready to heal families and marriages. While this event was taking place, Bentley was involved in an affair with one of his employees and shortly thereafter he and his wife got divorced. Some "prophetic proof" – dragging your children on stage and leading them into a future of shame and humiliation. And by the way, when he asked his wife to speak, she couldn't because she was "drunk in the spirit"; her eyes were glazed and she had to be held up by leaders on stage.

Bentley tells stories of remarkable healings. In fact, he claims that in his ministry thirty people have now been raised from the dead. Are these stories credible? Bentley claims that one man had been dead for forty-eight hours and was in a coffin. When the family gathered at the funeral home, the man knocked from inside the coffin to be let out. If any of these resurrections were true, every media outlet in the country would be reporting it. But to date, I have not seen one firsthand testimony.

At a revival in North Dakota, Bentley reports this event: "In the middle of the service I was in conversation with Ivan and another person when in walks Emma. As I stared at the angel with open eyes, the Lord said, 'Here's Emma.' I'm not kidding." Since the uproar over "Emma," Bentley has denied any knowledge or revelation of Emma.

Todd Bentley claims to have been taken to heaven by God and the angels several times, putting him in lofty company with the apostles Paul and John. On his website he claims he can teach people how to spiritually transport themselves from one dimension to another.

In Acts 8, the Bible tells a remarkable story of Philip baptizing the eunuch. Philip lowered the eunuch into the water and then disappeared, reappearing at Azotus. This seems to be a case of spiritual transportation, but if it was, it was an act of God, not something you can train people to do on their own.

> *The coming of the lawless one will be in accordance with how Satan works. He will use all sorts of displays of power through signs and wonders that serve the lie, and all the ways that wickedness deceives those who are perishing. They perish because they refused to love the truth and so be saved. For this reason God sends them a powerful delusion so that they will believe the lie and so that all will be condemned who have not believed the truth but have delighted in wickedness.* (2 Thessalonians 2:9-12)

Compare the fruit and teachings of Todd Bentley with the Word of God. Look at the fruit he bears: lying about Emma after being confronted; parading his children on stage, claiming they are prophetic proof of God healing marriages and families while he is having an affair, and later divorcing his wife; claiming dozens of miraculous resurrections from the dead without a single testimony from any of the "risen" ones; and claiming the gospel will not win any souls. Is this the fruit of a disciple of Jesus Christ?

Bentley is one of the higher-profile Signs and Wonders teachers out there today. Rick Joyner and Benny Hinn are two other notables. We hear miraculous story after miraculous story, but do we see one shred of proof to back up their incredible claims?

The greatest tragedy in all this is that it will bring into doubt any genuine miracle or sign or wonder one might see these days. As we approach the end of the age, I do believe God will pour out His Spirit in miraculous ways as He chooses, but He will not be at anyone's beck and call like a genie in the lamp waiting to appear when he is called. And all the false claims by people like Todd Bentley will not only lead immature Christians astray, but they will also cast a shadow on any real move of the Holy Spirit that believers or non-believers may hear about.

Events like these are often marked by chaos and uncontrolled emotion. People are screaming at the top of their voices, walking around "drunk," barking like dogs, and clucking like chickens. Bentley often goes into a near rage, calling down angels to come minister to those in attendance. Two points on scenes like this: First, according to scriptural accounts, angels are God's messengers. God usually sent them when an important message had to be delivered, and there are no indications whatsoever that there are angels of "finance" or "healing" as Bentley and others teach. Secondly, is chaos like this biblical or is God a god of order?

> *The acts of the flesh are obvious: sexual immorality, impurity and debauchery; idolatry and witchcraft; hatred, discord, jealousy, **fits of rage**, selfish ambition, dissensions, factions and envy; **drunkenness**, orgies, and the like. I warn you, as I did before, that those who live like this will not inherit the kingdom of God.*

> *But the fruit of the Spirit is love, joy, peace, forbearance, kindness, goodness, faithfulness, gentleness and **self-control**. Against such things there is no law.* (Galatians 5:19-23, emphasis added)

Fits of rage, drunkenness, and a *lack* of self-control are often evident at events by Bentley and others in the movement, yet countless thousands still consider them moves of the Holy Spirit. In 1 Corinthians 14:32-33, Paul teaches that worship should be orderly and that *the spirits of prophets are subject to the control of prophets. For God is not a God of disorder but of peace.* Order and peace are almost always absent from events that Bentley and other Signs and Wonders teachers conduct. They are usually marked by chaos.

The Bible warns us of many false miracles, signs, and wonders in the final days, and Christians should be careful not to fall for slick words or special effects. We must not let our feelings drive facts and faith. God gave us the Bible for a reason – so we could come to know His perfect nature and character and so He could show us a pattern of His works so we might be able to discern the real from the counterfeit. The Bible clearly teaches us that God is a God of order, not chaos, and this must be a guiding thought when we assess movements like this. Is God capable of doing something new that He has never done before? Yes, as long as it is consistent with His nature. The gospel is an account of what *Jesus* did, not men. And we should be very careful not to confuse the two. God is God and we are mere mortals – or are we?

Word of Faith Movement

Faith: Hebrews 11:6 says without faith it is impossible to please God. In Matthew 13 the Bible says that when Jesus returned to His hometown He did not perform many miracles because of the people's lack of faith. The Old and New Testament teach us not to be double-minded, but to have a strong, immovable faith in God.

So let's settle one thing first: Faith is what the Christian life is all about. Christianity is all about faith in Jesus Christ as the Son of God; faith in our eternal destination because of what Jesus did on the cross; and faith that when the whole world is crumbling around us, God has us in the palm of His hand. And I believe that our level of faith is very important when we make our petitions to God, whether they are for someone else or ourselves.

But there is a huge difference in *where* that faith is placed. Just what is it that commands and holds our faith? Is our faith in God or is it in our faith? God is capable of doing anything consistent with His perfect, sinless nature. Man is capable of nothing good according to Scripture.

God is to be worshipped, but not manipulated. And while *without faith it is impossible to please God* (Hebrews 11:6), faith is not a silver bullet for anything we desire. In John 5 Jesus healed the man at the pool of Bethesda even though he showed no faith, just a whiny attitude. And every day in this world men and women of strong faith pray for their children's lives to be spared after a tragic accident; they pray for their parents to survive life-threatening cancer; they pray for financial relief to stop foreclosure of their homes; and they pray for a lost friend to come to know salvation through Jesus Christ. Sometimes God answers "yes," but sometimes the answer is "no" or "not now." God will not be manipulated. He alone decides who to heal and who not to heal, and He decides who is blessed with wealth and who will struggle financially.

But some in the Word of Faith Movement seem convinced that if we just have enough faith and proclaim it loudly enough, every desire of our heart will be fulfilled. Some are convinced that sickness or even death has no power over us if we just have enough faith. Of course they cannot explain why eventually every one of us gets sick, and I am quite certain every one of us will die unless the rapture occurs in our lifetime. But hey, why quibble over details?

Rhonda Byrne wrote a best-selling book called *The Secret*. While some Christians read and embraced the book, once you study it thoroughly through the lens of Scripture, you will see that it is clearly a promotion of New Age theology and beliefs. The message basically is when you send positive thoughts into the universe, it reciprocates by sending positive things your way. So health, wealth, and prosperity are the results of positive thoughts, or "good vibrations."

Byrne lists her success formula in three easy steps:

- First, you must be clear about what exactly you want and then you need to make a command to the universe.

- Second, you must believe that you have received. You must know that what you want is yours the moment you ask for it. You must have complete and utter faith.

- Third, to receive what you believe, "You have to feel it!"

If life were only that simple and easy. And there is only one serious problem in Byrne's beliefs: They are completely contradictory to the Bible, even though Byrne has referred to herself as a "Christian." Well, if it is so simple and consistent with biblical teachings, why wasn't Paul, who had tremendous faith, rich and healthy? Why did he have to make tents to support his travels in spreading the gospel throughout Asia?

Rhonda Byrne is promoted and supported by Oprah Winfrey, and that should be a shock to no one. She is obviously a New Age proponent who believes God can be manipulated for our own personal gain. But just how closely are the teachings and beliefs of Rhonda Byrne lining up with Christian Word of Faith leaders?

Kenneth Hagin

Kenneth Hagin, considered the "Father of the Word of Faith Movement," seemed to tap into this mystic teaching long before Byrne discovered it. In his book titled *How to Write Your Own Ticket with God*, Hagin says that Jesus appeared to him personally and gave him the formula for faith. Hagin writes that Jesus told him, "If anybody, anywhere will take these four steps or put these four principles into operation, he will always receive whatever he wants from Me, or from God the Father. Say it, Do it, Receive it, and Tell it so others may believe."

Now even if you can get beyond the title of the book, there is another serious problem whenever people claim that Jesus appeared to them: *"So if anyone tells you, 'There he is, out in the wilderness,' do not go out; or, 'Here he is, in the inner rooms,' do not believe it. For as lightening that comes from the east is visible even in the west, so will be the coming of the Son of Man"* (Matthew 24:26-27). When Jesus appears again, it will not be just to Kenneth Hagin or Todd Bentley; everyone will witness His return in glory.

Another quote from Kenneth Hagin should curl your hair: "Man was created on terms of equality with God, and he could stand in God's presence without any consciousness of inferiority." Scripture tells us over and over again that God is far superior to man. Do Hagin and those who follow him violate the first commandment by claiming man is not inferior to God? Is this not worshipping ourselves as equal to God?

Hagin tells a bizarre story about a time when Jesus again appeared to him and they were deep in conversation. Hagin claims that suddenly a "demon monkey" jumped between them and began to shout down Jesus yelling, "Yackety, yack, yack, yack!" Hagin said he took control by telling the demon monkey to "shut up in the name of Jesus!" According to Hagin, Jesus told him, "If you hadn't done something about that, I couldn't have."

Are you kidding me? Jesus who cast out demons while He walked the earth was powerless to shut up a demon monkey, but Kenneth Hagin could with his words? Don't be too surprised because, as we will see later, Kenneth Copeland, a Hagin disciple, also believes Jesus is not very powerful.

Hagin wasn't the first Word of Faith teacher but he was arguably the most influential, as he spawned many disciples who are all over Christian television these days. We will touch on a few.

Kenneth Copeland

Ken and Gloria Copeland are on several Christian television networks including TBN and The Word Network. They are successful and quite wealthy. Reports say their personal mansion is worth several millions of dollars and they have a private fleet of jets to travel around the world. Are they building their wealth by their tremendous faith or on the backs of gullible followers?

> "I was shocked when I found out who the biggest failure in the Bible actually is…The biggest one is God…I mean He lost his top-ranking, most anointed angel; the first man He ever created; the first woman He ever created; the whole earth and all the fullness therein; a third of the angels, at least – that's a big loss, man…Now, the reason you don't think of God as a failure is He never said He's a failure. And you're not a failure till you say you're one."

I can hear it now – "You're misunderstanding Copeland and taking him out of context!" Even if we were to concede that point, the arrogance, even in jest, of calling God a loser is disrespectful at best and disgusting and vile at worst. It gets worse, much worse.

Copeland taught that Adam in the garden of Eden was God manifested in the flesh. This is exactly what the early Mormon church taught, that "Adam is our Father and our God." Also, according to Copeland, Satan conquered Jesus on the cross and Jesus descended into hell after His death and before His resurrection as an "emaciated, poured out, little wormy spirit" and wrestled the keys to heaven away from Satan. The Bible tells us Jesus' last words before His death on the cross were *"It is finished,"* meaning the sacrifice was complete. A rudimentary study of the original Greek words used in the New Testament along with reading and studying corresponding Scriptures clearly dispel this false teaching. The Greek words *sheol* and *hades* refer to the resting place of the dead, not the permanent place of hell where Satan resides.

Just before Jesus died on the cross He said, *"Father, into your hands I commit my spirit"* (Luke 23:46). It was finished and the battle against Satan was won. But not according to Copeland. First, Jesus had to go to hell as an "emaciated, poured out, little wormy spirit" to continue the battle against Satan. Is Copeland teaching a false gospel of salvation, denying the power of the cross?

Copeland also seems to be in tune with New Age theology when he says, "Any image that you get down on the inside of you that is so vivid when you close your eyes you see it, it'll come to pass."

Benny Hinn

> "When you were born again the Word was made flesh in you. And you became flesh of His flesh and bone of His bone. Don't tell me you have Jesus. You ARE everything He was and everything He is and ever shall be." (Benny Hinn)

There it is, folks. You are not being transformed into the *image* of Jesus –you *are* Jesus. What more needs to be said about Benny Hinn? Sadly, much more.

Hinn has made outlandish statements which he claims were revealed to him when Jesus personally visited him. For one, according to Benny Hinn, women were originally designed to give birth out of their sides.

Hinn predicted that instead of people burying their dead relatives and friends, they would one day sit them in a chair as they watched TBN for twenty-four hours and be resurrected. I'm sure Paul and Jan Crouch of TBN would love that, as they promote the same foolish thoughts frequently on air.

Hinn told his followers that Jesus would personally appear at one of his events in 2000. It didn't happen.

He also frequently visited the grave sites of mystics like Kathryn Kuhlman so he could "get the anointing from her bones." Deuteronomy 18:10-11 explicitly forbids God's people from necromancy, calling forth the spirits of the dead, and in verse 12 God states that *Anyone who does these things is detestable to the LORD.*

Benny Hinn is so outrageous and ridiculous you wonder how anyone can take him seriously. But millions do, watching him on television, continuing to line his pockets. P. T. Barnum was certainly right about a sucker being born every minute. But Hinn is not the only televangelist preaching the "name it, claim it" absurdity.

The list of participants in the Word of Faith Movement include Creflo Dollar, Marilyn Hickey, T. D. Jakes, Paul Crouch of TBN, Joel Osteen, Rod Parsley, Frederick Price, and Mike Murdock, who for $129 will send you your own personal prayer cloth to deliver money to you whenever you need it by praying over it.

One last example of how these teachers of health, wealth, and prosperity diminish God and elevate man: Jesse Duplantis, the lovable, jovial Ragin' Cajun. Duplantis must think God is really stupid. He teaches that when God created the animals He didn't know what they were, so He brought them to Adam. Adam then named them and spoke life into them. I suppose after that, Adam had to tell God who God was.

Many of these teachers do share some solid teachings from time to time, but they all share in the spreading of the prosperity gospel as our ticket to health, wealth, and prosperity. A common belief among them is that all that is needed for anything you want is enough faith. Arguably, the apostle Paul had more faith than any man who ever lived, and his faith in Jesus Christ was unshakable no matter what circumstances he faced. Perhaps if Paul had access to the teachings of these televangelists he might have escaped a life of poverty and that thorn in his side would have been removed, even though God told him He would not remove it. To many Word of Faith teachers, our faith can even override the will and final decision of God.

This, plain and simple, is an insult to God to teach that our will and faith can create things and override His perfect will for our lives, all for our own gain. This is putting ourselves on equal footing with God, or even worse, elevating us over God. Well, so much for the first commandment.

There is nothing wrong with asking God to provide us with physical health or financial blessings, and in fact scripture clearly condemns a lack of faith, but when these desires become an obsessive part of being a Christian and our motives is for our own gain and pleasure, something is wrong. Jesus never once told us to pursue treasure on earth. In fact,

He taught us it is futile. Instead, He taught us to store up treasures in heaven where moths or thieves could not take them from us.

Most of these televangelists live in multi-million-dollar homes, surrounded by luxury. Many of them own several private jets and stay in luxurious hotels as they travel. They are accumulating tremendous wealth on the backs of deceived poor and middle-class Christians who want to tap into the power of the prosperity gospel. You may disagree, but I think this is nothing short of stealing.

Whether it's the Signs and Wonders Movement or the Word of Faith Movement, we must recognize that many sincere Christians follow these men. These sincere Christians are genuine, loving people and born-again believers who will be joining us in heaven. They are not necessarily the problem; they are being deceived by teachers who are abusing Scripture for personal gain.

It is one thing to overexaggerate how our faith can manipulate God for our personal benefit, as if that isn't bad enough. But when these leaders claim personal visits from Jesus, and that Jesus had to go to hell to complete His victory over Satan, or that God cannot accomplish what He desires without our help, that is crossing the line. These claims clearly conflict with the Bible and define God as less than holy, perfect, and all powerful. Many are falling into this trap, and if they do not wake up and see the deception at hand, they are in for a big fall, either in this life or in eternity.

Religious Syncretism

I realize that since the book of Acts was written, every generation probably thought they would witness the return of Jesus. But when the Jews were returned to their land by God in 1948, the stage was set for the return of our Lord. It could happen this year or two hundred years from now, but it is a real possibility, perhaps a probability, that some of us will be around for the end of the age.

The Bible warns us of the Antichrist rising to power in the end times, accompanied by the false prophet, but world domination cannot occur without religious capitulation. The false prophet will thus succeed in leading the final great deception, somehow bringing all faiths into harmony. This seems implausible given the diverse beliefs of hundreds of religions, but it is not as difficult as one might think, as the early seeds are already beginning to sprout. So who are the participants, whether willful or ignorant, in this "end-of-the-age drama"?

The Bible speaks of a great falling away from the faith among Christians as the end of the age approaches. Second Thessalonians warns of God sending a powerful delusion to those who do not trust in the absolute truth of God's Word, and I believe we are experiencing that falling away and God's powerful delusion right now. When you look at the perversion of Christianity being taught by many of our influential teachers and leaders, and the number of pastors and Christians who are blindly following them, it seems obvious to me that many are under a great delusion.

The false prophet spoken of in Revelation will then unite world religions while Antichrist starts to gather political, economic, and military power. There is little doubt the United Nations will play a pivotal role as it has grown to where it has infiltrated every nation to some extent. Many of the social justice programs Christians fall for, including Rick Warren's PEACE Plan, work directly with the United Nations. The United Nations is an organization bent on world domination and intent on promoting secular humanism.

Many of the world's religions are comparatively small and have little influence beyond their small group of members. Some larger religions like Mormonism are based on New Age and universalism principles already, so they will be easy prey. Buddhism and Hinduism are more philosophical than religious and fit well into the growing New Age culture.

Only Christianity, Judaism, and Islam stand as strong, influential monotheistic religions. Sadly, most Jews are more cultural Jews than religious Jews, and even the religious ones deny Jesus as Messiah. They might well fall for a false god who shows miracles, signs, and wonders. So Islam and Christianity probably stand as the greatest obstacles to a world united on religion.

Allow me to speculate a little. Islam may be damaged severely by a nuclear war in the Middle East, perhaps the battle prophesied in Ezekiel

38. With Iran obtaining nuclear weapons and vowing to use them on Israel, war could break out there any day. This war, which might include nuclear weapons, could decimate the nations that are strongholds for Islam. We know that while Israel will certainly suffer heavy losses in that war, God will ultimately protect a remnant. If this speculative scenario occurs, Islam will be largely neutralized as a major religion.

Regardless of whether Islam will be severely damaged or not, the Chrislam Movement is making serious inroads to bridging a gap between deceptive Muslim leaders and naive Christian leaders like Hybels, McLaren, Wallis, and Warren. When watchmen like Elijah Abraham, Gary Kah, and yours truly sound a warning about Chrislam, we are largely ignored or dismissed as hateful. So be it.

If Muslim leaders can continue to deceive naive Christian leaders, these two religions might come to look very similar in the eyes of deceived or careless Christians, especially as biblical illiteracy continues to become a greater epidemic. We can blame Islam, world leaders, or anyone we want for this coming apostasy, but it is we Christians who will be held accountable by God when literally all hell breaks loose on earth. We have the Bible and the Holy Spirit to teach and guide us, but we are choosing to ignore them at an increasingly alarming rate.

The movement of Chrislam is leading naive Christians into religious syncretism with Islam, a religion of antichrist. The social justice movement led by people like Jim Wallis and Rick Warren preach the need for interfaith cooperation on issues of poverty and environmental issues. Evangelism takes a back seat to trying to solve the problems of human depravity by using human efforts and plans. Rarely if ever will you hear of these leaders calling out another religion as false. Syncretism for the sake of human efforts is replacing the sharing of the gospel with the lost.

The emergent church movement is building bridges between Christianity and Islam, secular humanists, Hinduism, Buddhism, and universalism religions. Nothing, including the Word of God, is sacred to these people.

The Catholic Church and the pope are always the usual suspects when it comes to ecumenism and social justice secularism, and no doubt the Catholic Church will play a huge role in the global spiritualization movement. In recent years the Vatican has made several overtures and statements that show a proclivity to embrace Islam as a true religion that worships the God of Christianity. But every denomination of Christianity is starting to embrace this apostasy. In fact, the official Roman Catholic catechism states this:

> **841: The Church's relationship with the Muslims.** "The plan of salvation also includes those who acknowledge the Creator, in the first place amongst whom are the Muslims; these profess to hold the faith of Abraham, and together with us they adore the one, merciful God, mankind's judge on the last day."

Yes, Catholicism teaches that Christians and Muslims worship the same God! The Vatican will be a player. Rick Warren is a player. And the growing social justice and emergent church movements are also players. Are these the players in the final act or just part of the warm-up before the big performance? Time will tell, but I think we are rapidly running out of time.

The clock is ticking. The game is winding down. It is what athletes call "crunch time"; the time when the cream is supposed to rise to the top. We know who wins the war. We think we are on His side, but with wicked and deceitful human hearts are we fooling ourselves? Could we really be pawns of the Enemy instead of warriors for God? This is a question worthy of prayer and internal assessment.

Chapter 10

Redefining God in Our Own Image

W e discussed earlier that inept leadership, combined with followers who care more about what they want instead of the truth,
are a toxic combination. It creates a vicious cycle with self-centered followers breeding weak leadership, breeding more self-centered followers.
Our growing love of money, comfort, and individualized morality has
led us to the edge of spiritual death.

In the last chapter we took a hard look at some Christian leaders and
explored their beliefs, methods, and motives. I realize what we covered
was tough, but I feel a tough critique of Christian leadership is necessary
in the midst of a growing adultery between American Christianity and
secular culture and humanism. If leaders are not willing to be open,
transparent, and accountable, they are unfit to lead. But we must also
be open to a tough, honest critique of our own hearts as people who follow these leaders. These leaders only represent the values and character
that we desire in our leaders. If they didn't, we would not be following
and elevating them.

The qualities we most want in our leadership these days seem to
be cultural trendiness, charisma, and an ability to avoid taking tough
stances. While leadership is crucial to any organization, we as rank-
and-file Christians are every bit as responsible as our leaders for this
slow march toward spiritual death. As Christians who have received
the Holy Spirit, we will not be able to blame leadership when we stand

before a holy God one day when every thought, word, and action will be judged.

Unless every Christian – leader and follower – allows God to reveal the deception in our hearts, it may be only a matter of time before God completely removes His hand of protection over the American church. Our hearts have grown cold to God's truth and unchanging nature as we slowly attempt to modify God to fit into our desired perception of Him.

The dangerous beliefs, selfish attitudes, and spiritual apathy that have infiltrated our hearts and minds are slowly killing us spiritually. We look at the world and feel sorrow or disgust over its beliefs and behaviors, but ours seem to be only marginally better at times. The behavior of the world is not surprising, since its people have not received the Holy Spirit, but we have the Spirit of the Lord and have been charged with being salt and light to this world. We are failing as a whole.

We are attempting to mold God into our desired image of Him, instead of allowing the Holy Spirit to mold us into the image of Jesus. This is, simply put, idolatry, worshipping a false God – ourselves! I submit for your consideration that this is no better than the Muslim or Hindu who worships a false god; in fact, it might be worse. We have the Word of God and the Holy Spirit in us and we should know better. This abominable action is at the root of every problem we face as Christians, individually and as a body. We are continually violating the first and second commandments of God, and as a result, our own efforts to obey the remaining commandments are futile. It's not that we are building and worshipping a physical golden calf like the Israelites did in Exodus, but in our minds and hearts we are doing something every bit as wrong and dangerous. We are picking and choosing the characteristics of God we like, and dismissing those parts of His stated character and nature that we want no part of. That simply will not suffice. We either acknowledge the complete character and nature of God and worship Him, or we worship a type of false god more to our liking.

Let's look at the subtle ways we attempt to recreate God more to our liking. As we explore, we need to be reflective, looking in the mirror. Every one of us is guilty of refashioning God to our desired image to some extent. You and I are part of the problem; it's not just "the rest of those Christians." As we discuss these topics, be in prayer, asking God to reveal what He sees in your heart, as David did: *Search me, God, and know my heart; test me and know my anxious thoughts. See if there is any offensive way in me, and lead me in the way everlasting* (Psalm 139:23-24).

"I Believe in Jesus"

We are taught as Christians that spiritual death is avoided when we believe in Jesus. I want to challenge that belief for a moment. *What* we believe about Jesus and *who* we believe Him to be is the crucial issue, not just that we believe in a shallow, indiscriminate way.

In the book of James the author challenges shallow believers. James 2:19 states: *You believe that there is one God. Good! Even the demons believe that—and shudder.* James refers to God as *one*, a tribute of faith to the mystery of a triune God: Father, Son, and Holy Spirit. One God manifested in three different persons is a difficult concept for humans, but we simply, by faith, choose to believe it.

James says the demons also believe, so are they saved? No, because while they believe God exists, they do not believe in Him as perfect love and justice, ruler of all created things. They do not accept His perfect nature and character as final authority over the entire universe and lord over their being.

Today too many Christians "believe" in a Jesus they do not understand, or they believe in a Jesus they are attempting to mold into their image and likeness. A "Buddy Jesus" who is their best friend but not their Lord and King. A Jesus who would never judge or condemn anyone. A Jesus who accepts you just as you are, a filthy sinner deserving of eternal death, with no requirement to turn away from your sinful nature and desires. *This is not Jesus.* It is a poor human substitute and an act of arrogance. To think we can worship God as we think He should be worshipped in lieu of worshipping God for who He is, is the height of arrogance and rebellion.

This false god is the god of this world. He is a god who serves us and conforms to our desires, and a god whom we judge instead of him judging us. We are worshipping the created instead of the Creator, an image of God we create out of convenience or greed because of our pride, self-righteousness, and extreme hubris. Will this lead us to eternal death? Perhaps, because God will not be mocked or minimized.

There is only one true God and our attempts to modify or change Him will not work. He is the same yesterday, today, and tomorrow, and no attempt to tweak Him for our convenience will work. We will all fall short of knowing His perfect holiness until we stand before Him in His glory, but if we attempt to modify His character and nature or substitute our own beliefs to create a god we prefer to worship, are we risking our eternal fate?

God Is a "God of Love"

There can be no doubt that God is perfect love. As Paul said in the famous "love chapter" of 1 Corinthians 13, love is patient, kind, not easily angered, and keeps no record of wrongs. These are certainly some of the characteristics of the perfect God we worship. But are we forgetting that in addition to being perfect love God is also perfectly just? Human beings have difficulty accepting things we do not completely understand. We may say we accept certain concepts, but deep down we continue to struggle with them. God is perfect in every way and His perfect nature means He cannot tolerate sin. Scripture is very clear that unrepentant sin is an abomination to God and that people who choose a life of unrepentant sin will face the most severe consequences: eternal separation from God. The fact that God is perfect love and perfectly just can cause confusion in the minds and hearts of people because as humans we cannot understand *either* concept.

Our love is flawed, imperfect, and often self-serving. We often perform acts of kindness for those we know or love in hopes that somehow we also may benefit. And when we love someone we usually hope we will be loved reciprocally. This makes many of the ways we express love conditional, as we hope to receive something in return. If over time our love does not bring us rewards, our love usually fades or disappears altogether.

Similarly, our idea of justice is often flawed, usually affected by our personal opinions and values. We have two issues within us that prevent us from understanding that God is perfect justice along with perfect love. The first is that as humans, we want to escape real justice so we are free to behave as we desire without consequences. Secondly, we do not understand the concept of perfect justice, since we will always judge others more harshly than we judge ourselves. So selfishness and ignorance combine to prevent us from understanding how God can be perfect justice.

You see an example of this when you attend a sporting event of a team you follow. The referee is in charge of making calls on fouls and handing out just penalties for infractions. Yet on almost every call made that is not clear-cut, both sets of fans see the call differently. If a close call goes against our team, our human reaction is to think the official either missed the call or he has an agenda to cheat the team we follow. When a close call favors our team, the opponents' fans react in the same way. So fans generally act out of ignorance of the rules, or their view of justice is tainted by their own personal desires. As a high school official for twenty years, I have seen this scenario played out hundreds of times.

A growing number of Christians seem to believe God is not a just God. They may believe God is perfect love, but they erroneously believe that His perfect love precludes Him from being just. This is clearly refuted by the Bible, but because our view of justice is ignorant or perverted by our personal desires, too many cannot accept that God is perfectly just and that His justice demands that He judge evil. This should cause us to ask a serious question: Would we want our eternal fate decided by a God who is not just? How could we have any eternal assurance if we were to be randomly judged by a God who is imperfect in how he dispenses reward or punishment?

God has clearly shown us how we can be assured of eternal life: Commit our life to Jesus Christ as our Savior *and* Lord. This and this alone overturns our guilt as sinners, allowing God to welcome us into His kingdom as His children. But when we share a gospel with the lost that is void of God demanding justice, are we leading the lost astray? And if we worship a God we believe does not demand justice, are we worshipping a false god of our own making? God will not tolerate any man's attempts to change His perfect nature, and that nature consists of perfect love and perfect justice. You can't have one without the other.

Obeying God? or Loving God?

True love fosters obedience, but obedience does not necessarily foster true love.

When I was a child, my father always assigned my brother and me the duty of cleaning the basement. At first, we approached our assignment enthusiastically to show our love and dedication to him along with showing him we could live up to his expectations. But no matter how meticulously we would clean, dad would always find some fault. We could never clean it to his standards, even though we spent hours cleaning while instead we could have been playing baseball or football.

So after about a year of busting our humps and missing a lot of time with our friends, we decided to go into "obedience mode." We would spend only a few minutes working on the basement, doing a poor job, so we could spend more time playing. Hey, we figured dad wouldn't be satisfied either way so we might as well have more playtime.

What we failed to realize was that dad had our best interests in mind when he pointed out ways we could clean the basement better. He was trying to build a strong work ethic in us, preparing us for life as adults. Now he certainly could have handled it better, encouraging while he challenged us to become excellent workers. But nevertheless, his intentions were good.

It is important that we look into our hearts and check to see if our relationship with God is obedience-based or truly love-based, and here is why: in our human nature we are rebellious and we always seek to serve ourselves over anyone else. Obedience does not come naturally to fallen man and even when we do obey, it is usually self-motivated. We obey in hopes of being rewarded.

Obedience also becomes conditional at times. If we do not see a sufficient reward for our obedience, resentment builds up. If we obey our employer but begin to believe there is little chance for the reward we think we deserve (better pay, a promotion, or recognition), we begin to rebel. We start giving less than our best effort because we see no incentive to work as hard as we did when we saw the possibility of greater reward.

This is what ultimately leads to the failure of every communist nation. Workers are told where they will work and what the state will pay them. There is little or no chance for greater reward, so workers become unproductive since they have nothing to gain from dedicated, obedient behavior. This is the attitude my brother and I developed with my father. We approached our relationship with our father from obedience, not love. As long as we did a decent job there would be no punishment, so why expend any more effort than necessary? These are the results of obedience-based relationships. We do what we have to do to avoid negative consequences, but we never fully commit to the job at hand.

Is this obedience mode infecting us as Christians? Our reward of heaven is secure by the blood of Jesus, so what further incentive is there for good behavior? Our works do not save us and neither does our strict obedience to the law, so why obey? This is what living in obedience mode does to us. If we cannot see a reward for our obedience, we tend to discount its importance.

When we get beyond obedience mode and enter love mode, everything changes. We no longer obey out of obligation or with selfish motives; rather, we obey out of perfect love. Our love for God propels us to new heights of obedience because we have no selfish human motive. We obey because we truly and deeply love God and want above all to express that deep love. While I have by no means made the complete transition from obedience to love, I find that when I am in love mode, obedience is much easier. I obey God because I deeply love Him and do not want to disappoint Him.

When Christian men, ordained by God as the leaders of our families, foster a culture of obedience instead of love in our homes, our wives and children act in similar manners. Their motivation is avoiding bad consequences or maybe even abuse. But husbands and fathers who lead from love and foster a culture of love usually receive love and find the obedience of their wives and children naturally occur out of that love.

As Scripture tells us, perfect love (not perfect obedience) casts out all fear, freeing us from guilt, shame, and our self-made prisons. Obedience can tend to be fear-based, keeping us trapped in a perpetual state of ups and downs. Obedience mode leads us to look at things selfishly, believing that if we obey we will be rewarded. But perfect love seeks no reward and gives of itself willingly and completely. When we enter into a state of perfect love of God we free ourselves from the desires of our flesh. And the eternal beauty is that the selfless love we carry out *is* rewarded for eternity by God!

As humans, we are incapable of obeying 100 percent of the time. Our self-serving human nature will prevail at times, even in the best of us. God knows this. As our High Priest and the sacrifice for our sins, Jesus knew every temptation we would ever face, yet He is perfect and we are flawed. God knows that too.

Paul eloquently expressed this in Romans 7, one of the most beautiful and telling writings in the Bible. Paul knew we are incapable of perfectly obeying God. That is why Jesus took on human form and became the perfect, necessary sacrifice to fulfill the justice of a perfect God.

When our relationship with God is based on obedience instead of a burning, passionate love, it cannot work the way God wants it to work. Since we cannot perfectly obey God, we will continually fail Him. God knows this and sent Jesus so that perfect obedience to the law would no longer be the requirement for eternal life with Him. While God no longer requires perfect obedience, He asks for perfect love. He has removed the penalty of eternal death as a payment for disobedience. Since He has done this, we no longer *have to* obey Him, but as His children we should want to.

While we are no longer under the penalty of a law we cannot live up to, nonetheless our perfect love of God should inspire us to obey His laws. Our love should propel us to a new level of obedience we were incapable of attaining when we worshipped God out of a mindset only of obedience. In turn, worshipping God out of love rather than out of obligation will propel us to greater intimacy with Him and bring us to a higher level of living in His Spirit.

We must change the focus of our relationship with God from one of obedience to one of total love. Obedience does not perpetuate love, but love does perpetuate obedience. When we can change our approach to God from obedience-based to one of total love, everything changes. The human desire to sin becomes overwhelmed by our desire to avoid sin because we love God. We are no longer fear-based, obeying to avoid punishment or negative consequences. Our total love of God leads to a more perfect obedience of Him.

To Know Him Is to Love Him

Remember the first time you fell in love? Not just a youthful infatuation, but a deep, burning love. You wanted to spend every waking moment with your new love, learn everything about him or her, and hang onto every word they spoke. The more you learned, the more you loved about them.

Almost every one of us has experienced this euphoric state. There is nothing quite like falling in love. The only thing better is *staying* in love, but too often that burning love fades and dies. Many a relationship fizzles as we begin to see that there is more to the person than we first realized.

We are exposed to the other side of that person, a darker side, starting with character traits that we didn't notice early on. Maybe we were just blinded by our early feelings, but often it is the result of the other person putting on a front, hiding characteristics and behaviors they thought would turn us off. We begin to see anger or selfish attitudes that we did not see early on, and these behaviors become annoying as our illusion of a perfect mate is destroyed.

Resentment sets in and perhaps we feel like we were victims of a "bait and switch." We feel we were deceived, thinking we were getting the perfect mate when in reality we got a flawed human, and our love fades with our perfect, unmet expectations.

The best marriages are those where God is at the center of everything, but also where both parties know each other, flaws and all, before they commit to marriage. When we are honest about our character, nature, and behaviors before a commitment, the chances of a successful marriage increase dramatically. No one wants to feel they have been a victim of a bait and switch.

One of the reasons Nancy and I have such a strong marriage is we know and admit our own flaws and accept the flaws in each other. She knows I usually do not wipe off the cupboard or stove after I cook dinner. When I do, she is pleasantly surprised but has no illusion that this will become habitual. Nancy is a pack rat and throws nothing away. This used to irritate the snot out of me until I realized this was so trivial compared to the wonderful characteristics she displays every day as my wife and friend. We have learned to accept each other, flaws and all, and even find humor in them. We constantly joke that we are a perfect match because no one else would want either one of us.

We knew these things about one another going into our marriage. There was no bait and switch involved that would lead to disillusion or resentment. But is American Christianity offering a bait-and-switch presentation to the lost about the character and nature of the God that we profess to lead them to?

How did you first come to know God? How was He presented to you? Did you respond to a weak altar call where Jesus was presented as a friend or a solution to every problem you faced at the time? Was He presented as a fire-breathing God waiting to consume you the moment you stepped out of line?

Christians who are raised early on to have an unhealthy fear of God – a fear that He is just waiting to punish us every time we mess up – often lead lives where they can never really learn to love God because they do not understand His perfect nature and character. They may never understand the depth of His love and His willingness to forgive when we repent of our sin. They remain in a perpetual state of defeat.

But Christians who respond to a Jesus presented as a ticket to earthly happiness with no responsibilities or trials are being set up for disappointment as problems continue and sometimes mount when they become Christians. When they are led to believe that Jesus accepts them just the way they are with no expectation of transformation, they become frustrated as the Holy Spirit begins to confront and convict them of lingering sin. When they are led to a Jesus who is more like their butler than their Lord, they grow disappointed and bitter as their financial problems linger or other problems in their lives do not instantly vanish.

Both of these sets of believers often go through life without really knowing the God they claim to love, and that is such a tragedy. The "fire and brimstone" Christians never experience the perfect love and mercy of God; the "feel good" Christians never experience the beauty of a God who draws you nearer to Him through discipline, suffering, and the convicting power of His Spirit. Is American Christianity participating in a tragic bait-and-switch trick on new Christians? We must present the complete character and nature of God to those who are seeking Him. They must understand just who they are worshipping and what they can expect. They can expect to come to know the God who loves us unconditionally in spite of our flaws, the God who is always willing to forgive when we ask forgiveness, and the God who will never forsake or abandon us.

But we must also present the God who insists on spiritual transformation and rebirth; the God who will not tolerate habitual sin in our lives and who allows consequences for that sin; the God who is not a butler, but rather our Lord and King; and the God who loves us too much to allow us to continue to flirt with the Enemy at the risk of eternal damnation. This is the God we must fully disclose to seeking people. Any other God is a misrepresentation that will lead people to disillusionment and frustration, stunting or even threatening their growth as true disciples of Jesus Christ. They must understand that God demands real change and He gives us His Spirit to facilitate that change. Is this the God new seekers hear of these days? Or do they hear about a God who is more of an addition to their lives to "complete" their happiness?

God never lies, as it is impossible, given His perfect nature. When He calls us to faith in Jesus and to a life as His disciples, there is no bait and switch going on. He is totally honest about His nature, character, and behavior, and His Word clearly spells it out. But do we take the time to really know Him before we say "I do" to Him? Or are we like love-starved teens seeing just what we want to see, setting ourselves up for disappointment and ultimately adultery toward Him?

Our view of God as a church is really confused these days. We fail to know, understand, or accept several aspects of His nature and character. We pick and choose which of His characteristics to believe about Him and discard the rest. The result is that one day we will be disappointed, either in this life or in eternity. Many professing Christians do not truly know God these days; they merely know a God of their own choosing, molded to fit their selfish agenda, and this is killing us as a church.

God Is Tolerant – Is He Really?

We are being taught that God tolerates sin, but nothing could be further from the truth because He hates sin. God cannot stand to be in the presence of sin because it is adultery against Him. It is His bride once again being unfaithful to Him in having an affair with the world. When we sin we are cheating on God with the world, rejecting God's love and faithfulness for our short-term pleasure. But that is not how American Christianity as a whole portrays it. We are taught that we are free from the law and can live as we choose to live, so why worry?

What did Jesus free us from on the cross? God's law? Responsibility? Doing as we choose? No, He died to free us from the power of sin in our lives. Satan no longer has power over us and our sins are totally voluntary, but we choose to commit them even though we should know better. The acceptance of sin has become the trademark of American Christianity. We don't talk or preach about sin anymore because it's become all about our happiness and having our "best life now." We do not confront one another with blatant, unrepentant sin because we fear we will also be held accountable for our own sins.

The apostle Paul gave the church the model of how to react to unrepentant sinners. It is a chilling teaching that cuts to the heart about how destructive sin is to the body of Christ.

> *It is actually reported that there is sexual immorality among you, and of a kind that even pagans do not tolerate: A man is sleeping with his father's wife. And you are proud! Shouldn't you rather have gone into mourning and have put out of your fellowship the man who has been doing this? For my part, even though I am not physically present, I am with you in spirit. As one who is present with you in this way, I have already passed judgment in the name of our Lord on the one who has been doing this. So when you are assembled*

*and I am with you in spirit, and the power of our Lord Jesus
is present, hand this man over to Satan for the destruction
of the flesh, so that his spirit may be saved on the day of the
Lord.* (1 Corinthians 5:1-5)

I always wondered why I had never once heard these Scriptures taught in
church, or even discussed by a single pastor I know. I ask you to slowly
read and pray over these verses as they are problematic for American
Christianity on several fronts.

- First, note that Paul chastises the church for accepting
  this sinner, even boasting about their tolerance of him.
  Unrepentant sin is widely tolerated in many churches
  these days.

- Second, note that Paul *judged this man*. We have been
  incorrectly told over and over again that we are not to judge
  others, but this is nothing more than laziness or corrupt
  theology. God alone is qualified to judge the eternal destiny
  of men, but we are clearly directed to judge sinners within
  the body of Christ. We will discuss in what and *how* we are
  to judge others a little later.

- The third potential problem, or at least something that
  should lead us to search the Scriptures more carefully, is
  when Paul instructs the church to throw this man into the
  hands of Satan so his sinful nature might be destroyed and
  his *spirit may be saved on the day of the Lord.* This points
  out another danger of having fake Christians in the church
  who are allowed to continue in unrepentant sin. They may
  have a false sense of security, believing they are saved, only
  to find out on judgment day that they are condemned to
  eternal hell. Paul says by handing this man over to Satan
  the hope is that his flesh might be destroyed but his soul
  may be saved.

One thing this Scripture confirms to me is this: God is patient but
not tolerant of sin, and His patience might well be wearing thin with
American Christianity.

"God Doesn't Judge Us" — Says Who?

This heresy is spreading through the church, compliments of leaders like McLaren, Bell, Wallis, and others. The arrogance of claiming that God accepts all men into eternity without condition is nothing short of a slap in the face to God. It attempts to minimize or even disqualify the painful sacrifice and death of the Son of God on a cross nearly two thousand years ago. This wrong teaching is arrogant and nothing short of calling God a liar. The Old and New Testament speak clearly of the death of Jesus as the only acceptable atonement for man to become righteous with God, and that this righteousness requires real faith in Jesus Christ as the Son of God. This is the essential cornerstone of Christianity.

Scripture also teaches that God will judge all men when they stand before Him. God has judged in the past and He will judge every man in the future when the Lord returns to reclaim His faithful people and usher in an eternity of true love and peace. How anyone claiming to be a Christian can read Matthew 25 or the whole book of Revelation and come to a conclusion that God does not judge is totally beyond me. It can only be the result of biblical illiteracy or extreme arrogance.

Did He not judge Sodom and Gomorrah? What about Jericho? And as stated clearly in the New Testament, He will judge again. I have seen tricky attempts by McLaren, Bell, and others to confuse young Christians by misleading or lying about supposed errors in translation. But if you take any amount of time with a Hebrew and Greek dictionary and study Scripture, you see their arguments are flawed and deceitful.

The growing lie that God does not judge might spring from several potential motives:

- A desire to justify our own sin

- A sincere but destructive desire to appeal gently to the lost since the true gospel is a "tough sell"

- A blatant agenda to deceive Christians

None of these reasons or excuses will hold water when we stand in judgment before a perfect, holy God. Jesus taught that no one comes to the Father except through Him. He also said you cannot know the Father unless you know Him. And He said this in Matthew 7:21-23:

> *"Not everyone who says to me, 'Lord, Lord,' will enter the kingdom of heaven, but only the one who does the will of my Father who is in heaven. Many will say to me that day, 'Lord, Lord, did we not prophesy in your name and in your name drive out demons and in your name perform many miracles?' Then I will tell them plainly, 'I never knew you. Away from me, you evildoers!'"*

The Bible is full of Scriptures telling us God is a God who will judge us.

> *In the presence of God and of Christ Jesus, who will judge the living and the dead.* (2 Timothy 4:1)

> *But they will have to give account to him who is ready to judge the living and the dead.* (1 Peter 4:5)

> *Marriage should be honored by all, and the marriage bed kept pure, for God will judge the adulterer and all the sexually immoral.* (Hebrews 13:4)

In Revelation 11:18 we are told that God will destroy those who destroy the earth:

> *"The nations were angry, and your wrath has come. The time has come for judging the dead, and for rewarding your servants the prophets and your people who revere your name, both small and great—and for destroying those who destroy the earth."*

In Hebrews 9:27 we are reminded that we only get one life (no reincarnation) and after that we face judgment: *Just as people are destined to die once, and after that to face judgment.*

For our Red Letter Christian friends, what about Jesus? When did He say He would judge anyone?

> *"If your right eye causes you to stumble, gouge it out and throw it away. It is better for you to lose one part of your*

body than for your whole body to be thrown into hell."
(Matthew 5:29)

"You snakes! You brood of vipers! How will you escape being condemned to hell?" (Matthew 23:33)

"But I will show you whom you should fear: Fear him who, after your body has been killed, has authority to throw you into hell. Yes, I tell you, fear him." (Luke 12:5)

The Bible consistently tells us that a judgment is coming. In John 3:36 it says this: *Whoever believes in the Son has eternal life, but whoever rejects the Son will not see life, for God's wrath remains on them.*

This dismissal of the clear teaching that God will judge all men one day is watering down Christianity to where it looks more like Unitarianism than Christianity. It is a clear distortion of the nature and character of God and serves to place us as our own judges of what is right or wrong. In essence, we become our own god.

Brothers and sisters, we can know *of* God, but still not *know* God. Satan and the demons know of God but do not submit to Him as the final authority of all creation. American Christianity claims to know God, but is increasingly denying His clearly stated nature, character, and attributes. We can know of God, but if we try to redefine Him to fit our desires, do we really *know* Him? When we attempt to change Him to fit our wishes, how can we claim to know a God who says He never changes and is the same yesterday, today, and tomorrow? To know Him is to love Him. To attempt to change Him is to deny Him. Which will we choose to do?

The Scourge of Biblical Illiteracy

In my previous career I was responsible for hiring dozens of people, and when our team was looking for new employees we would often receive hundreds of resumes. On one Friday afternoon a couple of us were winding down the workweek and we indulged in some humor at the expense of others. We grabbed a handful of resumes from college graduates and marveled at the poor grammar, misspellings, and overall effects of what college education seemed to have taught the younger generation.

One I recall vividly. A young man, a recent college graduate, sent in his resume, and under "Professional Goal" he wrote this: "Seeking a proffessional organation where I can use my skills and education to advance within a dynamic company." Obviously this young man either didn't know about or had turned off the spell-check feature on his computer.

Our public schools, in spite of incredible federal spending, have failed America. While I meet some young people who are still bright and can articulate a sentence without a string of "ahs" and "likes," many are almost illiterate if too many words have multiple syllables. They seem to lack basic reading and communication skills far too many times. This renders them functionally illiterate, and for the effect it has on everything from business to elections, it is killing this country.

Biblical illiteracy is killing the church. As noted earlier, Barna Group research found only one in three self-professed born-again Christians believe the Bible is absolute truth. This biblical illiteracy has led to an appalling lack of knowledge on many core teachings and beliefs of Christianity. And even if we know the core teachings, we are increasingly unable to articulate them to a world that desperately needs to know the truth of the Bible.

Rob Bell, as we discovered earlier, was the latest in a line of Christian leaders who could not answer a simple question of why there is suffering and death in the world. When we cannot explain the basic beliefs of our faith, the world laughs at us and rejects the message they desperately need.

When we cannot explain the very basics of our faith, just what does that say of our real love of God? If we do not take the time to really know Him and His story, I think it says that God is but a means to an end for us. He is our ticket to heaven, our "Get Out of Jail Free" card, and our "9-1-1" God when we find ourselves in trouble once again. Just how pathetic is it when we have a chance to explain why there is evil and death in the world, along with God's solution, and we cannot articulate it? But time after time Christian leaders drop the ball when given the opportunity to be God's instruments to release the scales from the eyes of the spiritually blind. What a sorry lot we have become.

"The Christian body in America is immersed in a crisis of biblical illiteracy," warns researcher George Barna. "How else can you describe matters when most churchgoing adults reject the accuracy of the Bible, reject the existence of Satan, claim that Jesus sinned, see no need to evangelize, believe that good works are one of the keys to persuading God to forgive their sins, and describe their commitment to Christianity as moderate or even less firm?"

Other disturbing findings by Barna document an overall lack of knowledge among churchgoing Christians that include the following:

- The most widely known "Bible verse" among adult and teen believers is "God helps those who help themselves," which is not in the Bible and actually conflicts with the basic message of Scripture.

- Less than one out of every ten believers possesses a biblical worldview as the basis for his or her decision making or behavior.

- When given thirteen basic teachings from the Bible, only 1 percent of adult believers firmly embraced all thirteen as being biblical perspectives.

Author David Wells puts the problem bluntly in his book *No Place for Truth*: "I have watched with growing disbelief as the evangelical church has cheerfully plunged into astounding theological illiteracy."

A major reason for biblical illiteracy and shallow theology today is the tremendous influence that unbiblical philosophies and worldviews are having on American Christianity. Liberal theology has questioned the authority of Scripture, assigning its teachings more to man than to God. Truth has become subjective, leading to abuse in biblical translation and interpretation.

Human emotions and feelings cause people to look internally for spirituality and truth instead of looking up to God or Scripture. The postmodernism culture we live in has convinced Christians to abandon the belief in absolute truth, leading an alarming number of Christians to seek truth in religious syncretism, picking and choosing beliefs from numerous religions to cobble together a truth that matches their desires and personal agenda. One needs to look no further than the emergent church movement to see this in action. Since traditional Christianity seems unwilling or unable to respond to the increase of this "cobble-stone religion," we are losing many younger Christians to a dangerous form of Christian universalism that abandons the truth of the Bible for a religion of convenience and selfishness.

In 2 Timothy 3:16-17, the apostle Paul writes: *All Scripture is God-breathed and is useful for teaching, rebuking, correcting and training in righteousness, so that the servant of God may be thoroughly equipped for every good work.* Only one in three born-again believers now believes that to be true. This puts Bible-believing Christians in the extreme minor-ity when compared to millions who refer to themselves as "Christians" in our nation. Experts fear the percentage will continue to decrease with each passing year, bringing American Christianity closer still to spiritual extinction.

I feel so sorry for people who do not think the Bible is absolute truth. Sure, you can survive without that anchor of truth when things are going well, but what happens when the world around us to which we have become accustomed starts to unravel? Where does one turn if not to the Bible when our nice little world starts to fall apart?

Once we are comfortable abandoning the Bible as the anchor of truth in our lives, it is a quick journey to sin and even apostasy. When we are the judges of our own morality, we are headed off the spiritual cliff at breakneck speed. It leads to many of the ills we now see regularly in American Christianity.

Matthew 7:1 Christianity

"Do not judge, or you too will be judged." This is a powerful message from Jesus, but its meaning has been twisted and has in essence served to nullify the remainder of the New Testament in the minds of illit-erate, misled Christians. "Matthew 7:1 Christianity" has become the newest denomination of Christianity. It is a fast-growing cult, no less dangerous than Mormonism, Jehovah's Witnesses, or Chrislam. Don't worry about the rest of what the Bible teaches, even the remainder of

that very chapter where Jesus goes on to tell us how to judge the fruits of another, or that He tells us the path to salvation is narrow but the road to destruction is wide. Jesus is teaching here about the dangers of hypocrisy. We are not to condemn a brother for a sin we are also guilty of committing.

Churches are filled with Christians claiming their love and compassion for others, but the truth is all they are doing is hoping to deflect attention from their own sin. They hope that if they do not have to hold a fellow Christian accountable for his life, no one will be looking to hold them accountable for their lives.

Matthew 7:1 Christians are cowards and unloving. Relationships and love involve risk. We risk that the one we love may not feel the same way about us. We risk our hearts and our reputations, and we risk losing a friend when we have to confront their destructive behaviors. And Matthew 7:1 Christians are afraid of risk. They would rather live and let live. And God forbid you should ever confront them on their sinful behavior! If you have the courage and love to do so, you will be made to feel like an unloving, ungrateful friend. "Hey, I am tolerant and understanding of you and you repay me by judging me? You're nothing but a legalistic Pharisee!"

Matthew 7:1 Christians are also enablers. They are no better than a friend who encourages an alcoholic to go out drinking or a friend who justifies his friend's physical abuse of his spouse. When a man is involved in a pattern of destructive behavior that will jeopardize his life, a real friend intervenes any way possible. He simply will not allow his friend to continue to behave in a way that could lead to his demise, doing whatever it takes for as long as it takes to straighten his friend out.

Might some Matthew 7:1 Christians one day be found guilty of manslaughter? Manslaughter can be defined as contributing directly or indirectly to the death of another by one's actions or inaction. If I supply the illegal drugs that my friend dies from through an overdose, I could be charged with and found guilty of manslaughter.

Some states now have what are called "Good Samaritan Laws," named after the story Jesus told in the Bible. Some of these laws permit charges to be brought if a person refuses to help someone in danger and it leads to serious injury or death. Can an argument be made that Matthew 7:1 Christians could be found guilty of this violation when they stand before God?

Matthew 7:1 Christians consider themselves loving people, but I would argue many are more hateful and selfish than they are loving. If we see a friend on a ledge ready to jump into a spiritual abyss and do not try to talk him off the ledge, is that loving or hateful? It may be the most hateful thing we can do to refuse to confront another with his sins. Just like God warned Ezekiel in his role as a watchman, if you do not warn the people and they die, their blood is on the watchman's hands.

Matthew 7:1 Christianity is spreading like wildfire, infiltrating every denomination of American Christianity. This new movement comes across as loving and caring, but it is actually lazy and self-centered.

Seeker-Friendly Christianity – Loving or Ashamed of the Gospel?

For I am not ashamed of the gospel, because it is the power of God that brings salvation to everyone who believes: first to the Jew, then to the Gentile. – Romans 1:16

The gospel is the power of God for salvation, not the fancy words we use, our marketing prowess, or our ability to relate to others. But American Christianity doesn't seem to think the gospel is sufficient anymore. We seem to think the gospel is losing power and needs an infusion of postmodern wisdom to bring it back to life. We believe that God can't reach the lost on His own anymore and He needs our help. What arrogance and foolishness!

The truth is, all we can do is diminish the power of the gospel when we try to add our earthly wisdom to it. Every time we open our mouths or act on our own strength, we add nothing, but risk diminishing the power of the gospel.

In the early church it was the power of the Holy Spirit that added to the numbers of the body, not the wisdom of man or clever marketing strategies. Paul witnessed the power of God on the road to Damascus and realized the folly of human efforts to apply the Word of God in a way we think is correct. Proverbs 14:12 teaches: *There is a way that appears to be right, but in the end it leads to death.*

Galatians gives us insight to one of the first recorded attempts at trying to be "relevant" instead of standing on the power of the gospel alone. *When Cephas came to Antioch, I opposed him to his face, because he stood condemned. For before certain men came from James, he used to eat with the Gentiles. But when they arrived, he began to draw back and separate himself from the Gentiles because he was afraid of those who belonged to the circumcision group. The other Jews joined him in his hypocrisy, so that by their hypocrisy even Barnabas was led astray. When I saw that they were not acting in line with the truth of the gospel, I said to Cephas in front of them all, "You are a Jew, yet you live like a Gentile and not like a Jew"* (Galatians 2:11-14).

Peter was guilty of hypocrisy by acting differently in front of Jews and Gentiles, depending on whom he was with at the time. He was trying to be culturally relevant to the Gentiles, yet he reverted to his legalistic behaviors when he was with the Jews, causing confusion within the Galatian church. This also confused Barnabas, leading him to join in Peter's hypocrisy. Peter, the man who told Jesus he would follow Him to the cross only to later deny he even knew Him, was at it again, giving in to pressure to be seen as loving and relevant to the Gentiles and righteous to the Jews. This confusion was destructive then, and it is equally destructive now, as we try to bounce between Christian teachings and being relevant to the secular culture. The gospel, not our words, has the power to change lives.

Paul was not interested in being relevant to the cultural norms. He spoke out boldly against them, standing firmly on the truth of the gospel. Greeks in those days openly embraced homosexuality as acceptable behavior, yet Paul warned them they would need to stop it or not inherit the kingdom of God. When the Galatians started to stray from the purity of the gospel, Paul got right in their face, calling them *foolish*. Paul would never make it in the church today, as he would be branded as uncaring, unloving, and even a hater. Are we ashamed of the simple truth of the gospel and believe it is powerless, needing our wisdom and marketing plans to succeed?

A few years back a couple of Christian friends asked me to help with an attempt to reach the unchurched. They put together a survey they wanted to mail to families who did not attend church, seeking to understand why these families were not attending. One of these friends still pastors a local church. As I sat with them reviewing the survey, I saw a pattern of questions trying to ascertain why the recipients were turned off by religion. We would be asking these people to be honest about what bothered them about the church, hoping to get insight as to why they disliked the church experience. I asked a simple question of the group: "So after we gather this information, what do we do about it?" My concern was that it might lead us down the dangerous road of compromising with the desires of the culture at the expense of the gospel. What if respondents said they were turned off by teachings on sin? Would we change the message to be more accepting of sin? The one pastor's response indicated to me he was more interested in compromising with secular culture instead of affecting it, accommodating to what people *wanted* from church instead of what they *needed*. I backed out of the project.

I cannot overstate the importance of this to the church: When we seek compromise with the culture, we lose! Nothing good can come from this unholy matrimony. When two diametrically opposed institutions like biblical Christianity and secular culture try to find common ground, all that can be accomplished is the watering down of the gospel because of our human nature.

Look again at Galatians 2:11-14 and Peter's attempt to bridge the gap between Jews and Gentiles. The only things that were accomplished were the Galatian church was confused and Barnabas was led astray into Peter's hypocrisy.

Seeker-friendly Christianity as defined these days is a joke, a very dangerous joke. Secular culture and its humanist beliefs are totally incompatible with biblical Christianity. They are the two sumo wrestlers we discussed earlier, intent on knocking each other out of the battle circle. The problem is the secular sumo knows its destructive purpose, but the Christian sumo seems to believe dialogue will attain a mutually satisfactory compromise. The Christian combatant believes if we just talk and seek common ground, we can learn to coexist.

The seeker-friendly disease has grown worse and worse. Progressive Christians refuse to acknowledge that abortion is murder and homosexuality is a sin because those words are just too harsh and condemning, and preaching on the depravity of man is just so belligerent and turns sinners off. Americans just want to feel better about ourselves and want assurance that we are a good people and that God loves us just the way we are. Well, God does love us, but He does not want us to stay just the way we are. He wants us to be transformed from our sinful nature to live a life of holiness and righteousness.

Jesus accepts us as sinners but He demands a real change by the power of the Holy Spirit. If there is no transformation in our lives, how dare we claim to be Christians? This is an insult to a holy God, rejecting His power to transform us into the image of Jesus and thereby acknowledging His lordship over our lives.

The pure gospel is the *real* seeker-friendly message. It is a message of real hope, in that man can be made righteous before God by the power of the sacrifice of Jesus, and that all a man must do is repent and turn away from his sinful nature, ask forgiveness, and accept that Jesus is the Son of God, his Lord, and his Savior. Friends, it doesn't get any more seeker-friendly than that!

But that's just not simple enough these days. Admitting we are sinners is just too much pride to swallow, and asking forgiveness is impossible unless you first admit you are a sinner. Oh, we want this Jesus to rescue us, but at what price? By admitting we are filthy, worthless sinners? Well, that's just too high a price to pay for a growing number of prideful men and too harsh a message for the church to deliver to the lost.

Not to worry, it's seeker-friendly Christianity to the rescue! Don't want to face your own human depravity? No problem. Jesus accepts you just as you are. Just ask Jesus into your heart and you are good to go. He is a loving, non-intrusive God who doesn't mind sharing space in your heart with evil and sin. He's just happy you've made Him a part of your life. You get all this for just saying a simple, halfhearted sinner's prayer.

And in a tribute to every other irritating infomercial out there,

"But wait, there's more! Invite Jesus into your heart in the next fifteen minutes and we'll include this permanent 'Get Out of Jail Free' card with your prayer. This card comes in handy when the Holy Spirit gets a little irritating, convicting you of sin in your life. So when the Spirit of the Lord beckons you to turn your back on sin, just sin anyway and flash your 'Get Out of Jail Free' card – it's that simple.

"So you get the instant, non-intrusive Jesus and the magical 'Get Out of Jail Free' card all for the price of one simple, halfhearted sinner's prayer! But act now and we'll throw in a set of non-judgmental, accepting Christian friends to make sure guilt or shame never become a factor in your life. A great addition to the spiritually dead life you've chosen."

If you don't think this is commonplace in American Christianity these days, wake up and smell the coffee. We are pandering to lost people by not confronting them on their sins, and if we do summon the courage to risk our friendship with them to share the gospel, it is a humanistic gospel that we are sharing, one that leads nowhere good at all.

God detests sin and we had better start to accept that fact. If we do sin and repent, He is faithful to forgive, but this requires us to acknowledge we are sinners in the first place. But *sinner* seems just too harsh a word today, and American Christianity is too weak, too uncaring, and too cowardly to speak the truth of the gospel these days.

Truth be told, which is not done enough these days, there is another reason we don't confront people and their sins these days, a selfish reason that hits too close to home. If we dare to confront people and their sins, we also open ourselves up to scrutiny about the sin in our own lives, and few of us want to go there.

Have you ever wondered why pornography is rarely, if ever, addressed from the pulpit and why so few churches offer any small-group discipleship and accountability systems for men struggling with it? And even if they do, will you find a pastor involved in the accountability system? Could it remotely be connected to the fact that Barna Group research found that as much as 80 percent of pastors confidentially reported that they are addicted to pornography to some degree? Is this merely a coincidence?

One of the Bible verses eliminated by the Matthew 7:1 Christian cult is in the very same chapter: *"Why do you look at the speck of saw-dust in your brother's eye and pay no attention to the plank in your own eye? How can you say to your brother, 'Let me take the speck out of your eye,' when all the time there is a plank in your own eye? You hypocrite, first take the plank out of your own eye, and then you will see clearly to remove the speck from your brother's eye"* (Matthew 7:3-5). We have no authority to speak to the sin in another's life if we also struggle with it, unless we are willing to admit to and repent of our own sin. If we do confess our sin we can then be in a position as a friend to be mutually accountable to one another, helping each other out of our sin by the power of the Holy Spirit.

Until our pastors and elders are willing to admit and confess their own sin, they have no moral or spiritual authority to perform their duties of shepherding the flock. They forfeit their authority as leaders. Until we as followers also admit our own sin, we are powerless to help our brother out of his sinful state.

We must take equal responsibility for this sad state of affairs. How many pastors feel comfortable coming to their elders or congregation and confessing their sins without the worry that they will be fired? And who are we as followers to condemn a man for the same sin we struggle with? Matthew 7:3-5 works both ways, folks!

We are in a deep mess that we cannot get out of on our own. Only God can rescue American Christianity before we spiritually kill our-selves. The solution is simple, but not easy. It's simple in that all it requires is true repentance and a commitment to worship the one true God we see in the Bible instead of the selfish piecemeal God we have manufactured in our minds and deceitful hearts. This is not easy from the view that this will require real humility and spiritual brokenness, and this is something we have not shown a proclivity to over the past couple decades.

In athletic competition it often comes down to desire: Who wants victory more? Well, pardon my pessimism, but it sure seems the Enemy wants spiritual chaos much more than we want spiritual purity and clarity these days. I hope I am proven wrong.

"I'm a Christian"

There was a time when words had clear and precise meanings. When a man or woman said, "I'm a Christian," we knew what they meant. They believed in God and that Jesus Christ is God's only begotten Son. They believed that Jesus took human form and died on the cross for our sins. They believed that if we put our faith in Jesus and lived as He taught us, we would one day enter heaven and live there for eternity in the presence of God. They believed that hell was a real place, reserved for those who rejected Jesus. They also believed that the Bible was 100 percent inspired by God and was His written Word and absolute truth. Finally, they believed we were called to lead a life of holiness, abandoning our sinful nature for a new and better spiritual life.

Every day I get to meet new people in my role as general manager at Q90 FM. In the past, when they would identify themselves as Christians, no further questions were needed. These days, I am forced to poke and prod a little deeper when someone calls themselves a Christian.

"Exactly what does that mean – you're a Christian?" That question alone is often met with a blank look and many people struggle to explain why they identify themselves as Christians.

"Well, I believe in God." I point out what it says in James, that so do the demons and they shudder in fear.

"I believe in Jesus." Which Jesus? A great teacher, a great man, or the only Son of God? Only a savior? Or savior *and* lord of everything, including our lives?

Assuming they survive these initial questions, I hit them with the big one: "What happens when Jesus returns at the end of the age?"

It is amazing how many Christians have not taken the time to see what God tells us about the final days of this world. Both the Old and New Testament are packed with biblical prophecy that has been proven to be 100-percent accurate every time. Many of these prophesies have been fulfilled, but some await us. The book of Revelation spells out the final years of this life, yet so many Christians ignore it or get confused, choosing to just set it aside. God is laying out His final battle plan, where He comes to rescue His children from a life of sin and death.

It is also amazing how many progressive Christians choose to read something into Revelation that just isn't there. Many have come to believe that man will rescue the earth and that when man conquers evil and brings forth justice, then Jesus will return and assume control of a world we have conquered for Him. People on both sides of the theological divide, conservative and progressive dominionists, actually believe we can change the outcome of biblical prophecy in spite of its 100-percent proven accuracy over the past several thousand years.

Saying "I'm a Christian" used to be self-explanatory. We knew what was meant and took it at face value. We can no longer afford to do this, as we have lost our cohesive identity as Christians and must return to the basics. Bear with me through one more football analogy . . .

In the sixties the Green Bay Packers were a dynasty. Winning championships was expected and losing a game was just plain unacceptable to their coach, Vince Lombardi. After a loss where the team was fundamentally beaten at every turn by the opponent, Lombardi called the players together the next day and announced, "Gentlemen, we stunk yesterday. We didn't block, tackle, catch the ball, or do anything well. We're going to return to the basics today." He held up a football and said, "Gentlemen, this is a football."

Max McGee, the class clown on the team quipped, "Slow down, coach, you're going too fast." This is a funny story but one that probably remains all too true when we look at American Christianity these days. Our leaders go on television and are thrown softballs like "How come God doesn't stop evil?" or "Why do bad things happen to good people?" They are given an opportunity to share the story of creation, man's fall, and his available salvation through Jesus Christ, and they stumble and fumble through an answer one might expect from a ten-year-old, but not a leader of the church.

I was at Power of One, a Christian music event, in 2011, meeting youth and parents. Six wonderful young ladies around the age of thirteen came to our booth and starting rattling off the names of their favorite Christian bands and telling us how much they enjoyed the music Q90 FM played. I felt an urging of the Holy Spirit to ask them a very unusual set of questions.

"Are you girls Christians?" They all said yes.

"Do you attend church?" They said they all attended the same church every Sunday and were participants in the youth ministry.

"Do you read the Bible regularly?" They all answered in the affirmative.

"One more question: What was Jesus' last name?" One said she didn't know; four answered "Christ," and one said she didn't think they had last names in those days because they were identified by their father and ancestors. So only one in six knew the correct answer, and these were young ladies who attend church and participate in their youth group.

Now, before we blurt out, "kids these days," how many adult Christians would know the answer to that question? And even if they did, are we taking the time to teach our children about Jesus and our faith? Are we equipping them for a Christian life in a world more hostile to God every day? Are we teaching them the foundations of our Christian faith or leading them to slaughter at the hands of an Enemy who seeks to kill and destroy?

The Narrow Path

"Enter through the narrow gate. For wide is the gate and broad is the road that leads to destruction, and many enter through it. But small is the gate and narrow the road that leads to life, and only a few find it." – Matthew 7:13-14

Jesus gives us a very stern warning here. The road to eternal life is narrow and few find it. A warning like this from our Lord and Savior should cause us to sit up and pay attention. He didn't say most or many would enter through the narrow gate, He said *few*.

I am fascinated with thinking and praying on this verse in Scripture. Just how narrow is the road to eternal life? Do 20 percent make it? Ten percent? Five percent? One percent? None of us knows, as God alone is qualified to judge the eternal destiny of each man. But we should not quickly gloss over this verse where Jesus says *few* find the narrow road to eternal life. It should cause us to analyze the depth of our faith and question whether our works reflect real faith and commitment to Him as Lord and Savior, or if our words and actions reflect a faith of convenience and mediocrity.

Narrow roads we drive on present challenges to us. They allow very little room for mistakes, as a momentary lapse in concentration can send us into a ditch. When I drive through a construction zone with a concrete barrier on one side and a ditch on the other, I am forced to concentrate on the road and my driving instead of being enamored with changing channels on my car radio or talking on my cell phone. I realize that a short lapse in concentration or letting my eyes wander could create a serious problem, as I could either crash my car or end up in a ditch.

Without getting into a discussion of whether or not we can lose our salvation, I wonder if we often take for granted that the road to salvation is an eight-lane superhighway where we can just coast instead of this narrow road Jesus mentions. We just put ourselves on cruise control and pay little attention to the traffic and conditions around us as our eyes wander to signs along the road or over to other drivers we encounter.

I think we set ourselves up for a very dangerous situation when we do not take these words of Jesus to heart. Narrow means narrow! Only a few find the road to eternal life. Is a simple "believing in God" enough? Not according to the book of James. Is a simple belief in Jesus enough? That depends on what we believe *about* Jesus. Acts 19 tells a fascinating story about certain creatures who knew Jesus:

> *Some Jews who went around driving out evil spirits tried*
> *to invoke the name of the Lord Jesus over those who were*
> *demon-possessed. They would say, "In the name of the Jesus*
> *whom Paul preaches, I command you to come out." Seven*
> *sons of Sceva, a Jewish chief priest, were doing this. One*
> *day the evil spirit answered them, "Jesus I know, and Paul*
> *I know about, but who are you?" Then the man who had*
> *the evil spirit jumped on them and overpowered them all.*
> *He gave them such a beating that they ran out of the house*
> *naked and bleeding.* (Acts 19:13-16)

These demons acknowledged knowing Jesus, so were the demons saved? No, because while they knew who Jesus was, they did not submit to Him as Lord. Simply knowing Jesus is not enough for salvation; He must also be Lord and Master over our lives. How many times a day do we not submit to His lordship in our lives? How many times do we willfully sin knowing we should not, as it is an affront to God? Is He really Lord over our lives? Is He Lord of every thought, word, and action?

I think this is something we really need to take to heart the next time we offer a bland altar call and a sinner's prayer. *What* we believe about Jesus is equally as important as believing He is the Son of God. I think this is what Romans 10:9 refers to when it says if we confess with our mouth and *believe in our heart*. Head knowledge of who Jesus is will not be enough. When we truly believe in our hearts, it is something deep, personal, and intimate. He becomes the sole object of our love and affection, not just an intellectual acknowledgment.

I make no judgment or definitive doctrinal statements in what I just wrote. I merely ask questions that will hopefully cause us to examine our hearts and minds and draw nearer to God. Jesus tells us that many who call Him Lord will be rebuffed with His words of *"I never knew you."* How sad for us if we hear those words when we stand before Him in judgment.

Let us not stop short of where God calls us to be as Christians. Jesus must be something more than an intellectual belief; He must reside in our hearts and rule us from there. Are we fooling ourselves with a type of phony salvation? Or do we truly belong to Jesus? Are we leading ourselves and others to a pot of fool's gold? Being led to something that looks shiny and valuable but is worthless and meaningless? If our commitment to Jesus never goes beyond a sinner's prayer, followed by a life without any fundamental change, let alone transformation, how will God judge us when we stand before Him?

These are the tough questions we must ask ourselves as American Christians. Questions like these lead to thought, prayer, and seeking God intimately. They lead to repentance when we realize we have been lulled to sleep by a faith that is shallow and deceptive, and they lead to revival in each of us and the church as a whole.

We must stop trying to redefine God into an image that He is not, an image that suits the selfish lifestyles of our flesh. God is the same yesterday, today, and tomorrow. We must see Him as the apostles saw Him – the apostles who were willing to give their very lives for Him. When each of us can do that we will see transformation, revival, and a moving of the Holy Spirit. Until that time comes, it will be "business as usual" and American Christianity will continue to decay.

Chapter 11

The Spiritual Abuse of Our Children

Training Tomorrow's Church Leaders – but for What?

I have breaking news for adult Christians: We will grow old and die one day. More breaking news: Today's Christian children will grow up to assume the mantle of leadership in the church over the next couple decades. How are we preparing them?

One of the primary responsibilities of a leader is to groom successors. An organization never faces a more critical time than when there is a transition in leadership. An institution as large and diverse as American Christianity faces an added challenge in grooming new leadership in comparison to a corporation.

A corporation will often see its key leadership responsibilities functioning in the hands of a relatively small group of centralized leaders. American Christianity, with its size and diversity, is a different animal. Leadership is not centralized; rather, it is fragmented and spread out among literally thousands of smaller entities known as denominations and churches.

This creates a unique challenge for the church. Leadership transition comes in smaller steps with subtle, incremental changes often not easily noticeable. No one leader, no matter how potentially dangerous or destructive, has complete influence, so leaders are easier to initially dismiss as more of a nuisance than a threat. But eventually a critical mass forms where enough potentially dangerous leaders come into power and become a real threat to the whole organization. American Christianity is in this critical condition.

For example, a few decades ago, one or two smaller Christian denominations came out and challenged the traditional teaching of homosexuality as a sin. Because they were insignificant in number when compared to the total number of leaders and denominations, they were easily dismissed as a fringe element. But look around today and see that the lie that homosexuality is not a sin has infiltrated virtually every denomination of Christianity with varying degrees of success. Because we did not act swiftly to counter the lies of these deceptive leaders and take appropriate actions, their camps began to grow.

Satan is evil, a liar, and the one who accuses the brethren. What he is not is stupid. He was the most brilliant angel created, the *morning star* (Isaiah 14:12). He is smart, crafty, scheming, and patient. He realized a full frontal assault on Christian leadership would fail, so he bides his time, lulling us to sleep as he claims small, incremental victories that seem insignificant at the time. But a lot of small victories eventually lead to a huge, decisive victory, and Satan is in position to gain victory over American Christianity. Satan has come to the brink of victory so subtly that most Christians do not realize it.

When you look at the landscape of leadership in American Christianity these days, you find that most of the leaders who stand on the principles of absolute biblical truth are advancing in years, while a growing majority of young leaders are far more liberal in their views about absolute truth. The elderly leaders are principled, but the younger ones are much more pragmatic. Elderly leaders view Christianity and God as consistent and never changing, while the younger leaders view God and Christianity as flexible to accommodate a postmodern culture's desires and dreams.

These younger leaders shun the belief of their predecessors that absolute truth exists. Absolute truth has become subjective truth – a truth that is subject to individual interpretation based on how a person feels. Experiences and emotions have replaced absolute truth as the guiding principle for this next generation of Christian leaders, and as this dangerous teaching spreads and becomes more accepted, we will soon be ruled and led by our human emotions rather than the truth of God. Once this happens there will no longer be any core doctrine that guides American Christianity. It will become a cobblestone of individual beliefs driven by how each individual feels about God, morality, and truth.

Well, fasten your seat belts because the "Young Guns" are just about ready to take control of the steering wheel that drives American Christianity, and the place to which they will drive the church is right into a ditch of secular humanism.

Satan has been working hard in the fields of media and education, both secular and Christian, to lay the foundation for this transition in leadership. He has succeeded in taking over the curriculum in our public schools over the past fifty years and is now making great inroads into some Christian educational institutions, promoting Christianity as more subjective to our individual feelings. As this continues to grow, the spiritual death of American Christianity will be near its completion.

"But I Send My Kids to a Christian School"

We know that secular education in the public schools is anti-Christian in the views and curriculum it shoves down the throats of our children. The NEA believes it has a responsibility to rescue youth from the archaic beliefs children learn from religion and their parents. As we noted earlier, this was shared by an NEA spokeswoman at the United Nations in 2011 as she appealed for mandatory sex education and transgenderism teaching for children as young as six years old.

In Wisconsin and around the nation, the NEA has successfully lobbied and bribed progressive politicians into blocking the expansion of Christian education at every turn. Through our tax codes the government has made Christian education a financial burden for parents who prefer a godly curriculum to one of secular humanism. The percentage of children attending public schools is at an all-time high and if the teachers unions have their way, Christian education will soon be extinct.

But the battle for the souls of our future leaders is not being waged just in public educational institutions; it is also occurring in Christian schools. Over the past fifty years there has been a dangerous trend showing that far too often Christian education is emulating and embracing the secular values and beliefs of public education. Here in Green Bay, a close friend of mine was shocked when his daughter told him the teacher who teaches the religion class in her parochial school taught that the flood in Noah's time was just a fable and not an actual historic event. He confronted the teacher and met with her and the school's principal. The principal backed up the teacher, telling my friend that our children needed to expand their thought process and embrace other views.

Wheaton College, an esteemed Christian university, consistently brings in pro-homosexual lecturers and social justice activists like Jim Wallis to lecture. They have also hosted homosexual activist Harry Knox to teach and speak. Knox, an avowed homosexual, calls his sexual orientation "an unchangeable gift from God for which I am very grateful. And it would fly in the face of my respect for God to give that gift back." Please try to square that up with biblical teaching and ask yourself why Wheaton College is committed to presenting views like this as Christian education. Several Wheaton professors are involved with anti-Israeli rallies like Christ at the Checkpoint, where the Palestinian cause is promoted and Israel is demonized as an aggressor in the conflict.

Richard Mouw and Fuller Theological Seminary

Richard Mouw is a former president of Fuller Theological Seminary. Many Christians believe Fuller left the camp of sound Christian doctrine a long time ago, and Richard Mouw has confirmed their beliefs on his own blog, written on March 15, 2011:

> "I told the *USA TODAY* reporter that Rob Bell's newly released *Love Wins* is a fine book and that I basically agree with his theology. I knew that the book was being widely criticized for having crossed the theological bridge from evangelical orthodoxy into universalism. Not true, I told the reporter. Rob Bell is calling us away from a stingy orthodoxy to a generous orthodoxy."

Note the "generous orthodoxy" reference, a tip of the hat to Mouw's friend Brian McLaren who wrote a book with the same title. Mouw is considered a darling of the emergent church and social justice movements and made sure his faculty taught these dangerous doctrines to Christian youth.

In a blog he wrote for CNN, Mouw disagreed with Christian leaders who called Mormonism a cult: "We evangelicals and our Mormon counterparts disagree about some important theological questions. But we have also found that on some matters we are not as far apart as we thought we were." There are *some* similarities in Christian and Mormon beliefs, but there are huge stumbling blocks to finding common spiritual communion between Christians and Mormons.

Mormons believe that God has not always been the Supreme Being of the universe, but attained that status through righteous living and persistent effort. They believe God the Father has a "body of flesh and bones as tangible as man's." Though abandoned by modern Mormon leaders, Brigham Young taught that Adam was God and the father of Jesus Christ.

Mormon leaders have taught that Jesus' incarnation was the result of a sexual relationship between God the Father and Mary. Mormons believe Jesus is a god, but that any human can also become a god.

So Richard Mouw, a president of Fuller Theological Seminary, apparently thinks these core disagreements do not disqualify Mormons as Christians. Are you seeing a trend here? Mouw also signed on to the "A Common Word Between Us and You" heresy a few years earlier that places Islam and Christianity on the same level. Now he is promoting Mormonism and Christianity as having common beliefs. Richard Mouw gives every indication that he is a universalist, and it is logical that he would hire faculty who reflect and teach those same beliefs.

These are just a couple short examples of how Christian education is being corrupted these days. Our next generation of Christian leaders and pastors are being trained to embrace dangerous movements that conflict with the teachings of the Bible, and soon they may comprise a majority of Christian leaders in this nation.

I want to stress that by no means have all Christian schools left the farm; some are holding on to sound biblical doctrine in their education programs. If you are a parent who will be sending your child into Christian education, I urge you to research the schools you consider very carefully. Thoroughly check into their curriculum and research the personal and religious views of the faculty that will be teaching and training your children. Many of them have personal blogs and Facebook pages and also write and post on other sites as well. Thoroughly investigate every aspect of their public life, along with their beliefs and opinions. You will be paying a very high price to send your children to Christian colleges, so do all you can to make sure you understand exactly what you are paying for.

Children and the Church

As education begins to systematically distort biblical doctrine, our churches must make sure they are teaching the Word of God to our children, beginning to establish a strong biblical foundation for them at a very early age. It is crucial that our children learn the fundamental beliefs of Christianity as taught in the Bible, to give them a fighting chance to survive the onslaught of secular beliefs they will be exposed to in our education system and in society as a whole. Unfortunately, our children do not seem to be a high priority in many of our churches these days. Instead of educating them we seem to be coddling or even dismissing them.

Throughout Jewish history, boys were often required to deeply know and even memorize the Torah by the age of thirteen. We hope by thirteen our children have recited a sinner's prayer. When a Jewish boy becomes a *bar mitzvah* ("son of commandment"), he is given greater authority to make certain decisions, subject to the Minyan, a group of relatives and adults who guide him and teach him. We give our youth over to a youth leader who may be more interested in entertaining them instead of teaching them the Bible. And if your church has a youth pastor who has been trained at a Christian college, this may be an additional danger to your children as we discovered earlier.

Jewish children sat at the feet of their parents and teachers, learning about the glory and commandments of God. Christian children spend countless hours on the Internet and Facebook. Their education is usually outsourced to a public school system that fights Christianity wherever it can.

A former commentator in our local paper composed a cartoon about twenty years ago that was more prophetic than he could have imagined at the time. A mom and dad were dropping their child off at kindergarten and told the teacher, "Educate him, feed him, entertain him, challenge him, and teach him morals and values. We'll pick him up when he's eighteen."

"The Children Are Dismissed"

At our former local church, every Sunday we started the service with three songs, then we made church and community announcements, followed by taking an offering. As the offering was completed another announcement was made: "The children are dismissed."

Sadly, there may be more meaning behind this statement than we realize. Are we dismissing our children, our future leaders, more and more these days? We send them off to children's church instead of having them listen to the sermon, learning the Word of God with their parents. We may do this for a variety of reasons that we have convinced ourselves are worthy motives. We think they will be disruptive and get antsy and bored, interrupting the pastor. Or, heaven forbid, our children might ask us a question about something the pastor said.

Sadly, we tend to treat our children as inconveniences sometimes. As parents, there are days when we just hope to survive until they become adults and are on their own. And the church, in spite of some dedicated teachers and youth leaders, often sends the same message to our youth. At a time when our youth need to learn the foundations of Christianity the most, we seem to be dismissing them as children, failing to recognize them as the future leaders of Christianity. Satan has a dangerous agenda in mind for them, and we must recognize that fact and begin to lay down a strong foundation in the minds and hearts of our children. Are we doing that?

I am quite sure that the intention of most pastors and church teachers is sound. They genuinely love and care for our children. But this status quo of how we are raising our children as Christians is leading the church down a dangerous road because there are dangers out there to our children. Dangerous education systems, a dangerous culture, and some dangerous Christian teachers who are appealing to our youth as we subconsciously dismiss them. That is ultimately why our ministry said we would not support the appearance of Jim Wallis speaking to youth at Lifest. He preaches a dangerously incomplete and false gospel, and there are enough enemies out there dismantling traditional Christian teachings these days without our youth hearing more from misleading Christian teachers.

What Are Christian Youth Learning These Days?

We know what our children are being taught in public education: God is an illusion and their only hope for happiness – even survival – is to embrace global citizenship. We know what they are learning from the secular culture. They are hearing that their only path to happiness lies in sex, substance abuse, and narcissistic behaviors.

As we unintentionally dismiss our children at home and in church, there are dangerous wolves out there waiting to destroy them. Satan has a dangerous agenda in mind for them and his tools include a secular American culture, a humanist education system, and the entertainment world of the Internet, television, and music that will destroy our youth if we do not counter their destructive messages.

We are tempted to just throw up our hands and give up, wondering how we could ever compete with these forces vying for the attention of our youth. All around us the world vies for the attention and allegiance of our children, so Christian parents turn to the church in hopes that their children will receive a solid foundation of biblical teaching to give them a fighting chance against a ruthless Enemy bent on their destruction.

We know what our children are learning from the culture, but what are they learning in church? Many Christian parents drop their children off on Wednesday evenings for youth group. Parents hope their children will learn about their Christian faith from a youth leader who will help reinforce the Christian values parents try to live out at home. Youth group is seen as a haven from the depravity of culture our youth are immersed in throughout the week. But just what *are* your children learning in youth group? Are they learning the Word of God?

Or something every bit as dangerous as the culture they are immersed in throughout the week?

On *Stand Up For the Truth*, a regular guest, Todd Friel of *Wretched Radio*, shared a website that listed the top ways Christian youth leaders are entertaining our children these days. Among the most popular activities listed and used were:

- The youth leader smears peanut butter in his armpits and the girls lick it out.

- The students drink Coca-Cola through each other's dirty socks.

- The youth leader has the boys dress in female clothes and makeup, with the girls judging which one is prettiest.

- The girls then dress up as boys, with the boys judging which one is the most handsome.

Pardon my strong language, but literally, what in God's name is going on here? Is this what constitutes youth group these days? What about teaching them the Word of God? What about talking about the difficult choices our youth face these days – sex, drugs, and peer pressure – and what the Word of God has to say to encourage them to make the right choices? Is this what our children really need – an enforcement of the secular culture they see all week with maybe just a little Jesus sprinkled in on occasion? These activities aimed at entertaining our children and showing them that our youth leaders can relate to the culture are very dangerous and destructive. They tend to reinforce the values of the very culture we are to disown as Christians.

Parents, I strongly urge you to find out what goes on in your church's youth group. If it is anything like this, you'd better find another church! Take the time to talk with your pastor and interview your child's youth leader, asking him tough questions about his Christian beliefs and hold those stated beliefs up against the Word of God. Find out which Christian leaders and pastors he admires. Failure to do so may result in you doing more damage to your children by sending them to youth group. We must hold our church leaders accountable for everything that is taught or reinforced within the church.

Our children's most influential teachers are not public school teachers or youth group leaders. The most influential people in the life of our children are right at home: their parents. The world will lead you to believe that your children find you boring and stupid, and that they do not care what you believe or teach them. Nothing could be further from the truth. Study after study shows that overwhelmingly, youth identify their parents as the most influential people in their lives. They may not express that overtly, but trust me, they are watching and listening, and they crave your attention and input as parents.

Research and studies conducted show that the average father spends less than four minutes per day having real conversations with his children. Four minutes a day, when they spend seven hours a day in public school being indoctrinated into humanism and they spend an average of five hours a day immersed in media.

Our children are the most precious investment we have as parents. God has given us the responsibility to raise them and teach them, grooming them to be the next generation of leaders in society and in the church. Is four minutes a day a worthwhile investment in the future of our nation and church? I say this not out of judgment, and from a confession that I fell far short of being the involved father I should have been in the lives of my children. I was guilty of working long hours, coming home tired, and watching television, missing so many opportunities to invest in my own children. Just a little more effort and a little less selfishness would have gone a long way. I missed so many opportunities to invest in them, wasting so much time on my meaningless hobbies and preoccupations.

Now that I have committed my life to God, I see the error of my ways and I hope I can help others who are raising children to avoid the mistakes I made. I encourage you to take the time to really invest in the future of your children and insist that your church do the same. Our children are the future leaders of America, and more importantly, of American Christianity. Every moment we invest in them today will pay huge dividends in the future. And every moment we ignore or dismiss them will be regretted if we see them become immersed in secular culture, walking away from the hope of Jesus Christ.

We are running out of time and cannot continue doing what we have been doing. If we as parents, along with the church, are unwilling to make a significant investment in our children as our future leaders, we deserve whatever happens to us. We will have only ourselves to blame and only God to answer to.

Chapter 12

A Spiritually Powerless and Dysfunctional Church

I ask you to read this chapter with an open mind and heart because I will be painting a very bleak picture of the American church. Some or all of it may or may not apply to the particular church you attend, and I am offering no indictment of any particular church or denomination. I am merely pointing out what seems to be happening in churches around our nation.

The odds are things are not as bad in your church as I point out in this chapter. But more than likely the church you attend suffers from parts of what we will cover next. Please do not put blinders on as you read what I am about to share, thinking none of this could be happening in your church.

I hope you will also ask God to speak to your heart about what we discuss in this chapter. Every one of us is part of a dysfunctional church because we and our leaders are human. But as a church we are called to be a pure, spotless bride and light and salt to the world we live in. And if you belong to a church that is spiritually powerless and dysfunctional, who is to blame? We can blame our leaders or we can look into our own hearts and ask God to reveal the ways we are contributing to a decaying church.

If you read this chapter and can honestly say none of this applies to you or the church you attend, then you are truly blessed. But do not allow the Enemy to deceive you. Satan wants what is happening in our churches to continue and he will constantly seek to convince us that we are "good to go" personally and that your church is doing a great job.

Why Are You Here?

I am blessed by having occasional opportunities to preach at various churches. When I was a young Christian I was being taught by a pastor who remains a close friend. He is a gifted teacher with sermons based solidly on God's Word that are challenging and interesting. I asked him how he was able to keep his sermons challenging and interesting. He answered that the best teachings were about subjects that he has personally experienced, some of which he stilled struggled with. He finds his mind sharpest and delivery most effective when he is passionate about the subject he is teaching on. Sage advice as we are most knowledgeable and passionate about the areas in God's Word where we are personally challenged the most.

A few years ago I was asked to preach at a local church and given six weeks' notice to prepare. With less than two weeks to go I still had not heard clearly from God as to what He wanted me to preach on. As I sat in my home church one Sunday, I heard that still, small voice in my head ask a question: "Why are you here?" Interesting question, and as I pondered my response, I felt the leading not only to answer God's question of me, but also to challenge the congregation I was to preach to the following Sunday. Why are we here in this place we call church?

Usually I really enjoy heading to church to worship God, learn from His Word, and enjoy great fellowship with other believers. I admit there are days, however, where I just want to stay home and curl up in my recliner with the Bible and seek God's voice. But God was challenging me this Sunday, forcing me to do some self-assessment on my Sunday ritual of coming to church. Over the next few days I came to realize that my progression from a child to a Christian adult, and the reasons why I came to church, were probably similar to most other Christians. Let me throw my thoughts out there and let you chew on them a little.

When I was a child I came to church out of obligation. Mom and Dad just told us we were going to church and that was that. Church was not optional and my reaction in church showed that. I would come up with little mind games to help pass the time until we could return home and get on with life.

When I became a teen I attended out of habit. I had become accustomed to just going to church on Sunday and so I continued to do so. Still not much more than passing time, but I was there nonetheless.

When I became a new Christian going to church became an act of obedience to God. That's just what Christians do: we go to church because we love God and want to worship Him. Now at least it became something more than habit, and I was there out of love rather than obligation. And there were times when listening to the Word was exciting as I sought to know more about God and His will for my life.

But I still approached church in a selfish sort of way. Church became a way for me to fill my spiritual tank. My hope was that I would get enough Jesus to get me by and perhaps find some special message or experience that would propel me through the following week of going to work and living the daily grind. Now this can be a valuable benefit in attending church, but is it any attitude to have when we enter into corporate worship of God with our brothers and sisters? Should we have an attitude of *gimme* or one of thanks, expressing the great love of God? Is attending church about me or about God? This is an important distinction.

I also noticed a pattern of behavior in me and my Christian brothers and sisters. When we were together at church on Sunday all of life was wonderful, at least if you listened to us talk. "God is good. Doing great! Praise God!" We were filled with joy, or so it seemed. You would have thought that our life was just one victory after another.

But as I would meet with these fellow believers in a small group setting I heard stories of struggles, failures, and at times downright depression. Life was hard and there were many more setbacks than victories, and I was no different. The unbridled but often phony joy expressed on Sunday was just a mask to hide the pain and struggles of everyday life. But we didn't dare be totally honest about our weeklong struggles when we met on Sunday because we just didn't do that at church. Something was wrong with that, *seriously* wrong.

I hoped church would fill up my spiritual gas tank and get me through the week. At times it did, but other times I was out of gas by Tuesday morning. The rest of the week would be a struggle to just survive spiritually, hoping I could hold on until Sunday, when it was time to refuel the tank again. I began to realize that in a way, going to church had become a detriment to my faith. I had come to depend on church to feed me spiritually, and it would for a short period, only to leave me high and dry by midweek.

Going to church had become my identity and badge of honor as a Christian. I searched the Scriptures and found nowhere that God identified His followers as people who attended church once a week. I looked in the book of Acts and found no requirement or teaching that instructed us to attend church every week. What I did see was that the first-century believers met daily. They gathered for dinner and gave thanks and glory to God. They served one another, offering all they owned to help others. They shared all the great things God was doing in their lives and celebrated their newfound freedom from the punishment of sin and its power in their lives.

We drag ourselves to church for one hour a week while *they* gathered daily, not out of obligation, but out of joy and wonder. Folks, we have it all wrong. Going to church identifies us as Christians, but the early believers *were* the church. I picture the early believers working throughout the day, eagerly anticipating their time together that night. They would spend time thinking about the sacrifice of Jesus, thanking and praising Him for all He had done for them. They were *filling* their spiritual tanks throughout the day, and came spiritually filled up for their time together as a family. We stop in for a quick fill-up on Sunday and watch helplessly as our tanks get drained throughout the week.

Once I realized how I had been looking at church as a crutch to lean on and get me through the next week, something started to change in me. I realized that every day, even the tough ones, were a cause for thanks and celebration. I started praying constantly throughout the day while I worked, thanking God for every circumstance that came my way. I realized that seeking fuel on Sunday that would be used up by Tuesday was an exercise in futility. God had given me a renewable energy source that could continually fill me up and power me through the week. I didn't have to run on fumes, hoping I could just chug and sputter into the gas station on Sunday. He gave me His Word and the privilege of approaching His throne in prayer. I could actually have a conversation with God and He would take as much time as I needed to teach and encourage me. I didn't have to wait until Sunday and hope in one hour I could get what I needed to survive the next week.

Sunday church service should be a time for families to gather in a celebration, a time to share the Word of God and all He is doing in our lives, and a time to encourage and challenge one another to elevate our relationship with God to new heights. Too often these days our churches look more like a meeting of the walking dead instead of Christians overflowing with joy and thanks that Jesus has delivered us from the punishment for sin, and is working in us to deliver us from the power of sin in our lives. In a sense we have developed an unhealthy dependence on church. It has become a house of escape from life instead of a house of worship where we celebrate life – a life of salvation and victory.

Imagine what would happen if a local church brought families together who were overflowing with joy and victory – I mean real joy, not the fake joy we Christians often express. Imagine how the power of the Holy Spirit would be unleashed through us if we came to church filled with love, joy, peace, and real faith. We might see healings, salvations, and miracles on a regular basis, and we might just witness the power of the Holy Spirit as we read about in the book of Acts. The church is God's instrument of bringing His people together in praise, worship, prayer, and celebration. But sadly, that doesn't look like the church in America these days.

The church should have fewer wounded soldiers and more victorious conquerors. When we come to know Jesus as Lord and Savior we come already having been wounded by the Enemy, and now we face a battle to overcome sin in our lives. We need healing from our past wounds before we can be effective in that next battle where we will surely receive more wounds. But too many soldiers are not being healed because they are not being treated with the truth of God's Word, or they choose to ignore His Word. They come to church, get a dose of

Jesus, and go back into the world where that dose starts to wear off and they face more defeat. This occurs for one of two reasons: either they are not being mentored properly, or deep down they choose to remain wounded, ignoring the cure. Neither reason is acceptable and must be addressed to foster a healthy church.

But this would involve a major paradigm shift in how we view success as a church. The lust for nickels and noses would have to be replaced by a passion for spiritually deep disciples. We might have to look for ways to shrink our numbers in the short term, allowing God to prune us for greater future growth. We would need to feel free to be open, honest, and transparent about our sins. We would need to give each other sincere permission to examine our lives at home and work, not just accepting the facade we put up when we attend church.

Do we have the courage and faith in God to ask Him to have His way in our lives and within our churches? Do we believe everything we proclaim from the pulpit, that God is in control and we need to surrender to His will for our lives? It may be time to put up or shut up. We either "do church" God's way, or we continue to die a slow death as sin and hypocrisy expand their foothold in our churches, eating away at her foundation.

We can continue to do things our way and hope things will change, or we can become the church God intends us to be. We can become a place where victorious warriors mentor wounded soldiers who want to join the ranks of the victorious, fighting side by side. A place that is always welcome to wounded soldiers who really want to be healed, but will not tolerate soldiers who continually fall into defeat because they will not allow themselves to be healed by the Word of God and His Spirit.

What Is a Successful Church?

"Pastor, tell me about your church . . . ." When you invite a pastor to tell you about the church he leads, he probably will begin with one of two responses:

- "We're a _____ denomination . . ." or,
- "We have about 125 members . . ."

Consciously or subconsciously we determine our identity and success by our denominational quirks or by how many people attend our church. Is this really what it should all be about?

So just what does constitute a successful church? Attendance? The size of our building? The weekly collection amount? Our outreach events? Or the depth of spiritual maturity the members exhibit, not just at church, but in their daily lives?

Let's be honest. America is the land of "bigger is better," gauging our success on numbers and size. We live in large houses that are more like shrines to our own achievements than functional homes of comfort, joy, and peace. Men often gauge our success on our salaries or work titles, and the family with the most toys is viewed as more successful than the family who lives a modest lifestyle.

We expect such superficial thinking from the world, but should we not expect better from ourselves as Christians? In reality, we are no better than the world, as the church with the largest attendance is envied by other pastors and held up as the gold standard in the community. Church members love to attend big churches because we feel we are a part of something big and important.

Pastors are just as human as you and me, suffering from envy and pride like the rest of us. How many times have we seen our neighbor or friend bring home a new car or boat and we secretly envied him? Pastors are no different, and, in spite of their denials, most desire a larger church, bigger collections, and greater influence. And even if they don't, the ruling elders probably will put pressure on them to define the church's success in these superficial terms.

Jesus invested three years of His life sharing the gospel with anyone willing to listen. His initial message was received eagerly by many looking for a savior. But as His teachings became increasingly difficult, such as John 6 where He says, *"Whoever eats my flesh and drinks my blood has eternal life,"* most fell away from following Him. Likewise, in American Christianity, the more difficult and challenging teachings of the Bible are often ignored out of fear that halfhearted "Christians" will be confused or offended and possibly leave the church. By today's standards Jesus might be seen as an ineffective leader, preaching too harsh a message and not being relative enough to people. He would probably be fired and His unemployment claim denied; and good luck when He tried to find another church to lead because He seemed to know nothing about how to grow a church! While there is nothing wrong with a large church per se, how that church grows in size is what really matters. Is growth based on avoiding the tougher verses in Scripture so more are "comfortable"? Or is growth accomplished by teaching the full counsel of God's Word, challenging members to live the life Jesus exemplified and taught?

Jesus knew that God's plan would be better carried out by a smaller group of committed disciples rather than by a large group who were only really focused on themselves. When Jesus said they must eat His flesh and drink His blood if they wanted eternal life, He knew the ranks of His followers would diminish significantly. All that would be left were those truly committed to Him. Do we fear losing church members for far less-radical statements than that? Do we fear if we preach on the conviction of sin in our lives that members will leave to find a gentler church? I say preach boldly and let them leave, and start trusting in God, not man, to grow the church. God can do more with eleven committed disciples than any man can do with five thousand self-righteous people who need to be coddled.

Sadly, we have bought into the lie that success in the church equates to a nickels-and-noses formula of success and into the "If you build it, they will come" mentality. Oh, that might work if you want to attract a large group of superficial believers who are dazzled by the newest and best building, but you will probably lose them to the next newest and best church building that pops up in your community.

In the Gospel of Matthew, before Jesus ascended into heaven He gave us our orders: *"Go and make disciples."* He didn't tell us to attract superficial church members. God doesn't care about the size of our church; He cares about the size of the heart and spiritual condition of however many people belong to your church. He is into evangelists who grieve for the lost, not catchy outreach programs. And I am quite certain our Lord is more pleased with a church of fifty strong disciples than He is with a church of five hundred shallow Christians.

But those standards are just not good enough for American Christianity these days. We need more people occupying our seats on Sunday to feel successful. We need bigger offerings to fuel God's work. And to accomplish those goals and better relate to the culture these days we are going to need a catchy slogan and a slick marketing plan.

We feel the need to meet the physical and emotional needs of the people, so we have to figure out what they look for in a church and overcome their objections to attending church. We need to craft a series of messages that will appeal to them and we need to let them know Jesus accepts them just the way they are. In other words, we need to sell out to the world.

Look, I understand the pressure to grow in numbers and finances. I lead a Christian ministry; I get it. While my performance review is partially contingent upon our audience growth and financial stability, the day those become the overriding judgment on my performance I will move on. My primary job as a leader is to challenge and encourage those I lead to draw closer to God, pursuing righteousness and holiness. If we can do that, everything else will fall into place. As a ministry, the Holy Spirit will equip us to accomplish what He wants accomplished.

I have been asked if we know how many people listen to *Stand Up For the Truth* every day. Because of limited resources and an inaccurate measuring tool utilized by the industry, I honestly cannot tell. And to be honest, I don't worry about it. Our job is to love and obey God by boldly standing on the absolute truth of His Word and challenging Christians to go back to reading the Bible. Our job is to obey what God commands and the results are up to Him. As we have pursued this, God has more than provided for our needs in spite of our message being a tough one for wishy-washy Christians to swallow.

At the risk of sounding arrogant, I wish more church leaders would come to understand the freedom we receive when we stop worrying about results and just do what God wants us to do. It takes the pressure off, freeing you from undue stress and self-imposed performance standards. God asks for love that leads to obedience. When we love and obey Him, He takes care of the results according to His perfect plan.

Finding a Proper Balance

The saved and the lost, disciples and superficial Christians, and victorious warriors and defeated soldiers – the church has any number of combinations of all these members. A church is like a quilt, a patchwork of patterns and designs woven together into one blanket.

The church is also like a classroom of students. Some are more intelligent and advanced, wanting to be challenged with greater depth and knowledge, while others need the basics and would get lost if we jumped right to advanced studies. Imagine, for a moment, you are putting together the curriculum for the coming school year for incoming freshmen in high school, and since math is a required course to get a high school diploma, you list available classes for students but you simply list these classes as "Math."

Students sign up and come to class on the first day, where you lay out the yearlong agenda and goals. Some are expecting basic math studies, others algebra, and still others advanced trigonometry. They all are expecting one thing that fits their needs and agenda. So you announce the class as advanced trigonometry, and 90 percent of the students gasp in horror. They have not even mastered the basics of math and they are being thrown into advanced trigonometry, and they fear they may not survive the course. Or you announce that the study will be basic math – addition, subtraction, multiplication, and division – the bare essentials. Some are shocked and saddened, already knowing these basics, and they want something more challenging so they can grow in their understanding and preparation for college and life beyond. They sit in class, bored stiff, as the other students learn what these advanced students learned eight years earlier. Either of these scenarios leads to a dysfunctional class with some interested students and some who have checked out emotionally and intellectually.

Welcome to the American Christian church: a patchwork of biblical students at varying levels of knowledge and wisdom. Some can memorize entire chapters from the Bible while others don't know the first thing about terms like *justification* and *sanctification*. Some read the book of Revelation and see God revealing wisdom and blessings, and others give up reading it after the first attempt because their head is spinning.

Some coming to church need milk – the basics of our faith; others desire meat – the pursuit of righteousness and holiness. But the only class posted on the sign is "church." *Church* means a lot of different things to different people. To some it is a place to attend out of obligation, and to others it is a place to worship and glorify God. Some come to give and others come to take. Some come to serve and others come to be served. Some come for the basics while others come for advanced studies.

And "church" as a whole is just not working. We seem confused on what to preach, what to teach, how to train up children, and what to do with a diverse blend of mature and young Christians. If a pastor preaches on the basics of the faith, many sit back bored and unchallenged. If he preaches on advanced issues of the faith, he might just lose about 80 percent of the people by speaking over their heads. If he preaches on sin and hell, look out! Someone might be offended and leave the church, affecting our nickels and noses. If he continually feeds milk to the congregation, Christians wanting to learn about righteousness and holiness become bored and consider moving to a church where they can be challenged to go deeper in their faith. What is the solution to this difficult problem? It may be easier than you think if we are willing to set aside our paradigms about what constitutes a successful church and concentrate on making disciples, not just "members," for Jesus.

Surviving Algebra Class

I was one of the students described earlier who expected my freshman studies of math to be more elementary. I came in, quite frankly, looking for three easy credits, as simple math always came naturally to me. Then I signed up for algebra class. I quickly realized I was in over my head. All the x and y symbols and calculations just shut down when they entered my brain. I started to fall behind in the class and failure became a real likelihood. I began to think I should just drop out and take an easier class. But my friend and next-door neighbor stepped in and helped. He would sit with me and explain things in a way that, while they still didn't make a lot of sense to me, would at least get me through with a passing grade. I limped through class and ended up passing algebra.

As I think back, I probably felt about algebra like a lot of new Christians feel about the Word of God – confused by the advanced studies and feeling like we might never understand it. But a friend and a mentor gets us through it. New Christians may not yet realize that the Holy Spirit is ready to remove the scales from their eyes and reveal the power and beauty of the written Word to us, perhaps because we just don't teach a lot about the Holy Spirit these days. It's all about Jesus and the sacrifice on the cross. Now certainly the cross is the central teaching of Christianity, but as the book of Hebrews states, it is the *milk* we start off with in our journey as Christians. We need to teach more on the solid food of righteousness and holiness and the role the Holy Spirit wants to play in our journey as Christians.

So imagine a new Christian sitting in a small group or listening to a sermon and hearing the meat of the gospel but feeling lost. Many either just shut down or bluff their way through it, pretending to understand the power and teachings of the Bible. But deep down they just don't get it and are restricted to a life of defeat and mediocrity. So is the answer to dumb down the gospel message and just stick to the basics of the cross, salvation, and the resurrection? Will that turn things around?

> *In fact, though by this time you ought to be teachers, you need someone to teach you the elementary truths of God's word all over again. You need milk, not solid food! Anyone who lives on milk, being still an infant, is not acquainted with the teaching about righteousness. But solid food is for the mature, who by constant use have trained themselves to distinguish good from evil.*
>
> *Therefore let us move beyond the elementary teachings about Christ and be taken forward to maturity, not laying again the foundation of repentance from acts that lead to death, and of faith in God, instruction about cleansing rites, the laying on of hands, the resurrection of the dead, and eternal judgment. And God permitting we will do so.* (Hebrews 5:12-6:3)

Ouch! If this is not an indictment of American Christianity, I don't know what is. We choose to remain on milk – good milk – but milk all the same. Notice that milk is described as repentance, faith, the resurrection, and eternal judgment. We spend way too much time on these elementary beliefs of our faith and little or no time on the solid food: the pursuit of righteousness and holiness. We have too many children suffering from spiritual malnutrition. And then we wonder why we cannot find victory in our lives or effectively witness to the lost.

I would guess that as much as 90 percent of church members are still stuck drinking milk. So we continue to offer milk to the congregation over and over out of fear we will challenge or offend new Christians or people who want to stay in their infant stage. The members who want solid food are forced to find it in small groups or even give up and just accept mediocrity in their faith.

We need to understand that victory is ours if we just surrender to the Holy Spirit. He will deliver us from the power of sin in our lives if we just trust in Him and allow Him to take us where He wants us to go. However, this requires us giving up those strongholds of our flesh that we too often still desire. We gain victory through total surrender.

Discipleship

"Therefore go and make disciples of all nations, baptizing them in the name of the Father and of the Son and of the Holy Spirit, teaching them to obey everything I have commanded you. And surely I am with you always, to the very end of the age." – Matthew 28:19-20

Jesus commanded us to make disciples, not members. He told us to teach them to obey everything He commanded, not just the things He taught that we feel like obeying. If we cannot get beyond the milk, how will we ever obey the Great Commission? If we pander to the fear of challenging believers to become disciples and obey everything Jesus commanded lest we lose members or offend the lost, we are stuck in neutral and simply treading water.

Now some churches do offer small-group discipleship meetings for members who want to go deeper, and while that is a good thing, in some ways it is also a cop-out and a surrender to seeker-friendly Christianity. Are we asking too much for members who claim to be Christians to

241

become disciples instead of remaining on milk forever? The last thing we need is more halfhearted, self-centered Christians. We need disciples who are on fire for God and true disciples who seek holiness and righteousness, who hunger for the truth and grieve for the lost.

The church has become more of a country club than a family. A country club where we put on our best face and behavior so we can impress other members with our piety and spiritual depth; a country club where we behave well when we are in the club in order to impress those around us. But how do we behave when we are away from the club? Do our lives reflect God when we are at home or work or are alone?

Setting the Bar Too Low?

The church needs to become more of a family. When we host a Christmas or Thanksgiving dinner, whom do we invite? We dine with our family. On occasion we may invite friends, but they are select friends, not just strangers off the street or casual acquaintances.

The early church was a family, not a social club. Christians came to learn more about the Word of God. They shared meals and possessions when necessary, and they challenged one another and together raised the corporate level of Christian spirituality. They were committed Christians, not curious strangers. They didn't send out fliers announcing cleverly disguised outreach events that are just ploys to attract new members. If you weren't serious about knowing the gospel, you stayed away. The Word was not reduced to the lowest level of common understanding, allowing the spiritually weak to drag down those who wanted to pursue holiness and righteousness.

When we do join an organization or country club, we pledge to behave according to the standards written. If we violate acceptable standards of behavior, we are first warned, but if we continue to behave outside the rules, we are asked to leave the organization.

Not at church. Rules and behavioral expectations are just too harsh. A person can usually stay in a church as long as they show up and throw a few dollars in the offering plate. If you tithe, well, you can pretty much do or say whatever you want. And if you bring a large tithe, heck, you can even tell leadership anytime you are offended by a message or unhappy with how something is handled within the church. Leadership will often bend over backwards to make sure you and your tithe remain a part of the church.

We have also become a church of enablers. Struggling with sin? No problem, because Jesus loves you just the way you are. No need to repent in a truly meaningful way; just say, "I'm sorry" until the next time you sin. Struggling with pornography? Just keep that to yourself, mister, because we don't want to know about it. Hey, if we start to address issues like that, we will have to confront our own similar temptation and sin as leaders and members, and we aren't going there. And if a brave soul looks for help and confesses an addiction to pornography, infidelity, or homosexuality, they will receive condemnation. Condemnation from the same men who watch pornography at home or nearly break their necks every time a beautiful woman walks by.

The early church in the book of Acts was a place open to anyone seeking the complete truth of the gospel. Sinners were welcome but they dared not get comfortable in their sinful state or accept it as normal behavior. Look at Ananias and Sapphira to understand how pride, hypocrisy, and lying were handled by God within the church.

The early church was an exclusive family dedicated to learning the solid fruit of the gospel and learning about righteousness and holiness. They thanked and praised God for all things, and came to church with a heart and mind to worship God instead of just escaping the world and its troubles. And in doing this, they attracted a visitor, a visitor of great power – the Holy Spirit. The Holy Spirit added to their numbers daily as they gathered, performing signs, wonders, healings, and miracles. Many new disciples came to the Lord and the church grew despite persecution and vicious rumors.

Does that even remotely look like American Christianity these days? Are we a church of power or are we a powerless church eating table scraps that the Enemy and culture throw our way? Are we seeing lives transformed or lives that look no different than those of pagans?

If we have the courage and wisdom to believe that by setting higher standards for church membership God will first prune, then grow the church, our churches can be like the church in the book of Acts. Lives will be transformed, the sick might be healed, and addictions broken. But if we remain content to let the Enemy and culture define the membership rules, forget it. We will continue to die slowly but surely. It simply comes down to this: Will we do things God's way or our way? But isn't that what it always comes down to?

Summary

The church is the bride of Christ. But by any objective look we are not a spotless, beautiful bride. We are flirting with the Enemy, and our eyes are more often on him than on our husband-to-be. We are committing adultery with secular culture, risking our intimacy with our future eternal husband. How much "cheating" can we continue to do before He decides we are not truly committed to Him? We should be purifying ourselves in preparation for the blessed union, but instead we are polluting ourselves by accepting sin in the name of tolerance. We are showing we have wandering, adulterous eyes for the world.

This is not just a leadership problem, nor solely a problem due to followers who want their ears tickled. Both parties are responsible. We are insulting God, just like the moneychangers in the temple, turning His house of worship into a den of inequity.

God never gives up on us. And if we turn back to Him, acknowledge our sins, and repent with a commitment to never stray again, He will make us beautiful once more. We must crucify our flesh daily and purge ourselves of our delusional definitions of success as a church. It will not be easy, but then I am still searching for that quote in the Gospels where Jesus promised us that being His disciples would be easy.

Chapter 13

Loving People to Death

There is no stronger emotion than love. God created us to love Him and to be loved by Him. The gospel is the greatest expression of love in history, in that God loved us so much He sent Jesus to rescue us when we were totally unlovable.

But like all perfect gifts from God, man has continually perverted what we call love. Men have murdered in the name of love, left their wives and children in the name of love, and fought wars over love. The famous Trojan War was fought between the Greeks and Trojans over the love of a woman, leaving thousands dead and an empire in ruin. The love of God is perfect while man's love is far from perfect. Man cannot understand perfect, selfless love because in our human nature we are only capable of acting selfishly and loving ourselves.

When we become a new creation by salvation and rebirth through Jesus Christ, we begin being transformed into the image of Jesus, and we can show occasional glimpses of true love. But the Spirit in us is still in competition with our flesh and we can easily revert to our selfish human understanding of love.

As Christians, Jesus commands us to love all men, even our enemies – men like Hitler, Stalin, and Osama bin Laden who act out of malice and hatred. This is not an easy thing to do.

We should also have a special love in our hearts for the lost. Once we have experienced life in the light of God we should desire to love the lost so much that we would do anything we can to share the true gospel with them. We should also have a deep love for our brothers and sisters in Christ Jesus. We are now family, united in love and purpose to support one another in any way possible.

The previous two paragraphs describe the perfect love of God. Unfortunately, we continually fall far short of that perfect standard. So we do the best we can to love one another, all the while trying to manage the internal battle between our new spirit and our flesh. Given that we all will continue to fall short of perfect love in this lifetime, it is a good idea that we continually assess our human understanding of what love is and is not. We must understand that the temptation will always be there to define love selfishly, from a perspective of what is best for us in our flesh. It is obvious that what we currently define as love in relationship to both our fellow Christians and the lost is often not really love at all. If it were, we would not be in the mess we are in as a church and there would be millions more in our ranks.

I Love You, Brother, but Keep Your Problems to Yourself!

As my mother continued to poison herself with alcohol and cigarettes after surviving breast cancer, it grieved me deeply. She had been given a second chance at life but continued to slowly kill herself. Her typical breakfast was a Brandy Manhattan and a few Pall Mall cigarettes, and maybe half a piece of toast. She would nibble on food throughout the day in between downing on average a half-quart of brandy. Before bed she would consume a triple dose of NyQuil to help her fall asleep, and she would wake the next morning, continuing her cycle of slow death.

Our initial attempt at loving her during this time was to meekly suggest that perhaps she needed professional help, but then she would start to cry and lay a guilt trip on us about how hard her life had been, asking why we could not understand that and just love her. We backed down and "just loved her" as she continued to slowly kill herself.

One night I received another in a series of regular calls around 10:00 p.m. Mom was intoxicated and crying about how sad she was over any one of a series of circumstances that was depressing her that evening.

She hinted that maybe she would be better off dead, a sentiment she had previously shared, but this time I sensed she was much more serious. I suggested that if she did not stop her pattern of self-destruction I would be forced to have her checked in to the local mental health center to get professional help.

My mother panicked and called her best friend, a true enabler and fellow alcoholic. This friend drove her to a secret location where we couldn't find her, and for about three days I was worried sick. Mom would still call, drunk and depressed, asking how I could want her committed after all she had done over the years as my mother. I backed off my threat out of fear she would commit suicide. She returned home to my father, who was livid at me over how I had confronted Mom. Both of my parents were quite mad at me for the next few weeks.

My mother was in serious trouble and I had made the decision that she needed to be confronted with the cold, hard fact that she was destroying herself. She reacted with hurt and anger. I risked my relationship with my mother because I loved her and she needed to hear the truth that she was killing herself physically and spiritually. It was painful and difficult to confront my mother but it was the right thing to do.

If we truly love someone who is headed off a cliff, we will risk our friendship to confront them with the truth. When we start to stray into dangerous spiritual waters, God loves us so much that He will do anything He can within the confines of our free will to warn us. When we see a fellow Christian start to stray, are we willing to be God's instrument to reel them in before they fall into the hands of the Enemy? Usually not, because we have fallen into the trap of thinking love means having an attitude of accepting someone right where they are, even if that place is leading them to destruction. Friends, this is not love; this is closer to hatred than it is to true love.

When I asked my pastor the hypothetical question of whether he would throw me out of the church if I admitted to having a sexual relationship outside of my marriage and was not repentant, and he answered no, he thought he would be showing great love for me by allowing me to stay in the body. But Paul taught we should throw the unrepentant sinner out of the church and into the hands of Satan so he might see the error of his ways and repent. Paul knew the real meaning of love, while my pastor, with the right intentions, was buying into the world's definition of love. He was exhibiting tolerance and de facto acceptance of my sin.

Now we must exhibit caution and discernment when we confront a fellow Christian so that we are not going on "witch hunts." There is a big difference between sinners who seek holiness but have not yet found freedom from their sinful bondages, and unrepentant sinners who refuse to admit their sinful ways and do not attempt to walk away from habitual sin. The day we decide it is best to throw every sinner out of the church is the day no one will ever enter church again. And as Jesus taught us, we must first remove the plank from our own eye before we try to remove a speck from another's eye.

But a habitual pattern of unrepentant sin must be addressed firmly for the sake of the church and the individual. We must preach the full gospel. Not a gospel where we tell people Jesus accepts you as you are with no requirement to walk away from habitual sin, but a gospel of confession of sin, sincere repentance, and a desire powered by the Holy Spirit to lead a life of righteousness and holiness.

To me it is funny and sad how Christians will hammer on a person who still smokes or has an occasional drink as "defiling the temple of the Holy Spirit," yet they will not confront people on the serious sins of pride, gossip, sexual sin, gluttony, and a hardened heart. Of course, smoking or excessive alcohol is not good for you, but to condemn a Christian for smoking while allowing serious sins to go unchallenged within the church is the height of hypocrisy. We love to point to people who have an occasional beer or glass of wine as "causing others to stumble," but we think nothing of how we cause others to stumble when we gossip or ignore sexual sin, pride, and gluttony. Which do you think defiles the temple of the Holy Spirit more – a Christian who is honest, sexually pure, kind, loving, and generous but who still smokes cigarettes, or a non-smoker who is a gossip, addicted to pornography, stingy, and spiteful?

Gluttony in particular is a sin that is affecting virtually every Christian in America. We just cannot get enough food or enough of the latest gadgets, clothes, or trendy items that we desire in our flesh, yet an alarmingly small percentage of Christians tithe or give any significant amount of their income to God's work. We have become slaves to our desires of the flesh, ignoring the blessing God wants us to be to others.

How we show love to our Christian brothers and sisters these days looks more like enablement and cowardice than it does true love. We fail to understand that loving someone often involves risk. We risk being called judgmental when we confront another on their sins; we risk our reputation as a kind, loving person when we take the time to confront them with disturbing things we see them doing; and we risk being branded as a Pharisee when we talk about the need for us to pursue a life that is holy and pleasing to God. And if we do not back down once we have confronted them and been rebuffed, we risk losing a friend.

A close friend of mine stopped in to see me about two years ago, distraught and feeling the need to get something off his chest. He had fallen into the habit of frequenting local strip clubs without his wife's knowledge. One isolated stop at a strip club when he was on a business trip had opened the door for his flesh to again seek pleasure in looking at naked women. When he returned home the attraction to strip clubs became greater and greater until he gave in and visited a local establishment. It grew into a habit and he was now visiting them once or twice a week. He had managed to hide this from his wife and friends, but the guilt and shame were now welling up and he had to confess to someone and he chose me.

I listened as he cried and expressed the shame he felt over the addiction he had fallen into. He was truly sorry for opening that door in his life and didn't know what to do. I asked if he was willing to repent of his sin. When he answered yes, we prayed together asking for God's forgiveness and restoration. I then asked him if he was willing to confess this to his wife and ask her forgiveness. "No, that would be horribly painful for her and me!" As he left, I gave him my cell phone number and told him he could call me anytime he felt the temptation again so we could meet and pray.

A couple weeks later he came back, having fallen again to the same addiction. We prayed together again asking God to forgive him and release him from this terrible addiction. This time when we finished I told him he needed to confess this to his wife, asking for her forgiveness and help. He refused to go there, so I took a risk. I risked our friendship by telling him that if he did not confess this to his wife within twenty-four hours, I would tell her.

The look on his face was one of feeling betrayed by a close friend and wondering how I could claim to be a friend and be so cruel and heartless. He shot back, "You wouldn't do that!" But I assured him I would if he did not talk to his wife. He promised he would summon the courage to do it and tell her to call me so I could also support and encourage her by telling her that I understood the addiction he was fighting and would walk by his side to help him any way I could. She called me the next day and was hurt, but appreciative. She told me she had a feeling something was going on by his behavior and his coolness toward her lately, and every time she asked if something was wrong, he deflected. She thanked me for risking my friendship with him to help him.

She loves him very much, and when she got over the initial pain, she committed to helping him in building a stronger marriage. Was I bluffing when I told him I would talk to his wife if he didn't? Would I have really called her? I think I would have but I am not 100-percent sure. I may have cowered when push came to shove, but I hope not. I hope my love for him would have overpowered my fear of losing a friend or seeming like a meddler.

Nancy and I have found greater trust and intimacy by opening up to one another and confessing if we felt an attraction to another. On the rare occasion it would happen, we talk about it, pray together, and commit to helping each other. We try to look internally to see if we are doing something, or not doing something, that is contributing to the potential problem. Am I providing the emotional and spiritual connection she desires? Am I not taking the time to hold her hand and tell her how very much I love her? Is she taking my acts of service for granted, opening a door for resentment?

I love my wife more than anyone except God, and I thank God every day that He gave me such a wonderful wife. But when I allow my flesh instead of the Holy Spirit to rule my heart, I am susceptible to temptation and start to find my eye wandering and my neck twisting and turning to take one more look at the beautiful woman who just walked by. I am every bit as capable in my flesh of doing exactly what my friend did, and if you think you are beyond it, then you do not realize the depravity of your human condition. I hope if I ever succumb to temptation and walk into a place I shouldn't, that a true friend will love me enough to confront me and make sure I do the right thing.

Our churches need to become safe places once again. Places where we can be honest with one another and confess the temptations we face before they turn into sin. We need to develop real friendships with Christians we can trust; Christians who will not enable, but correct and rebuke when necessary. There is, of course, a difference between temptation and sin.

> *Therefore, since we have a great high priest who has ascended into heaven, Jesus the Son of God, let us hold firmly to the faith we profess. For we do not have a high priest who is unable to sympathize with our weaknesses, but we have one who has been tempted in every way, just as we are—yet he did not sin. Let us then approach God's throne of grace with confidence, so that we may receive mercy and find grace to help us in our time of need.* (Hebrews 4:14-16)

Jesus was tempted in every way that we are but His connection with the Father was so strong that He was able to remain sinless. We as humans do not yet have that perfect connection to the Father as we face the civil war in our hearts between the Spirit and our flesh. We need Christian brothers and sisters who love us enough to not let us continue in a state of destructive sin; friends who are willing to risk much for us – respect, reputation, and friendship. If we are not willing to put ourselves at risk for another, are we truly a friend?

When we find the courage and love to be at risk to confront a brother in sin, we do more than just help him – we also strengthen the local church. Our relationship with God is personal *and* corporate, and just as Paul wrote in 1 Corinthians 5:6, a little yeast infects all the dough. When one of us is in a state of unrepentant sin, it also damages our corporate relationship with God as a church, and the power of the local body is diminished. But when we seek individual and corporate holiness and will not tolerate unrepentant sin that God hates, God will bless us individually and as a church. We will see greater strength, and yes, maybe even greater numbers. We will witness the power of the Holy Spirit. We might just see more healings and more miracles, and we will certainly see more joy and peace as together we form a bond that just will not allow a brother or sister to walk through this world of temptation and sin alone.

We have a choice as the church. We can continue doing what we are doing and expect different results (the unofficial definition of *insanity* by the way), or we can choose this day to be a body that is committed to real fellowship and corporate strength. I guess it comes down to asking ourselves one question: Are we satisfied with the direction and power we see in our church today?

Loving the Lost Right to the Gates of Hell

Jaye and I rose from our knees at the conclusion of the prayer. Along with a dozen other Christians we had prayed asking God's blessing as we prepared to head in to the festival. We were preparing to be a witness to about four hundred people gathered for what has become an annual event in Green Bay: the "Pride Alive" event. It was a public gathering of homosexuals, transgenders, and their friends, proclaiming their pride in the lifestyle they had chosen.

As Jaye and I walked together approaching the festival, a lady caught up to us and asked why we were going in. We told her we were here to share the gospel with some lost people. She started into a three-minute tirade, chastising us for being unloving and intolerant of others. She told us her church accepts homosexuals as part of the church because Jesus taught us to love all men and because Jesus told us we were not to judge another.

I told her I agreed with her that we are to love all men, but I asked her to define the word *love*. She said it was "accepting people just as they are." I asked if that was what she was taught in church, and she said yes, that message was taught constantly. This is a lady who attends one of the larger churches in our area. If what she said is accurate, that the church teaches that love is accepting people just as they are, she and the church could not be more misguided or more wrong. Love is quite the opposite in most instances. Love is not being willing to accept people just as they are if they are headed into the abyss of eternal destruction. However, when I gave her my definition of love, "a willingness to be at risk for another," she just waved her arms at me in disgust and walked away.

Jaye and I continued in and entered the Pride Alive event. I must say that I saw no blatant sexual acts or perversion committed. A few couples were holding hands and shared an occasional short kiss, but that was the extent of it. What I did see were a number of local and national companies who had paid money to be sponsors of the event, supporting gay rights and gay marriage. I saw vendors selling beer, soda, snacks, and crafts. One vendor was a man who is a Christian, yet chose to attend the event as a paid vendor. I approached him and asked if he felt he was doing anything wrong in supporting a movement that was clearly sinful in God's eyes. His answer was short and simple: "No. I'm just here to make some money."

We continued on through the grounds, stopping at various booths and asking a few questions of people regarding their beliefs and attitudes about God. Some told me they didn't believe there is a God; others said they believed in a God who accepts all people just as they are. (Boy, where did I hear that before?)

We approached a church booth of a national denomination, asking a man why they were there, and his response was to support equal rights for all people. When Jaye asked him some questions about God and the Bible, the man said, "Let me bring my life partner over; he can better answer your questions." He brought the man over – a liberal Catholic priest, complete with the priest collar. Jaye asked him to please square up his beliefs on homosexuality with the Bible and the man tried to tap-dance around the questions, continually citing a few select verses many Christians use to exonerate and justify their beliefs on homosexuality.

Jaye kept pressing but kept getting the same old tired response – that God loves all men and accepts them just as they are. The man started to get a little irritated but kept his composure.

I went to a booth manned by the Unitarian Universalist Church. They had this catchy banner with a quote that read: "Don't place a period where God intended a comma." This was an obvious reference to how they believed man had twisted God's beliefs and writings. I asked the two men if they attended the church and they said they did. I asked them just where in the Bible we had replaced God's comma with a period. They looked at each other and one said, "I don't read the Bible." The other nodded in affirmation. I asked why not, and his response was, "Because it isn't important; we know what we believe."

It was quite a day. No "conversions" that I know of and no sinner's prayer recitals. But it gave me a little more insight into the world of homosexual beliefs and the attitude of too many Christians like the lady who approached us – that love is all about just accepting people, even if they are headed over a cliff. That love means never having to say, "You're wrong." That love means just letting people live as they see best regardless of what the Bible says. How very sad that love has been twisted into such an attitude of covert hatred.

It is not just homosexuality that Christians take a live-and-let-live approach to. It is virtually every sin and cultural behavior that exists these days. Abortion? Just "love on people." Adulterers? "Who are we to judge?" Greed and selfishness? "Hey, it's my money and I'll spend it as I want."

The sad truth is that deep down most Christians don't truly care about the lost. Hey, we've got our salvation, so we're good to go! Our actions, or rather inactions, define love as selfish, uncaring, and tolerant of just about anything, and that is a cowardly love. We just can't handle the rejection of being seen as unloving or intolerant, and would rather watch countless millions go to their eternal deaths than risk being seen as intolerant or "Bible thumpers." Whether we admit it or not, we act ashamed of the gospel.

Ashamed of the gospel. What does that say about the depth of our love of God? We are like a man who says he loves his wife but never takes her out of the house because other men might think she is ugly. We tell her she's pretty, but our actions belie those words.

If we truly loved God and the gospel, we would not be able to contain our joy or our desire to share it with everyone we know. If we truly loved the lost, we would do anything we could to share the gospel with them.

Hanging On for Dear Life

We have all seen the movies where a man is about to fall to his death, hanging on for dear life by his fingertips. The friend reaches out to pull him up and for a moment we are left wondering if he will be able to pull his dangling friend to safety. Well, what would happen if the rescuer did not have a firm hold of the ground on which he stood as he attempted to rescue his friend? What if he did not have one hand firmly grasping a well-anchored object while he reached out with his other hand? Both would fall to their deaths. Welcome to the seeker-friendly world of progressive American Christianity.

Organizations like Sojourners and Red Letter Christians are cowards, ashamed of the gospel. They present a facade of "love and tolerance" as the preferred means to reach out to the man hanging on by his fingertips. They think they care for the lost, but they are like the ill-fated rescuer who is not completely anchored on a solid object that will allow him to really attempt a rescue. So they either convince themselves and the dangling man that he is not really in danger, allowing him to fall to his death, or they do something even worse. In their attempt to rescue him, they fail to remain anchored to something immovable, the Word of God, and they fall to their death just like the man they are trying to rescue.

God will not be mocked. He gave us the gospel as the sole means by which man can be rescued from eternal death. It is the power of the gospel, not our feeble, cowardly attempts at love that can save a man. But aren't we mocking God by saying our ways are better than His? Are we not diminishing the power of the gospel when we put our own little spin on it? Do we think that God needs to change His formula for reaching the lost in this postmodern era? That God just cannot relate to the world and culture as it is today?

Seeker-friendly Christianity as it is presented today is arrogant and ineffective. It is telling God He is less than able to reach the lost without our help and our ability to relate to the culture. God just doesn't get it, and we need to intervene. Just how foolish and arrogant is that?

Summary

Just like Vince Lombardi had to take his football team back to the basics to get them on track, we need to return as a church to a basic understanding of what love is and what it isn't. God's love is perfect while ours is flawed. Unless we identify love as God defines it there is no real hope of restoring unrepentant Christian sinners or reaching the lost. We may see an occasional victory here or there, but as they say, even a broken clock is right twice a day.

Don't tell me you love someone when you lack the courage to put yourself at risk for them. And leaders, stop teaching our children that love means tolerance and unbiblical acceptance of people just as they are. Fool yourself if you want, but stop taking our children down with you as you enter very dangerous territory.

Love is sacrifice, total commitment, and a willingness to put yourself at risk of harm. Love is the cross. It is not what we have come to define it as.

Chapter 14

The Heart of the Matter

Chrislam, New Age Christianity, and social justice; the emergent church movement, weak leadership, mushy followers, and an evil secular culture. There are plenty of battles to fight these days and no shortage of challenges facing Bible-believing Christians today. The world hates God more each day, and too many Christians are defining God and Christianity on their own terms.

But none of these opponents or challenges should be a match for the body of Christ. We have the truth and the Holy Spirit in our corner, so any opponent should be easily vanquished. But they are not being vanquished and they are winning the battle. We must reverse this, but how?

The first key to winning a battle is to understand that we are in a battle to begin with. Unless we realize that and understand the full scope of the battle, we are unprepared to engage the opponent.

The second key is to make sure we are an army whom an opponent would never want to fight in the first place. The greatest deterrent to an enemy attack is when the enemy fears the outcome. It is obvious that the culture does not fear American Christianity as an opponent. It views us as weak, scattered, and willing to compromise rather than engage in battle, and they are correct.

Before World War II, Hitler began to annex territory and build a military force even though both were forbidden by the surrender treaty Germany signed after the previous world war. He started testing the resolve of European leaders in small ways, and when they did not oppose him, his confidence and boldness increased. He saw weakness in his opponent and exploited it masterfully. With each additional move he made he assured the Allied Nations it would be his last.

He signed a nonaggression treaty with his enemy to the north, Russia, effectively neutralizing the greatest single threat he might face. He continued to annex land and build his military force while his opponents continued to hope that peace could be maintained and war averted.

Then he invaded Poland and crossed a line which the Allied Nations could not excuse, so they declared war on Germany. But by this time Germany's military might was formidable. The allies declared war but their weakness resulted in a war that would leave more than fifty million dead and Europe all but destroyed.

Aggressive enemies prey on the weaknesses and fears of others. They use our passive attitudes and lack of commitment to our mission to exploit and manipulate us. They chip away, taking small bites out of us until we are weak and ineffective, and then they strike. If their opponent does not have a heart for battle, the enemy will prey on that weakness and gain incremental victories until they are ready for an all-out attack.

The Enemy we face, Satan, is no different in his methods. He chips away at us in many ways, convincing us of lies and half-truths that weaken our position. He tells us that love means accepting all people right where they are instead of helping them out of a life of sin. He convinces us that we deserve the good things in this life even if it means compromising truth and righteousness. He convinces us that God is tolerant of our sin, and he convinces us that the sin in our life has no real consequences for us, individually or corporately, as the body of Christ.

Our sins do have consequences. They draw us away from God and take our eyes off Him, placing them on ourselves. Sin is also addicting, and once you give in once to a particular sin it becomes progressively easier. We continue down a destructive path until God intervenes by allowing the consequences of our sin to catch up with us. When that happens it often comes with a very high price as our lives are shaken by the accumulated sin that God finally decides has gone too far. To a married man who is unfaithful to his wife, with another woman or through pornography, the price might be a severely strained relationship that takes years to restore. If this happens to a Christian leader it might also mean an end to his ministry work. Sin also gives others one more excuse to shun the Christian faith.

We must take a strong stand against the sin that has sadly become too commonplace in American Christianity. We must take a stand against the unrepentant sin of others, but most importantly we must take a strong stand against our own sin that we hide in our hearts away from public scrutiny.

Defeating Sin in Our Lives

Have we given up trying to purge sin from our lives? It sure seems so. Righteousness and the pursuit of holiness have been replaced at the forefront of Christian teachings with less-challenging messages used as excuses for our continuing to sin before a holy God.

"We're all sinners, saved by grace." No doubt this is a true statement. There is no one who is righteous except by the grace and mercy of God through Jesus, but this true statement has morphed into a popular excuse to not walk away from sin and pursue a life of holiness.

How we view ourselves makes all the difference sometimes. If I see myself as decrepit and unlovable, I will probably start to behave that way. But if I read Scripture, particularly Romans 7, I can see myself as God sees me.

Romans 7 is a perfect definition of how Christians should see themselves. We tend to look at ourselves as a singular entity, but Paul describes two entities living within himself: the Holy Spirit of God and his own flesh. These two inhabitants are in the midst of a civil war, battling every moment of our day. The Spirit within us longs to love and worship God, but the other inhabitant, our flesh, lives to serve only our sinful desires. It is very important that we see ourselves as Paul did, with two competing inhabitants fighting every moment for ultimate control of our lives and our eternal destiny. If we simply look at ourselves as a singular entity, we are setting ourselves up for trouble.

If we view ourselves as nothing more than decrepit, worthless sinners, we begin to live out that by which we define ourselves. We subconsciously give up, resigning ourselves to a life of sin, depending on the grace and mercy of God. Conversely, if we think of ourselves as singularly holy and righteous, we can become arrogant and deceitful. We start to justify our every action by the fact that we have accepted the mercy and forgiveness of Jesus, and we abandon a pursuit of holiness because we think it is unnecessary.

However, if we understand that God hates sin and that we are a dual entity, part of us hating sin and the other part loving it, we can frame up the battle in a way where we can start to fight and attain victory. We also come to understand something very crucial: the most powerful enemy we face in restoring biblical Christianity in our churches resides in each of us. We must first find victory in this internal battle before we can have any real hope of defeating the Enemy who seeks to discredit and destroy American Christianity.

Chrislam, New Age thought, or emergent theology are powerless threats if we could only conquer the enemy residing in each one of us, our own desires of the flesh. Once we conquer our internal enemy, the external enemies can be vanquished.

The Battle in Our Mind and Why We Are Losing

There have been some excellent books written by Christian teachers on the important battle we fight daily in our minds. Good and evil fight it out in the midst of memories, thoughts, and temptations, pulling us in two directions. Our flesh desires to feed its lusts and desires, while our love of God calls us to lead a life of holiness. The apostle Paul eloquently writes of this internal civil war in Romans 7.

When we first become Christians, we carry all the baggage of our sinful past with us. We are immediately justified by our faith in Jesus, but sanctification, the pursuit of holiness, takes a long time. Years of living in the world and under its influence battles against our newfound love of God that calls us to lead a pure life. We have become creatures of habit in choosing sin, and our sinful human nature does not give up easily. Our mind becomes a raging battlefield where we make decisions to honor God or continue to feed our flesh. Despite our best efforts, the old baggage we still carry often wins out and we give in to temptation and sin.

In Philippians 4:8 we are taught to think on things that are right, pure, lovely, and praiseworthy to help us ward off our desires of the flesh and the Enemy who seeks to steal our new love of God. Our minds are like the muscles of our body, needing to be trained and exercised to maximize their potential. When we train them properly they become strong and fruitful.

As new Christians we learn about receiving the Holy Spirit and allowing Him to comfort us *and* convict us of sin in our lives, but fully understanding how to do this takes time. We receive the Holy Spirit but our minds have not yet been weaned off our sinful habits, and memories and past experiences still have a hold on us, influencing our decisions and acting as impediments to living a life of holiness. As we continue to read the Word of God and draw nearer to Him, we slowly learn the sources of the baggage in our minds that hold us back as Christians. We find Scriptures that teach us about being a new creation and rejecting the sin and hurt in our past that impedes our progress.

As we grow in our maturity as Christians, God exposes the dangerous programming that has infiltrated our minds, causing us to turn time and again to our sinful nature in spite of our new life in Him. This programming is similar to a virus on a computer, causing glitches and breakdowns in our mind – the computer hardware of our bodies. God's Word helps us understand these viruses, and once we identify them we can begin to isolate them by the power of the Holy Spirit. But while we isolate them they are still ever present and surface time and again. Once we know what these viruses are, we are now able to wipe them from our minds if we understand and follow the Word of God.

Hardware, Software, and Virus Firewalls

If our brain is the hardware, our heart is the software. The heart creates an emotional reaction, feeds it to our brain where a decision is made, leading to an action. This is consistent with how computers work, and the human brain is the greatest of computers, capable of millions of instinctive reactions that control every part of our body. The software tells the hardware what programs to run and the hardware carries out the command.

The Bible mentions the heart six times more than it does the mind, identifying the heart as the proverbial source of our emotions. In 1 Timothy 1 Paul encourages us to stay true to the gospel and reject sin. In verse 5 he states, *The goal of this command is love, which comes from a pure heart and a good conscience and a sincere faith.* However, we are not born with a *pure heart.* In Jeremiah 17:9 God tells us, *The heart is deceitful above all things and beyond cure.* So Paul tells us that love comes from a pure heart but in Jeremiah we are told the heart is deceitful. Obviously this presents quite a challenge for us as Christians. How do we develop a pure heart from one that is deceitful above all things? We cannot – we need a heart transplant.

> *I will give you a new heart and put a new spirit in you; I*
> *will remove from you your heart of stone and give you a*
> *heart of flesh. And I will put my Spirit in you and move*
> *you to follow my decrees and be careful to keep my laws.*
> (Ezekiel 36:26-27)

There is your heart transplant, your new software. The old heart is gone, wiped away, and your new heart, complete with God's Spirit, now runs on the hard drive of your brain. This new heart replaces your deceitful human heart, eliminating the garbage we carried since the day we were born. But even this new heart we receive is not immune to new viruses.

Unless we eradicate the viruses we have accumulated in our hearts and minds over many years of painful experiences, we will continually fight a losing battle in our minds. When God gives us a heart transplant, replacing our human heart of stone with a new heart that includes His Spirit, the viruses can be wiped out. We are no longer ruled by our past failures and fears; instead, we are truly a new creation and are "born again."

In John 3:3, 5-6, Jesus told Nicodemus, *"Very truly I tell you, no one can see the kingdom of God unless they are born again. Very truly I tell you, no one can enter the kingdom of God unless they are born of water and the Spirit. Flesh gives birth to flesh, but the Spirit gives birth to spirit."* Unfortunately, Christians have been misled to think that saying the sinner's prayer equates to being born again. But until we accept the new heart God offers in Ezekiel, complete with His Spirit, we are not truly born again. We remain flesh, fighting against overwhelming odds to become holy in the eyes of a perfect God. But once we accept God's offer of a new heart *and His Spirit*, we truly *are* born again and can start living as a new creation, freed from all the baggage of our old lives. Without our new heart it is virtually impossible to live a holy life, as the viruses of our previous life pollute our minds, leading to continuous sin.

Fighting the battle in our minds will produce some victories but many more defeats, as our minds are already infected with viruses from our old heart. But when we allow God to install new software via the heart He offers, complete with His Spirit, we start clean. Our hearts, the proverbial residence of all our emotions, are now virus-free, capable of saturating our minds with a deep love of God. This gives us the power to turn our backs on our sinful nature and achieve real victory over sin.

So our brain is the hardware, and our new heart the virus-free software installed by God. But hackers are very cunning, always looking for ways to infect computers and wreak havoc. Satan is the most cunning and brilliant of all hackers. He knows our vulnerabilities and will always seek to install new viruses on our new heart and mind. But God has an answer for that challenge.

A Fool-Proof Firewall and Anti-Virus Protection

"When an impure spirit comes out of a person, it goes through arid places seeking rest and does not find it. Then it says, 'I will return to the house I left.' When it arrives, it finds the house swept clean and put in order. Then it goes and takes seven other spirits more wicked than itself, and they go in and live there. And the final condition of that person is worse than the first." – Luke 11:24-26

Satan never gives up. Our new heart from God is still subject to viruses that Satan will send to prod our defenses, looking for weaknesses. He is committed to disrupting and polluting the new heart God has given us, stopping at nothing in his quest to rob us of our joy and pursuit of holiness. He will redouble his efforts to infect the new heart God has given us so we must not be lulled into a false sense of security.

Firewall and anti-virus software is critical to protecting a computer network from hackers and viruses. It is no different with our human brain, the hardware, or our new heart, the software. God provides the perfect virus protection that can detect attacks before they infiltrate our hearts and minds, causing serious problems: His written Word.

> *No temptation has overtaken you except what is common to*
> *mankind. And God is faithful; he will not let you be tempted*
> *beyond what you can bear. But when you are tempted,*
> *he will also provide a way out so that you can endure it.*
> (1 Corinthians 10:13)

The Bible tells us a lot about the hacker and Enemy we battle. It tells us Satan is like a lion, constantly prowling in search of his next victim. He is also the *father of lies* and the master of the half-truth. We just saw that when a demon is rebuked, he can return with allies to break back in if we do not securely lock our hearts and minds. However, if the anti-virus program and firewall of God's Word is properly utilized, the Enemy has no entrance to gain a foothold.

With our new pure heart from God, His Spirit, and the anti-virus firewall of His Word, we can attain greater victory than we ever could by fighting the battle in our minds that have been corrupted with many years of viruses. There is a real battlefield in our minds, seeking to spoil our new life in Jesus. If we fight this battle without the new heart and virus protection of the written Word, we are bound to fail far more than we succeed. God wants us to lead lives of victory and has provided a way to do so, but this will require a real commitment from us; a commitment too few Christians seem willing to embrace in these wicked times.

The only way to successfully win the battle between our spirit and the flesh is to wipe away the corrupted software infecting the hardware and reinstall good software. And the only way this can be accomplished is by a spiritual heart transplant from God. When protected by the perfect firewall, the Word of God, we are now able to lead a life of victory and holiness.

Chapter 15

Now my closing thoughts . . .

The number and ferocity of the enemies fighting American Christianity are large. But none are more destructive than the internal battle we fight every minute of every day. If we find victory personally, and then corporately in the church, the remaining enemies will be powerless. Any attack they launch will break like waves on the rocks.

We as Christians are continuously making choices. We choose to love God by obeying Him or we choose to reject His perfect will for our lives, diminishing our ability to fight the external enemies dismantling the church. Every decision we make has consequences, and every time we choose righteousness we strengthen ourselves and the body of Christ. But when we choose sin, even if it goes unnoticed by anyone else, we weaken the body as a whole. Unless we gain victory internally, within our own heart and mind, we will never achieve victory against the external enemies of the church.

We are the greatest enemy we will face this day and our human sinful nature is our greatest threat. I am as capable of doing damage to the body of Christ as any heretical movement, weak leader, or cultural cancer out there. When I choose sin, I weaken not only myself but also my Christian brothers and sisters who with me compose the body of Christ. Until each of us understands and accepts this fact, we are acting as hypocrites when we speak out against false teachers and movements.

We must first remove the plank from our own eye so we have the ability and moral standing to point out the speck in our brother's eye.

Victory is ours if we have the courage to grasp it, but it will not be easy given our current state of deterioration. Do we have the courage to walk away from our sinful habits? Do we have the courage to truly love one another and risk everything to confront our brothers and sisters in their habitual sin? Do we have the courage to redefine success for the church from nickels and noses to an army of real disciples? Do we have the courage to respectfully challenge everything a Christian leader says or does if it seems to conflict with the Word of God? Do we have the courage to stand up to the secular culture and say, "No more!"

If we do, we can restore and renew American Christianity. If we lack the courage, we will slowly die at our own hands. All that will remain of American Christianity is a remnant, and much will be lost. The choice is ours and God awaits our answer.

Can We Come Back from the Brink of Spiritual Death?

The world is rapidly deteriorating into chaos because of sin. When Adam and Eve chose to know sin instead of trusting God, our Creator wound the clock and started the countdown to the end of the age. An exciting, new eternal life awaits those of us who truly know Jesus as our Lord and Savior. But in the meantime, we have work to do.

We cannot save our world. No source of renewable energy, no politician, no world leader, and no peace treaty can stop the inevitable end of the story. We cannot stop the rise to power of the Antichrist or the false prophet. They will rule the majority of the world one day.

We cannot change biblical prophecy. No amount of social justice or dominionist theology will alter the fate of this world spelled out in the Bible.

We cannot change the declining culture. It will grow more evil and hateful of God. We may be forced as church and ministry leaders to choose between our nonprofit status or continuing to preach the gospel without compromise. We may face a decision one day soon to stop calling homosexuality a sin or face imprisonment for promoting hate speech.

Our public education system will never again be a place where our children hear the Christian values we teach as parents supported or reinforced. Instead, our children will increasingly be marginalized, perhaps even bullied, for standing on their Christian beliefs.

The secular media will never again be friendly to us as Christians. It will continue to marginalize us and lie about God and those of us committed to Him. Christian media will continue to slide toward mushy theology, scorning anyone who has the courage to call out false teachings and false teachers. It will begin to look more and more like the secular culture with each passing year.

Feeling depressed yet? Don't be, because I can think of no greater time to be a Christian. We might well be witnesses to the final days before our King returns to take us home, when we will see the arrogance of Satan shattered as he is defeated decisively and eternally. We are seeing history unfold right before our eyes, witnessing the time when Jesus said there would be a great falling away. We might be witnessing the strong delusion God promised to send in Romans 1 and 2 Thessalonians.

We live in a world where the harvest is great but the workers are few. What a time to work those fields! We can be the select few who stand strong until the end no matter what the Enemy sends our way, leading many to the light and hope of the true gospel.

There is work to do and all is not lost by any stretch of the imagination. We can salvage American Christianity. Perhaps our numbers will decrease, but Gideon only needed three hundred to conquer a much larger army because the Lord was with him. Moses delivered his people with nothing more than a shepherd's staff because the Lord was with him. All we have to do is repent of our apathy and recommit ourselves to the Lord's plan for our lives. Whether we are three hundred, three thousand, or three million, when has the size of an army ever mattered to God?

When the world starts to fall apart and others begin to panic, we can be God's instruments to bring the lost home to Him. We can shine the irresistible light of the risen Christ right through the darkness of this world. It can be a bright beacon for millions of lost ships. What a time to be alive!

But it will take genuine repentance and a total commitment to the

Lord's agenda, abandoning our own selfish ways. It will take real love and not the phony "love" of cowardice and tolerance. It will take courage to speak out boldly, compassion for those in troubling times, and a willingness to abandon everything of this world that we have come to love. We cannot do it, but the Holy Spirit can do it through us if we give Him permission and total control. That's asking a lot and Jesus told us it would not be easy. As my wife often says, "Jesus asks only one thing from us: everything." Are we willing to surrender everything to Him?

Become a good Berean and take everything you hear from anyone to the Word of God. It is the only source of eternal truth available to us. Paul commended the Bereans for checking everything *he* taught against the Scriptures. If our Christian leaders are unwilling to be scrutinized in the same manner, then shame on them. If you are willing to gamble your eternal soul by blindly following any man instead of God, you deserve the fate that awaits you. But if you are committed to trusting God and His Word, your future will be secure.

Meet the Author

M ike LeMay is an author, biblical apologist, radio talk show host, and general manager of Q90 FM, a Christian radio station in Green Bay, Wisconsin. He has extensively studied and reported on news, issues, and trends pertaining to the Christian life, pointing people to the truth of God's Word.

His books have received critical acclaim for their insight in bringing news and topics of the day into correct biblical context and understanding, helping Christians see the big picture of what is happening around them. His latest book, American Christianity's Slide into Apostasy: What We Must Do before It's Too Late, points out the growing disparity between Biblical Christianity and an "American Christianity" that is integrating secular beliefs, thoughts, and processes into the church, leading people further away from God and His eternal truth.

Mike is also owner of Christian Thought Consulting, LLC, and he helps families and business professionals find peace, joy, and purpose in their increasingly busy lives. He can be reached at 920-676-7083 or www.michaeldlemay.com.

Visit Michael online at:

www.michaeldlemay.com

Also by Michael D. LeMay

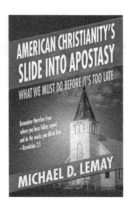

Always remember this: If your church is drifting from Biblical Christianity to American Christianity, your church leaders may not even realize it. In all probability they are not purposely leading the church away from God and His Word. The subtle and dangerous deception Satan has mastered along with ignorant but dedicated allies in public education, media, entertainment, and government create a powerful yet subtle deception that is well masqueraded. Unless we are completely immersed and grounded in God's Word, we may even be deceived into thinking we are serving God when in reality we serve His enemy.

This book is a call to professing Christians to examine their beliefs and actions and to compare them to God's truth and standards in His Word. It is an attempt to help every professing Christian understand the deception perpetrated by the father of lies that infects both the secular and professing Christian institutions in our nation, such that in the final days one will not be able to distinguish between evil human government and religion. And it is a call for truly born-again, spirit-filled Christians to spot deception and lovingly but firmly confront church leaders who are leading congregations away from true Biblical Christianity.

Available where books are sold

We are being lied to—and many professing Christians are buying the lies. Your eternal soul may be at stake. The Bible foretells a great deception and falling away from the faith in the latter days where absolute truth is discounted and moral relativism is elevated: Humanism!

The clever deception of Humanism has completely taken over government, media and public education, and has infiltrated the visible church so strongly that many churches differ little in their beliefs and teachings from the humanist views of the world.

This book will open your eyes to the rampant deception around us and help you correctly interpret the Word of God so you can stand strong in your faith to the end. It will help you open the eyes of family and friends who fall for the deception of Humanism, and point them to the eternal hope of Jesus Christ. It will teach you how to take your thoughts captive in obedience to Christ and live a life of joy, peace and obedience to God.

You will see how God designed our brain, heart and conscience to work, and how the truth of the Bible and the Holy Spirit can help you live a life of joy and peace as the world continues to spin out of control.

Available where books are sold

"Are You Really Saved?" is a book that will challenge everything you think you know about God, eternal life and hell. Far too many professing Christians cannot explain why they believe what they claim to believe, relying on others to explain the teachings of God. Jesus Christ is very clear that the path to eternal life with God is very narrow, and few people find it. Yet most professing Christians do not think twice about these words of Jesus. They think because they were baptized as a baby, or attend a certain church, that they are destined for eternal life in heaven. But the Bible tells a much different story. Jesus said unless we love Him with all our heart, mind and strength, we will not enter eternall life with Him. Yet most professing Christians know more about their favorite sport team or television show than they do the teachings of the One who came to save us. This book will challenge you to the very essence of your soul.

Available where books are sold

Also by the publisher

There are consequences when God's people take the path of least resistance and back out of culture. One only needs to look at our society to see we are living with those consequences today.

- Why do you think so many Christians pursue comfort over commitment to Christ?

- Do you sometimes feel overwhelmed by the darkness and moral decline in society today and wonder what happened to the salt and light?

- How have we reached a point where Christians who do preach the gospel and speak up about sin are called hateful, intolerant, or judgmental?

Christian in name only, America has become an epicenter for the culture war as too many of us keep ducking the issue of sin. Due to decades of Christians being silent, failing to preach the gospel and speak the truth in love, we've reached a tipping point in which political correctness refuses to coexist with religious freedom. Why do you think Christians who defend God's Word are often called hateful, intolerant, or judgmental? There are consequences in this life and for eternity, when Christians take the path of least resistance. We cannot reverse the moral decline, but we can choose to stand for righteousness as we pray for revival and be the salt and light Jesus called us to be while we're still here.

Available where books are sold

To have found God and still to pursue Him is a paradox of love, scorned indeed by the too-easily-satisfied religious person, but justified in happy experience by the children of the burning heart. Saint Bernard of Clairvaux stated this holy paradox in a musical four-line poem that will be instantly understood by every worshipping soul:

We taste Thee, O Thou Living Bread,
And long to feast upon Thee still:
We drink of Thee, the Fountainhead
And thirst our souls from Thee to fill.

Come near to the holy men and women of the past and you will soon feel the heat of their desire after God. Let A. W. Tozer's pursuit of God spur you also into a genuine hunger and thirst to truly know God.

Available where books are sold

There is no situation in life for which you cannot find some word of consolation in Scripture. If you are in affliction, if you are in adversity and trial, there is a promise for you. In joy and sorrow, in health and in sickness, in poverty and in riches, in every condition of life, God has a promise stored up in His Word for you.

This classic book by Dwight L. Moody brings to light the necessity of studying the Scriptures, presents methods which help stimulate excitement for the Scriptures, and offers tools to help you comprehend the difficult passages in the Scriptures. To live a victorious Christian life, you must read and understand what God is saying to you. Moody is a master of using stories to illustrate what he is saying, and you will be both inspired and convicted to pursue truth from the pages of God's Word.

Available where books are sold

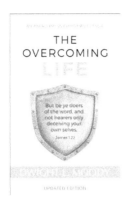

THE OVERCOMING LIFE

But be ye doers of the word, and not hearers only deceiving your own selves.

James 1:22

UPDATED EDITION

Are you an overcomer? Or, are you plagued by little sins that easily beset you? Even worse, are you failing in your Christian walk, but refuse to admit and address it? No Christian can afford to dismiss the call to be an overcomer. The earthly cost is minor; the eternal reward is beyond measure.

Dwight L. Moody is a master at unearthing what ails us. He uses stories and humor to bring to light the essential principles of successful Christian living. Each aspect of overcoming is looked at from a practical and understandable angle. The solution Moody presents for our problems is not religion, rules, or other outward corrections. Instead, he takes us to the heart of the matter and prescribes biblical, God-given remedies for every Christian's life. Get ready to embrace genuine victory for today, and joy for eternity.

Available where books are sold

CPSIA information can be obtained
at www.ICGtesting.com
Printed in the USA
LVHW020840250219
608648LV00022B/256/P

9 781622 451043